LAKEFRONT BILLIONAIRES

LAUREN ASHER

Bloom *books*

Published by Bloom Books, an imprint of Sourcebooks
1935 Brookdale RD, Naperville, IL 60563-2773
(630) 961-3900
sourcebooks.com

Cataloging-in-Publication Data is on file with the Library of Congress.

Printed and bound in the United States of America.
VP 10 9 8 7 6 5 4 3 2 1

PLAYLISTS

Love Arranged by Lauren Asher

Scan to listen

+

Love Arranged
Playlist >

Flower Shop Pop
Playlist >

Road Trip Requirements
Playlist >

I Hate Running
Playlist >

Dancing Around In The Kitchen
Playlist >

AUTHOR NOTE AND CONTENT WARNING

Love Arranged is considered a standalone novel, but events in this book coincide with those in *Love Redesigned* and *Love Unwritten*, the first and second books in the Lakefront Billionaires series.

This love story contains explicit content and topics that may be sensitive to some readers. For a more detailed content warning list, please scan the QR code or visit https://laurenasher.com /lalbcontentwarnings/

To those who dream of falling in love.
And to anyone who fears it.
Love is one of life's greatest rewards,
so long as you're prepared to work for it.

Welcome to Eros

An anonymous dating app inspired by Cupid's lesser-known Greek counterpart.

Not familiar with the best love story in Greek mythology? No worries! We'll give you a quick summary of what happened to the god of love.

Long story short: a mortal woman named Psyche fell in love with Eros without ever seeing his face, proving that beauty isn't skin-deep (and inspiring our "love is blind" twist).

Get Started →

Login

Before you aim arrows at possible matches, upload a photo of yourself.

This photo will **not** be revealed until **you** choose to do so.

A match can request to see your photo, but there is a mythology-inspired catch that would make Aphrodite proud, so proceed with caution (seriously, brush up on your Greek myths and see what happened to Psyche before considering this option).

Upload Your Photo

Continue

Now that your photo is uploaded, share a few facts about yourself.

When's your birthday?

What's your gender?

Who are you looking to match with?

Who's your favorite Greek god or goddess?

Choose at least three interests

Reading	Movies	Music
Fashion	Cooking	Nature
Traveling	Cars	Animals/Pets

Submit your answers

You're all set!

Now all you have to do is read our community guidelines below and click *I Agree* to start your love story.

I Agree

August

Nearly One Year Ago...

LAURENCE

Have you ever done something bad?

ANA

I can't tell if you're trying to flirt with me or scare me into never using Eros again.

LAURENCE

And if it's the first?

ANA

Well, if I have done something bad, then I'm not about to disclose it in a chat that some random IT guy could read when he's bored.

LAURENCE

And if it's the second option?

ANA

Then I have a feeling we're not talking about traffic violations or borrowing my sister's favorite sweater and shrinking it by accident.

LAURENCE

Most definitely not.

ANA

Good to know.

ANA

Then as your unofficial legal counsel, I need to advise you against continuing this conversation.

LAURENCE

Are you a lawyer?

ANA

After all the dramatized detective shows I've seen, I could run a law firm.

LAURENCE

Straight into the ground?

ANA

I'm wounded that you think so little of me.
Have a little faith.

LAURENCE

I have some.

ANA

Just not the good kind?

LAURENCE

Exactly.

ANA

You are aware this is a dating app and not a
crisis hotline, right?

LAURENCE

It's easy to forget given the state of your
love life.

ANA

Mine? What about yours?

LAURENCE

It was DOA years ago.

ANA

Aw. Did someone break your heart?

LAURENCE

Who said I have one?

ANA

Well then now's my chance to drop a clichéd
"everyone has a heart, even if yours is a bit
broken" line.

LAURENCE

You've got a real talent for words.

ANA

Really?

LAURENCE

No.

ANA

Maybe it's time for me to delete this anonymous chat and find someone who appreciates my charm AND has no problem meeting up in person after spending the last few weeks messaging nonstop.

LAURENCE

Giving up already?

ANA

Your sunny disposition is starting to wear on me a bit.

LAURENCE

Your jokes are improving. I nearly laughed.

ANA

Is there hope for me yet?

LAURENCE

I hate to break it to you, but I have about as much hope as I do faith.

ANA

You know what I learned from fostering animals?

LAURENCE

Hurt dogs don't holler. They bite.

ANA

Sometimes I think about packing my bags and going somewhere else.

LAURENCE

I don't believe you.

ANA

You're right. I love Lake Wisteria and plan on spending the rest of my life here. It's part of my whole thirty-year plan to buy a cottage, have a few kids, and start a bee sanctuary in my backyard.

LAURENCE

That's...oddly specific.

ANA

I've had a lot of time to think it over.

LAURENCE

I wouldn't have guessed.

ANA

Don't you have a thirty-year plan?

LAURENCE

No, and even if I did, I don't think it would include this town.

ANA

This place will warm up to you eventually. Mark my words.

LAURENCE

Nearly impossible with the brutal winters.

ANA

I take it you're not from somewhere cold.

LAURENCE

Hell is known to have the same temp year-round.

ANA

You're funny.

LAURENCE

Your bar is far too low.

ANA

At least it's easier for you to hit.

LAURENCE

You should expect more from people.

ANA

Why?

LAURENCE

Because if not, then you'll end up with someone like me.

ANA

Is that supposed to be a bad thing?

LAURENCE

You have no idea.

September

ANA

Do you ever feel lonely?

LAURENCE

No.

ANA

Let me guess: You enjoy your own company way too much.

LAURENCE

You'd understand if you heard the voice in my head.

ANA

You struggle with that too? I thought I was the only one.

ANA

Does yours always tell you to treat yourself to a sweet treat or new outfit when you've been mildly inconvenienced?

LAURENCE

No.

ANA

Oh.

ANA

That's disappointing.

ANA

Perhaps you should seek professional help then.

LAURENCE

Why do you feel lonely?

ANA

Forget about me. We're focusing on you for once.

LAURENCE

If I answer your question honestly, will you tell me?

ANA

Aw. You care about my feelings that much? I'm touched.

LAURENCE

More like I'm curious how someone like you could ever feel lonely a single day in her life.

ANA

I can't tell if you're insulting me or not.

LAURENCE

You'd know if I was.

ANA

Would it kill you to compliment someone from time to time?

ANA

And by someone, I mean me.

LAURENCE

And risk you expecting more of them?

ANA

The horror!!!

LAURENCE

Answer my question.

ANA

It might seem silly to someone who doesn't care for other people's company.

LAURENCE

I like yours.

Ana is offline.

Ana is online.

ANA

Sorry for the delay. I had to check if I accidentally fell asleep at work and started dreaming.

LAURENCE

And how did you do that?

ANA

It's best you don't ask.

LAURENCE

You're...

ANA

The most special woman you've ever met?

LAURENCE

No.

LAURENCE

You're the most special *person* I've ever met.

ANA

That better not be an insult.

LAURENCE

And if it wasn't?

ANA

Then you might end up proving this anonymous app isn't such a silly idea after all.

ANA

So, you're shipwrecked on an island and you can only bring three things. What are they?

LAURENCE

Things or people?

ANA

We both know you'd never willingly choose to be trapped with another human being.

LAURENCE

True.

LAURENCE

Or at least it was until I met you.

 **October**

ANA

There's a Halloween party tomorrow at Last Call. I think it would be fun.

LAURENCE

Nice. Enjoy.

ANA

You should go.

LAURENCE

I'm busy.

ANA

Your blood sacrifices can wait.

LAURENCE

Tell that to the full moon.

ANA

I hope you're joking.

ANA

Please tell me you're kidding.

ANA

It's been five minutes and I'm still waiting for an answer.

LAURENCE

Let's leave it up to your imagination.

ANA

How about we don't since it tends to run a bit wild.

LAURENCE

This is your daily reminder that I'm not some vampire or werewolf.

ANA

Except that's exactly what someone would say to get me off their trail.

LAURENCE

Right.

ANA

Please come to the party.

ANA

Don't make me beg.

LAURENCE

I'd rather you didn't. I find submissiveness
rather unattractive.

ANA

Funny because I feel the same way about
someone running scared.

LAURENCE

I'm not scared.

ANA

Right. Sure you aren't.

LAURENCE

Why are you pushing for us to meet up?

ANA

I'm done giving you time to get to
know me first.

ANA

Tomorrow is your only chance. I'll be dressed
like a cowgirl. Pink hat. Lots of sparkles.
Most likely to be found out on the dance floor
with a passion fruit vodka seltzer in hand.

LAURENCE

I won't be attending.

ANA

What a shame. If you don't show up, then I
plan on going home with someone else.

LAURENCE

Are you threatening me?

ANA

If you took it as one, that means you care more about me than you want to admit.

LAURENCE

I don't.

ANA

Then prove it.

Ana is offline

LAURENCE

When you see this tonight, run.
Laurence attached a photo

ANA

Run where? Straight into your arms?

LAURENCE

Why am I not surprised?

ANA

How did you get a mask like that on short notice?

LAURENCE

Don't worry about it.

ANA

Please. The only thing I'm worried about is the way I'll react in public once we finally meet.

Ana is offline

Lorenzo

Up until yesterday, I loved a good challenge. I *thrived* off them, but then Ana came along, calling my bluff when she threatened to go home tonight with another man should I not show up.

I knew it then that I lost the game, and after tonight, I'll lose her for good.

She was never yours to keep.

Ignoring the knot of unease growing in my chest, I slip my mask over my face and enter the crowded bar. I've never seen Last Call this packed before, the entire space full of people wearing a variety of costumes, all of which required far more effort than my plain black shirt, jeans, and light-up mask with neon blue stitching for the eyes and mouth.

I search the room full of people for the woman who has plagued my mind since she first messaged me. I've spent two months wondering if every woman I talk to is *her*.

Two months of overthinking. Of *denial*. Of me trying to distance myself from Ana, who was someone I had no business pursuing once I determined I would never choose her to be my fake fiancée.

I *couldn't*.

I tried to let her go, but I failed. Then I tried again, only to end up right where Ana wants me, searching the dance floor for a woman dressed in a pink, sparkly dress and matching cowboy hat.

I tell myself to stick to the perimeter. That if I don't find her in five minutes, I'll take it as a sign.

Fate must enjoy making a mockery of my life, because the moment I start the countdown, the crowd begins to part. It's as if someone drove an invisible wedge down the center of the dance floor, separating people to reveal Ana at the center, a glow from a random spotlight shining down on her.

Or should I call her *Liliana.*

My heart, which has been acting up ever since I walked into the bar, picks up speed, the bass from the loud music adding to the intense pulsing sensation in my ears.

I take a step back, and then another, only to stumble on my third when Lily locks eyes with me.

Everyone else fades away, as if they were banished into darkness as her bright, carefree smile grows, stretching her perfectly plump lips. I'm stunned, my useless body on standby as she heads over to me.

Her steps are confident as she walks in my direction, all while I stare, trying to make sense of the fact that my Ana is none other than Liliana Muñoz.

It must be a trick. It doesn't make sense that someone who attracts positive attention and exudes kindness with every interaction likes *me.* If it weren't for Lily clearly recognizing my mask, I would've thought her costume is only a coincidence.

In all the scenarios I've imagined, Ana wasn't the same ethereal woman whose smile dazzled me nearly a year ago when she slid into the empty seat beside me at church, her brown eyes warm and welcoming as they swept over me.

"So you're the one everyone is talking about this week," she says.

"I feel like I'm at a disadvantage because I have no idea who you are."

Her smile remains, somehow even brighter than before. "Lily Muñoz." She holds her hand out, and I hesitate to reach for it. I don't like to touch others unless necessary, but the longer her hand hangs in the air, the more inclined I am to grab it.

When I do, an excited current of unfamiliar energy shoots up my arm, zapping away all worried thoughts about physical contact.

"Lorenzo Vittori." My voice drops an octave.

"Nice to meet you, Lorenzo," she replies, my name sounding like pure sin from her luscious lips.

"So," I whisper. "I feel compelled to ask: What exactly are *people saying about me?"*

She laughs—a sound that makes me feel closer to heaven than any religious service or gospel. "I don't like to gossip."

"You just enjoy listening to it, then?"

"Guilty as charged." She winks, and all hell breaks loose in my stomach as—I can't believe I'm saying this—butterflies take flight.

The memory shimmers away, but that same wild feeling in my stomach remains as my past and present blend together.

"Well, well. Look who decided to show up after all." Lily traces a line up the center of my chest with her index finger, leaving a path of heated skin in her wake.

I stay quiet because I'm unsure if she'd be able to recognize my voice from all the mayoral ads showing on local TV.

"Are we playing the silent game?" She teases the bottom of my mask with her thumb while her pinky tickles my throat.

I shiver, the reaction far from subtle.

Her smile grows impossibly large. "Fine. It's a good thing you don't need to talk while dancing."

She laces her fingers with mine and drags me onto the dance floor, making me forget all about my boundaries as I get lost in the music.

Where I get lost in *her*.

I hand over my control for ten minutes. Ten, all-too-short minutes that fly by before I'm promising myself another five. But then fifteen turns into thirty, and next thing I know, Lily is fully in charge of our ruin as she tows me through the crowd and down a back hallway.

All she needs to do is throw me a secretive smile from over her shoulder, and every previous reservation I had about taking this further disappears.

People don't pay us much attention, either because they're too busy hooking up or too distracted by their friends while they wait to use the restroom.

I have no idea where she is taking me, but we somehow end up outside. The emergency exit door slams shut behind us before she cages me against it.

Since when are you the type to relinquish control? The anxious voice bleeds into the moment, threatening to destroy it.

This isn't you, my instincts scream.

Run now before it's too late, the voice reminds me as Lily closes the gap between us until our chests touch.

There is a playful glint in her eyes as she slips her hand under my mask and teases my bottom lip with her thumb. A tingle erupts from a single pass, and before I think better of it, I nip at the pad of her thumb.

Her smile is captivating as she cups my chin and drops a kiss on my plastic mask, proving that she doesn't even need to touch my lips to send a zap shooting down my spine.

At first, it is a pleasant tingle, but soon the sensation transforms into a full-blown paralyzing shock as I process how I want to rip my mask off and crush my mouth to hers, devouring her in a way that leaves her desperate for relief.

A relief I desperately need as well.

An image of her in my bed, wrapped up in my sheets, wearing nothing but my marks on her neck brings my fantasies to a screeching halt.

A fake relationship can't work between two people who desire each other. Too many lines would be blurred, and every limit I've set would be challenged.

Maybe even destroyed.

So, no, I can't pursue a real relationship. I don't *want* to, even if I tricked myself into thinking it was a possibility for the last couple of months.

Not even with someone as incredible as Lily.

Especially not with her.

I'm about to put a stop to all this, but then she traces a path of kisses down the column of my throat, stealing my breath and the words right from my mouth.

Pathetic, the same voice returns, louder than before.

My hands find her hips, not to keep her at a distance like I originally intended, but to drag her closer.

She smiles against my pebbled skin. "Are you going to hide behind a mask all night, or are you going to finally show me who I've been dreaming of for two months?"

Fuck. Me.

Her body molds to mine as she wraps her arms around my neck, teasing the strap keeping my mask in place. "Because as much as I'd love to explore this new mask kink of mine, I have a different idea about how I want tonight to go for us."

"Like?"

"I'd rather show you." Her eyes are so bright, so full of hope as she lifts my mask up. I don't have a chance to stop her, or maybe I didn't make enough effort to as Lily finally comes face-to-face with *Laurence*.

Her eyes widen, and her lips part with a gasp.

"Lo—"

I crush my mouth to hers.

One kiss to remember her by, I promise myself, embracing the rush of energy coursing through my body as she single-handedly ruins every future kiss for me.

She might as well be my first and my last because no one from my past compares, and there won't be a single person who ever will.

It's the least I deserve for the pain I'm about to cause her. Because the man she has spent two months *dreaming of...* The one she wants for a thirty-year plan... I'm not him.

I hope you never forgive me for hurting you, I think to myself when she returns my kiss with equal enthusiasm. She tastes of passion fruit and sweet temptation, a forbidden combination that I could become addicted to.

I hope you find every reason to hate me and hold on to it, I silently add as I slide my hands through her hair and tilt her head back so I can better plunder her mouth.

And I hope that one day, I'll stop hating myself for letting you go.

When I break away, I know it won't be possible because I don't *just* hate myself.

I *despise* the weak person I am and the anxiety I struggle with. The same anxiety that demands for me to push Lily away, not because she deserves better, but because I won't *be* better.

I don't know how. Don't want to figure it out either, in part because I'm scared. I'm selfish. I'm too damn focused on my goal to get distracted by some fantasy that was never mine.

I gently spin Lily around so she has her back to the door before I release my hold on her waist and take a step away.

And another.

My third is smaller thanks to the crushed look on her face, but I manage a fourth and a fifth without tripping.

"Where are you going?" Her voice gives her distress away, making my stomach churn.

"This was a terrible idea." I keep my tone flat. Emotionless. No room for misinterpretation about where I stand on the asshole spectrum.

"What?"

"You. Me… We were a mistake."

She flinches, adding to the dark cloud of hatred following me everywhere I go.

A feeling of self-loathing that I'm all too familiar with, and one that will eat away at me until all I'm left with are a bunch of regrets, but none as big as this one.

I can feel it from the very first step I take.

ANA

Are we going to talk about last night?

ANA

Or the fact that you're Lorenzo fucking Vittori?

Laurence is offline

ANA

Don't be an asshole. Talk to me.

Ana is offline

ANA

Seriously? You're going to keep reading my messages and ignoring me after we spent the last two months talking every single day?

Laurence is offline

ANA

Are you pushing me away because of Julian and Rafa? They're overbearing at times but completely harmless. Trust me. They stopped getting involved in my love life long ago.

Ana is offline

ANA

I could pull you aside in public and force you to talk to me about all this, but I'm afraid of what you might say. I hate to admit it, but it's true.

Ana is offline

ANA

When you saw me at the animal shelter and acted like you'd never met me before in front of the volunteer team, it felt like you took my heart and smashed it into a thousand pieces to match yours.

ANA

If you want to pretend we're strangers, fine. I'll be sure to do the same.

Ana is offline

Ana is offline

Ana is offline

🥲 November

ANA

It's been a while since I sent a message, but I'm a little drunk.

ANA

By a little, I mean wastedddd.

ANA

Sloshed. Hammered. Borracha.

Ana is offline

ANA

My sister tried to take my phone away but I'm back and here to say I miss you.

ANA

I just...

Ana is offline

ANA

My phone died. Whoo0pps.

ANA

I didn't want to pretend anymore. Just like I don't want to pretend now. I don't care if you're Lorenzo or Laurence. I like you despite all the reasons I shouldn't, and it makes me hate myself.

Ana is offline

ANA

Well, talk about embarrassing, but not nearly as bad as how I looked when you walked into my shop and asked me to make you a bouquet for another woman.

ANA

I finally realized that I was a challenge rather than the endgame.

Ana has deactivated her account

secret garden studio

WWS ???
wildflower wishes studio

petal + cross

The Pressed Petal

CHAPTER ONE

Lily

With an unbelievable amount of self-restraint, I resist turning the shocking letter I read into paper confetti. Instead, I toss it inside my thrifted shoulder bag and lock my office.

On my way to the sales floor, I pass by my mom's empty office. Her door is shut—a more frequent occurrence since her doctor said she needed to take it easy because of her high blood pressure—and the plastic box nailed beside the white door is full of a few days' worth of mail.

I spot the matching envelope to the one I received with the town's crest on the upper left-hand corner. My vivid imagination gets the best of me, and I'm overwhelmed by images of my mom reading the notice tomorrow before she opens the flower shop for the day.

I can picture her breaking down when she learns how a

condemnation act works. She'd spiral once she figures out that local governments are allowed to buy properties regardless if someone wants to sell or not, so long as there is appropriate, fair market compensation.

My mom and dad poured everything into turning this shop into their legacy, and I'll fight anyone, including our small-town city council, who thinks they can buy out a few small businesses because of some antiquated amendment and turn them into fancy new storefronts.

Not wanting to second-guess my decision, I steal my mom's letter and throw it inside my purse. It's heavy from the weight of my rash choice, but I'd rather be the one to deliver the bad news.

Ditching the scene of my crime, I push on the swinging door that separates the offices, break room, and storage area from the sales floor. I'm hit with the fresh scent of flowers first, followed by the sound of soft music streaming from the hidden portable speakers.

The comfort I always feel whenever I walk into Rose & Thorn is quickly replaced by an emotional gut punch as I take in everything I stand to lose. My eyes well with tears as my watery gaze wanders around the small shop bursting with different roses, carnations, and other popular summer blooms.

The pristine shop is kept organized, allowing customers to navigate the endless amounts of color-coded buckets full of flowers and foliage so they can easily create their perfect custom bouquet—a Rose & Thorn experience I suggested five years ago—along with description cards placed in front of each bucket describing the name, origin, and possible meanings.

Our newest Rose & Thorn employee, Jane, picks the perfect time to look up from the flowers she's rearranging at the front of the store. She is a sweet, young woman who moved here from Lake Aurora, a neighboring town that's only a thirty-minute drive away.

"Everything okay?" Her brows knit together with worry.

I quickly smooth out my sour expression. "Yup. Got some mail from the IRS."

Even if I wanted to tell Jane about the letter, I shouldn't. Given the notice's emphasis on discretion, I'd only anger the people who control our shop's fate.

As a sign of good faith—I use the term loosely—the Ludlow family is willing to offer a hush-money check in exchange for a signed NDA. It is meant to be a bonus that encourages people to stay quiet until January when the forced sale is finalized and announced to the town.

Assholes.

Jane's nose twitches. "I'd suggest shredding the envelope and pretending you never got it, but I believe that's a crime."

I laugh, but it rings a bit hollow. "Don't tempt me."

She brushes a hand down her Rose & Thorn embroidered apron. "I won't tell on you if anyone comes knocking."

"Your loyalty is appreciated."

She returns to fixing the flowers while I stare out the window at Lavender Lane, which is ground zero for the city council's reconstruction project.

The sun is slowly setting outside, casting our run-down street in a golden glow. It might not be the nicest, most popular part of the Historic District, but at this time of day, the hues of pink and orange make our humble little side street look like the most beautiful part of town.

"Are you sure you're good with locking up later?" I ask, only to delay my departure.

Jane offers me another reassuring smile. "Absolutely. You don't have to worry about me. I've got everything covered."

I get going, but instead of heading to my car right away, I pause outside the store to take it all in.

While the other four storefronts need a serious makeover, Rose & Thorn stands out with its pink-painted bricks and striped awnings. My dad installed the window coverings himself, and it was one of many improvement projects he worked on in the store.

This season's window display, which took me eight days to assemble, might be my favorite one yet. The melting ice-cream cones are made completely out of flowers, and they've been an absolute hit since I unveiled them last week, driving up foot traffic, sales numbers, and social media buzz.

My plan of having *Visit Rose & Thorn* on everyone's Michigan bucket list is slowly coming together, and I'll be damned if the city council thinks they can shut our doors for good.

Ignoring the ache in my chest, I turn away from the window and walk to my parked car located across the street. It's stuffy inside thanks to the faded upholstery and constant exposure to the hot June sun, but it's nothing that blasting the AC can't fix.

I plug my key into the ignition and turn it, only for my heart to drop at the telltale clicking sound.

"No." I groan while turning the key again.

The dead battery doesn't respond to my second or third try, so I spend the next few minutes researching tips and tricks. By my fifth failed attempt, I give up on Google and pop the hood open.

My long, dark hair sticks to the back of my neck as I check out the engine. I'm not sure why I bother since I know next to nothing about cars, but I at least need to *try* to diagnose the issue before I text the family group chat asking for help.

I shoot daggers at the engine until the sound of shoes clapping against the sidewalk steals my attention. I'm about to wave the person down, only to stop when I find a pair of dark brown eyes already focused on me.

If eyes are the window to the soul, Lorenzo Vittori must lack one, because his blank stare gives absolutely nothing away. It remains emotionless as his eyes ever so slowly rove down my body—a reaction he can't seem to help whenever I'm around.

Today's outfit is bland at best, like most of my neutral colors lately. Ditching my bright clothes didn't happen overnight, but rather it felt like I slowly turned the saturation down in my life.

Fashion is my favorite form of self-expression, and lately I want to keep that part of myself hidden away. I'm not sure for how long, but at least until I stop worrying that I'm *too much*.

After being vulnerable with one too many assholes, I'm done wearing my heart on my sleeve—both literally and figuratively.

My choice to dim my personality isn't a confidence issue.

It's a trust one.

If a man wants to get to know me, he needs to work for it.

Then, once they earn my trust, I'll whip out the pastel dresses, crochet tops in every color yarn, and my custom-painted sneakers with satin ribbons for laces.

Like usual, I expect Lorenzo to carry on with his day without acknowledging my existence, but I'm surprised when he heads directly toward me.

Something in my chest *flutters*, and I swear to God I've never hated the sensation more. Swooning over *Laurence* was one thing, but feeling lightheaded in his alter ego's presence?

"Need some help?" he asks, the deep timbre in his voice sending a vibration rolling through my body.

"Nope." I lean over and start fiddling with a cap of some sort.

He stops beside me, standing close enough for me to see the one tiny speck of dirt on his shoe.

How out of character for the perfectionist.

"I haven't given it a try myself, but maybe if you turn that cap the wrong way long enough, it'll finally come off," he says, his amused tone grating on my fraying nerves.

My composure slips at the stupid smirk on his face, and my irritation flares. "Don't you have somewhere to be?"

He checks his fancy platinum watch, which must be worth more than my monthly salary. "Not yet."

A rarity coming from the man who is busy juggling a mayoral campaign and his small but growing venture-capitalist portfolio.

His gaze dips. "You've got a stain on your pants."

I take a jump back with a gasp, the muscles in my neck

spasming from how quickly I look down to assess the white linen material. "Where?"

He effectively slips through the gap and starts tinkering around underneath my hood. I never allow my stare to linger on him, but today I'm taken aback by his nearness.

Laurence—or should I say *Lorenzo*—once told me he liked cars, but I didn't know he could *repair* them.

His dark hair falls in front of his eyes as he leans over to see something, and I'm tempted to comb it back.

Have you learned nothing?

I blame my lack of impulse control on his proximity. It's disarming, being this close to him after months of avoiding each other, so my head is a mess.

I *try* to refocus on his actions. The ease in which he twists knobs and assesses engine parts with his phone's flashlight distracts me temporarily, only for me to become entranced by how his bespoke suit bunches up around his muscles when he bends over to get a better look at something.

The view of his backside...I swear the man's physique could've inspired Renaissance sculptors with a body like his.

His voice startles me, but it's his narrowed eyes that make me want to die of humiliation.

Shit. My face turns hot.

What did he say?

When I don't reply fast enough, Lorenzo raises a single brow. "When's the last time you got an oil change?"

Oh.

I'm quick to look down at the metal stick in his hands. "Uh...let me see."

I take the opportunity to add some distance and get a hold of myself. It's a valiant effort that's ruined when I accidentally brush against his back with my shoulder, sending sparks down my arm.

He bristles at the contact, adding to my embarrassment as I dart around him to check the sticker on my windshield.

I climb back out of the car with the grace of a newborn foal. "Looks like I went in May."

"Of this year?"

I shake my head. "Last."

"I guessed as much." His lips, which look deceptively firm, mash together, and I'm reminded of what it felt to have his mouth pressed to mine.

The way my body *tingled* as soon as we touched.

I'm overwhelmed with an urge to flee him and the memory, but then he beckons me closer with a quick flick of his hand. "Come take a look."

With shaky legs, I step forward until I'm close enough to smell the crisp, clean scent of his cologne. I'm a glutton for punishment, so I take another sniff because why the hell not? It's not like things can get any more awkward between us.

"See this?" He holds up the stick with tiny markings.

Even with contacts, I need to squint to read it. "What am I looking at?"

He points at one line with an *F*. "This is where your oil should be." His finger travels down the stick until it nearly reaches the end. "And this is where it is now."

"I'm guessing that's not great."

"Unless your goal is to kill your engine, no. It's not."

I look up at the sky and pray for patience when Lorenzo shifts the stick so I can get a better look.

"See how it's dark?" he asks.

"A bit hard to miss." The bead of oil at the end of the stick is nearly the same shade as his eyes, hair, and today's suit. He skipped out on wearing a tie, but I imagine it would match his doom-and-gloom aesthetic.

"That means you need to get it changed, along with your serpentine belt, which looks like shit, by the way."

"I knew you loved collecting cars, but I had no idea you knew how to fix them too." The comment slips out. Typically I pretend we hardly know each other, especially around my family, but I forgot myself.

He puts the metal stick back where it belongs before he stands to his full height and assesses his stained hands. "Do you have a rag or something?"

I pluck his fancy pocket square from his jacket and hand it over. "This looks like it could work."

He grabs it with a fake smile. I ignore the way the tips of my fingers tingle when his brush against mine, just like I ignore the small jolt in my chest when he stares at his hand too.

He wipes engine grease from his well-manicured fingers and tosses the stained silk square into the trash bin next to us before asking, "When's the last time you changed the battery?"

"Recently."

"Are we talking in the current decade?" His smile grows, along with the pain in my chest. Countless times I've seen *Vote Vittori* lawn signs, street banners, and local television ads promoting his mayoral campaign, so I *should* be used to it.

My gaze drops to his mouth before I look back at the engine. "I'm going to grab my phone and call the mechanic. He can come out and take a look."

"The shop's closed already."

"Great," I mumble to myself.

He shuts my hood. "I can give you a ride home."

"I'd rather walk."

"In the middle of a heat wave?"

I give his suit a quick pass. "I don't see you struggling."

"This is nothing compared to Vegas."

"Huh. And here I thought you spent the last two decades in hell."

"Sure felt like it sometimes." His light tone doesn't match the dark, intriguing look in his eyes.

"Hm," I reply while chanting *We don't care enough about him to ask what he means* in my head.

"Do you want a ride or not?" He pulls out his key ring from the interior pocket of his jacket. "I don't have a lot of time before my next meeting."

I stare at him without saying anything.

"I'll even call Manny on the way and ask him to come here first thing tomorrow morning."

My brows rise. "I wasn't aware that you're on a first-name basis with the town's mechanic."

"He didn't give me much of a choice."

"Aw. Look at you making a friend. Should I warn him about what happens when anyone gets too close?"

"You and I were never friends."

A sharp pain shoots through my chest. "Great. Since you

cleared up that misunderstanding, you'll understand why I don't accept rides from strangers." I curse to myself, knowing I revealed way, *way* too much about how hurt I am.

Feeling both embarrassed *and* annoyed at myself, I reach inside my car and grab my purse from the passenger seat. The white envelope peeking out makes my bad mood even worse, so I need to get out of here before I say or do something I'll regret.

"Thanks for the help." I lock up my car without looking at him.

"You hate me that much?" he says, low enough for no one around to hear us.

I start walking in the opposite direction without replying.

I don't look back because I'm too afraid of my eyes revealing the answer to his question.

CHAPTER TWO

Lorenzo

like clockwork, I stop by Rose & Thorn every week to pick up my two bouquets. The task has become an essential part of my routine and, frankly, something I've looked forward to since I moved to Lake Wisteria almost two years ago. My schedule of campaigning and never-ending meetings can be taxing at times, but something about the floral shop located in the town's quiet Historic District and the carefree florist who runs it breaks up the monotony of my life.

The same florist who chose a grueling, thirty-minute walk in the middle of a heat wave over my offer to drive her home.

I'm reminded of Lily's decision as I step out of Rose & Thorn with my order. Her car is still abandoned across the street—if I can even call the hunk of metal she owns a *car*.

Lily claims the billionaire Lopez cousins are like family

to her, but if that's the case, why are they allowing her to drive around in a rusting metal death trap with a rear bumper held together by prayers and duct tape? Or better yet, why hasn't her sister, who is a wildly successful interior designer, gifted her a car?

From my point of view, it seems like no one cares enough about her safety to step in and send the car straight to the junkyard.

I try to remind myself that Lily isn't my problem—how I made sure she would never become one either—but then I remember the state of her testing dipstick, worn tires, and serpentine belt, which looks one rotation away from breaking.

Given her stubbornness and general dislike toward me, I don't trust Lily to follow up with most of the concerns I noted, so I'll take it upon myself to make sure her car gets the full workup. If the Lopez cousins get pissed off about it, even better.

I grab my phone and reach out to Manny, the mechanic who became my friend after I hired him to service my twenty cars. Before he inserted himself into my life, I only had two friends in town—Willow, who I pay to help me with my campaign, and Ellie, who happens to be her best friend.

ME

Will you do me a favor?

MANNY

For my best friend? Of course.

I roll my eyes.

ME

What's the going rate for a new battery, serpentine belt, and an oil change?

MANNY

For you? A day driving your Ferrari.

ME

No.

MANNY

Okay. I understand. What about the superbike?

ME

Do you even know how to drive a motorcycle?

MANNY

No, but I'm thinking about having you park it outside Last Call so I can stand by it and hope a woman takes me up on a ride.

ME

And if they do?

MANNY

I haven't thought that far ahead yet.

ME

It's a real mystery why you're single.

MANNY

Is that a no on the superbike?

ME

Yes.

MANNY

I take it the Lambo is also off-limits?

ME

You guessed correctly.

MANNY

Fine. I'll send an invoice for the battery and belt, but friends and family get free oil changes.

ME

Thanks. The tow truck will drop off Lily's car in an hour.

MANNY

Lily...Muñoz?

ME

Yes?

MANNY

Interesting.

MANNY

You sure you don't want to ask her out on a date?

I ignore his question and ask one of my own.

ME

Fix the car first thing in the morning?

MANNY

Morning? I plan on heading to the shop now and getting started once it arrives.

My good deed is quickly spiraling into something else thanks to Manny's ability to romanticize the mundane.

> **ME**
>
> That's unnecessary.

> **MANNY**
>
> Nonsense. Can you imagine what she'll think about you if she wakes up to find out you already had her car fixed?

Doubt anything will change her opinion of me, but Manny isn't aware of what happened between Lily and me. No one is.

> **ME**
>
> I'd rather we not find out.

> **MANNY**
>
> Please. It'll be part of my best man speech when you get married because of me.

Manny is both a romantic and a certified yapper—two qualities I'm uninterested in exposing myself to—but he is also thoroughly up to date on all the town gossip, so I've accepted his quirks in exchange for information.

> **MANNY**
>
> For the record, my full name is Emanuel, so feel obliged to name your first kid after me.

I pocket my phone and ignore the way it vibrates from whatever ridiculous messages Manny is sending me right now about Lily.

During the charity softball game two weeks ago, he caught

me checking out Lily, but he didn't say anything until after he saw us having a little *chat* at Last Call after the game.

Should Manny decide to make a big deal about this, I'll remind him and anyone else how I'm helping someone in need…even if that someone happens to be the woman I pushed away because falling in love with her isn't an option.

I take a seat in front of the one-way mirror as Willow, my publicist, campaign manager, and unsolicited friend, sits beside me. We both watch as a campaign volunteer walks into a conference room full of townspeople. She asks the focus group to have a seat at the long table before she reviews today's payment and the rules.

"Please feel free to be as honest as you'd like while answering the questions. Your paperwork will remain anonymous, and anything you say in this room will be kept private."

The ten people fill out the paperwork full of questions. A woman I once politely turned down after she asked me out on a date looks up from her clipboard and clocks the one-way mirror, but thankfully she doesn't say anything to the rest of the group.

Once an elderly man with a pocket protector and aviator reading glasses finishes his set of questions, the volunteer asks the first one.

"In your opinion, what are the three biggest problems facing Lake Wisteria today?"

A few people share similar responses: property taxes increasing, the growing class divide, a similar concern I have about a billionaire real estate developer named Julian Lopez turning older homes into summer houses for the new and more affluent residents.

I'm not surprised by everyone's answers to the next set of questions, although I'm bothered by how they respond to the volunteer asking, "If you had to pick between Lorenzo Vittori and Trevor Ludlow, who do you think would do a better job protecting the town's interests?"

It's nearly a clean sweep in Trevor's favor despite his family playing a significant role in all their concerns, and it makes me question what I'm doing wrong because I'm campaigning in their best interests.

Trevor Ludlow—like his father, who is retiring this election season—comes from a long line of town mayors, so his nepotistic connections run deep. Their family is a pillar in the community, while I'm still viewed as an outsider despite my Lake Wisteria birth certificate.

Maybe if people knew more about the man vying to replace his father, they'd reconsider, but that's one of my biggest problems with this campaign. No one knows the truth about Trevor and what he cost my family, so they have no problem voting for him.

"Does anyone want to expand on their answer?" the volunteer asks.

The elderly man with five different pens inside his front pocket readjusts his glasses. "Trevor Ludlow is the best choice—even if he's new to the job. His family has run the city council since it was founded, so I trust him to uphold our values and traditions."

LAUREN ASHER

A woman with pink stripes in her hair nods. "And he's one of us."

People easily forget or ignore how I spent the first decade of my life growing up in this town until I became an orphan.

Another man in his early forties talks next. "Yeah, I agree. There's something about Lorenzo that I don't trust."

Next to me, Willow scribbles on her notepad, jotting everyone's points down as if we haven't heard them countless times before.

"What do you mean?" someone calls from the corner of the table.

"Doesn't anyone find it strange how he came out of nowhere two years ago and decided to run for mayor? It's not as if he has deep ties to the town, and he isn't like Trevor, who has a legacy he wants to protect, so what's his deal?"

Revenge. Simple as that.

I look forward to dismantling life as the Ludlows know it, and it all starts with removing them from their century-long position of power. For a family who values their pride, reputation, and social status, losing the election will be a huge blow they probably won't recover from.

"And what about a family? I heard Lorenzo hates kids, so it's not like he plans on settling down here," the woman with pink hair adds.

"He'd have to be open to dating to want that," the woman I rejected says while looking at the mirror.

Safe to assume I'll never get her vote.

"Maybe it's for the best. We don't need him bringing his

family's mafia business here," the forty-year-old man with a blue ball cap on says.

Another person chimes in with "Oh, I heard about that. Do you think that's why he sold his shares of the family company?"

"He did?" someone else asks.

"Yeah. A random article I read online mentioned how he and his uncle would get in arguments during board meetings. Nearly came to blows once."

Yes, while that *is* accurate, I would've put up with my uncle if it weren't for how he hid the truth about my parents' accident. After I found out what really happened, I quit my job as the director of operations, sold my Vittori Holdings shares, and walked away without looking back.

A quiet member of the group speaks next. "Apparently his uncle hired a hitman to kill Lorenzo's father, which is why they never found the person responsible for the hit-and-run accident."

Yet another lie.

"I always thought it was strange how the Vittoris mostly kept to themselves. Lorenzo's mother was nice and involved in the church, but there was always something…off about his father," the same man in a ball cap says.

If by *off* he means diagnosed with obsessive-compulsive disorder, then fuck him very much. My father was a good man, although his struggle with OCD could be downright debilitating—a daily mental battle I'm all too familiar with thanks to my own diagnosis.

I want to barge in there and say *No, I don't hate children* and *No, I'm not involved in the mafia, although I can't say the same for my uncle and cousins who are in the casino business*—a fact the Ludlow family likes to remind everyone all too often.

My teeth grind together, and I reach inside my pants pocket and pull out my lucky dice. I roll the glass cubes between my fingers, the familiarity of the indentations soothing me until I'm no longer seething.

The volunteer scrambles to get the session back in order, but the focus group quickly goes from gathering useful intel to people making the most inaccurate assumptions about me.

After spending the last year campaigning on ideas like preserving the town's historic character and improving local services for the youth and elderly townspeople alike, it's frustrating to be typecast as something I'm not.

If I don't find a way to improve my image and give people the confidence to vote for me, I'll never be able to catch up to Trevor Ludlow. And if I don't do it soon, my nightmare scenario will quickly become an unbearable reality.

secret garden studio

WWS ???
wildflower wishes studio

petal + press

the Pressed Petal

CHAPTER THREE

Lily

When I get home after my walk from hell—seriously, I question if my pride was worth the extra cardio—I take a cold shower before heading to our garage.

My mom encouraged me to convert it into a small work area last year, although I don't know how much longer I can keep using it. I've outgrown the space, and our neighbor's band practicing their set list in the garage across the street gives me a headache.

Somehow I tune out the negative thoughts and electric-guitar sounds, focusing instead on the beautiful, all-white bridal bouquet with tulips, snapdragons, and calla lilies I designed for a Lake Aurora bride.

Once my back starts to hurt from being hunched over for too long, I keep myself busy by folding the mountain of dark clothes on my bed.

In the middle of organizing my closet, I send a cardboard box toppling off the top shelf. Colorful clothes fly past me and land in a scattered mess at my feet, a mix of fabrics ranging from frilly and impractical to vibrant and eye-catching.

Ruffles and bows galore, satin skirts in every shade of the rainbow, neon athletic clothes that can be spotted a mile away in the dark, and shoes with hand-painted flowers and butterflies.

My heart painfully clenches as I shove everything back into the box and return it to the shelf before checking my vibrating phone.

I open the Kids' Table group chat I have with my sister, Dahlia, her boyfriend, Julian, and his cousin, Rafa, who shared a photo of him, Nico, and Ellie, Nico's nanny, snorkeling in Hawaii. Nico's dark hair is sticking up in all directions, similar to his father's, while Ellie looks like a blonde mermaid.

It's the smiles on everyone's faces that make my chest ache in the best kind of way. I don't remember the last time I've seen Rafa or Nico look so happy, especially not together, so I comment on how cute they look before sending an SOS message.

ME

Can anyone help me jump-start my car?

RAFA

Again?

JULIAN

Isn't this the second time in a month?

ME

Yes, but it's my car this time. Not the company van.

RAFA

In that case, no.

ME

You're not even in Lake Wisteria right now!

RAFA

I'm speaking on behalf of Julian and myself.

ME

Julian is a strong, independent man who can think for himself.

RAFA

Well, he *thinks* your car is shit, but he's too nice to say it.

ME

That's rude.

JULIAN

Maybe, but he's not exactly wrong...

JULIAN

Your car IS a road hazard.

ME

For who?!

RAFA

Anyone who might be driving behind you.

ME

> Unlike some of us who have been in an accident recently, I'm a good driver.

JULIAN

> That might be true, but your bumper does fall off if the tape gets too hot.

ME

> You know what? Forget I asked for help.

Julian sends me a private message, apologizing for taking his joke too far before offering to pick me up in twenty minutes. I only agree because I can't survive another walk across town in this weather, although my pride stings a bit at him calling my car shit.

Julian drives around in his dad's old truck, so I expected him to understand my inability to let mine go, but I guess my Corolla doesn't have the same appeal as the vintage truck he restored.

Dahlia, who never responded to the group chat, waltzes into my room. "I've got some new ideas for the expansion!"

My stomach drops, and my smile along with it, when I see the thick binder in her arms. It's full of design ideas for Rose & Thorn's spin-off business—a venture I dreamt up with her a few years ago.

She jumps into big-sister mode as soon as she notices the look on my face. "What's wrong?"

Everything, I want to answer, but the thought of talking to her about the condemnation notice feels impossible, and not because of the NDA.

The pressed-flower business has been on my vision board for three years, ever since I created an art piece for a client who wanted to preserve the bridal bouquet I made her, but it finally became an achievable goal once Rose & Thorn's sweet, elderly neighbor offered to sell me her shop last month.

Now, thanks to Mayor Ludlow, there won't be a store on Lavender Lane to buy anymore.

At least not for *me*.

After spending a year scouting locations around town and being outbid on multiple properties I loved, I can predict that finding a new one won't be easy. Rental spaces are impossible to come by, and any available properties to purchase are way too expensive to justify the cost.

Hence my predicament.

I take a seat on the corner of my bed. "I'm stressed."

"About the car?" So she *did* see our messages.

I nod.

She places the binder on top of my desk before leaning against it. "If you want, we can go visit some dealerships together this weekend. It could be fun to take a few out for a joyride…"

"I don't want a new car."

"No, but you *need* it."

My gaze drops to the carpet.

She talks when I don't. "If it's about money—"

"It's not, and even if it was, it's *your* money, not mine." I make a good salary managing Rose & Thorn, and I live at my mom's house, where I only need to chip in for groceries and utilities, so I save most of my income.

"I want to help you."

"I appreciate it, really, but I love my car."

She grimaces. "But you know Dad would want you to have a new one if he was still here."

But he's not, I want to say.

Similar to Rose & Thorn, the car he bought Dahlia and me is one of the last memories I have of him, so replacing it isn't an option, even if it's firing on its last cylinder.

She shakes her head. "Getting a new car doesn't erase his memory."

Her comment hits way too close to home, and I look away because I don't trust myself not to cry.

My sister stands and pulls me into a hug. She's slightly shorter than me, so her dark hair tickles my nose.

Her arms tighten around me. "I only bring it up because you deserve a car you can rely on."

"But they don't make them like they used to anymore."

"Are you twenty-eight or eighty-two?"

I push her away with a laugh. "Now enough about my car."

"Fine." Dahlia heads back to the desk to grab the binder. "Let's talk about the Pressed Petal."

"I never agreed on an official name."

"We'll keep workshopping it." She flips the binder open to the first page.

My eyes mist as I check out the mock-ups she created of a showroom full of pressed-flower art pieces. Her design brings the gallery idea I had to another level, telling a visual story of how I turn wedding bouquets I design into works of art for newlyweds.

"It's…wow." I clear my tight throat and flip to see the next page, which is a mock-up of the hidden work studio located on the other side of the sales floor-slash-gallery.

Dahlia's voice cuts through my fantasy turned unachievable dream.

"I still need to figure out what floor and paint samples you like best and what kind of wood species Julian will use for all the custom frames he'll make, but it's starting to all come together." She smiles, and I match it with a much weaker one.

It's hard not to feel guilty about the entire project given how invested my family is in making it happen. I try to brush the feeling off, but doubt lingers in the darkest shadows of my mind, never letting me fully enjoy my sister's hard work.

Tomorrow you'll figure it out, I tell myself.

But today… Today, I can't.

Julian shows up and invites Dahlia to tag along with us as we head to the Historic District. It's not a long drive, but it quickly becomes an annoying one when I can't go more than thirty seconds without being reminded of the mayoral race.

Many lawns are adorned with signs supporting either Lorenzo or Trevor Ludlow. Trevor's signs outnumber Lorenzo's, and he probably used his dad's connections to hang a particularly large banner across the most popular street in the Historic District.

To be honest, I don't like either candidate for different

reasons, although Lorenzo has a lead over Trevor since the former isn't trying to tear down my shop and all the history that comes with it.

After seeing one too many *Vote Vittori* signs, I decide to shut my eyes until Julian pulls to a stop.

"Did you forget where you parked?" Dahlia asks.

I sit up and look out the window. "No?"

I'm confused by the vacant spot where my car was parked earlier this afternoon.

"Don't tell me your car got stolen." She sounds a bit too excited at the idea.

"I doubt it," Julian mutters.

"Hey!" I poke him in the shoulder. "I'll have you know my car made it onto the Top Ten Most Stolen Cars list."

"In the nineties?"

Dahlia giggles, earning a small smile from Julian. My heart responds with a twinge, followed by the usual sense of yearning.

I want to have a connection like theirs with someone else, but nothing I've done has yielded promising results. I tried a running club (loved the cute outfits, hated the actual running part), I signed up for different dating apps (which I swore off after my experience with *Laurence*), and I agreed to a few blind dates (not all of them sucked, but none of them ended with me meeting the love of my life either).

So here I am, a witness to everyone else's love story after spending so long wishing for mine.

Dahlia breaks through my pity party and asks, "Should we file a report with the sheriff?"

"I guess?" I have no idea who would go through the effort of stealing my car given its current state, but maybe they wanted the parts.

Five minutes later, I follow Dahlia and Julian into the police station. A few people working the phones look up and wave, while two deputies seated at their desks stare at Dahlia and Julian like they might need their handcuffs.

"I hope you two aren't here to cause trouble." The sheriff sizes Julian up.

"No, sir." Julian turns red, and I enjoy the sheepish look on his face too damn much. After he and Dahlia got arrested last year for public indecency, I'm surprised he agreed to walk inside here.

"We're only here to report that Lily's car was stolen," my sister says with a grin, clearly enjoying the way Julian tries to make himself look smaller. Best of luck since the man is built like a linebacker.

The sheriff's white brows crinkle in my direction. "Where did you last see it?"

"Outside Rose & Thorn."

Using the radio strapped to his shoulder, the sheriff relays the information to his deputies before asking us a few more questions.

"You two aren't playing a prank on her, are you?" Suspicion bleeds into his voice.

Dahlia and Julian both shake their heads, and the sheriff reports back to his team. The three of us talk about the latest episode of our favorite reality dating show while we wait for an update.

Finally the sheriff's radio beeps with an incoming message from one of his deputies. He listens before looking up with raised brows. "Your car is at Manny's shop?"

I blink twice. "How did it get there?"

The sheriff asks his deputy to get more information, and we all wait to figure out what the heck is going on. It takes the deputy a few agonizingly slow minutes, but he returns to let the sheriff know the car was being repaired at Lorenzo Vittori's request.

Julian looks irritated at the mere mention of Lorenzo's name, while Dahlia's stare is shrouded in suspicion as she turns to look at me.

A few people whisper behind me, probably questioning why I would have anything to do with Lorenzo, and I don't blame them. In their eyes, we're like two puzzle pieces that don't fit together.

I need to do some serious damage control—and fast—but I have no idea where to start.

Thankfully the sheriff breaks the tension by asking, "Would you like to press charges?"

"What?" I ask, completely taken aback by the question.

"Yes," Julian answers for me.

Dahlia tugs on his shirt. "Julian."

"He stole Lily's car without her permission."

I rub my temple. "He didn't *steal* my car."

"Technically, he did take it without your permission," the sheriff clarifies.

"You're not helping," I mutter before speaking louder. "He was trying to do something nice for me."

Three sets of eyebrows rise, and instantly my plan to pretend that I hardly know Lorenzo goes up in flames, and he has no one to blame but himself.

X secret garden studio

WWS ???

wildflower washes studio

petal + press

the pressed petal

CHAPTER FOUR

Lily

There aren't many people inside the police station, but my face heats from the ones looking over in our direction as Julian slowly turns his body away from the front desk and faces Dahlia and me. "Since when does Lorenzo care about your car?"

"He saw me struggling with it and came over to help," I answer.

My sister rubs her forehead in confusion. "Which led to him sending it to the mechanic without you knowing?"

"Yes. It's a sweet thought, right?"

Her mouth presses into a flat line, as if to say *No.*

"What was he doing at Rose & Thorn anyway?" She switches up her interrogation, and I scramble to keep up.

"He comes by every week to pick up his flowers."

"What flowers?"

I look down at my shoes. "The two bouquets he orders."

"Oh my God." Her eyes bulge. "He's still doing that?"

"Yes?" It comes out like a question rather than a fact.

"Why?"

"I don't know."

"Are they for another woman?"

"They'd better not be." My tone is a hint too icy, and my sister frowns.

Julian scowls at the visible sign of her unhappiness. "I didn't know he was bothering you, but I'll talk to him."

"He's not *bothering* me, and no, don't you dare make a big deal out of nothing." My cheeks feel hot.

The sheriff and the secretary working the front desk pretend to be busy, but I catch them stealing glances.

"Why is your face turning pink?" Dahlia asks me point-blank.

"Because you're asking me a bunch of questions."

She grabs my arm and pulls me toward the front door while Julian says, "I'll get back to you on filing the report."

"No, he won't," I call out before I'm dragged outside.

Dahlia's nails dig into the flesh of my arm until we're standing by Julian's truck. "Okay. Spill. What's going on between you and Lorenzo?"

I look at her with raised brows. "There's nothing to spill."

"You're hiding something." She crosses her arms.

I do the same. "I'm not." *Outside of keeping a two-month situationship a secret, that is.*

"Then why can't I say Lorenzo's name without you turning two shades pinker?"

"It's nerves."

"Since when do *you* get nervous?"

I shrug.

"Do you like him?" she asks without any prelude.

"*No*." I sound genuine, but my incriminating face doesn't help matters.

"Hm," she says unconvincingly. "Does *he* like *you*?"

I can't help laughing at the absurd question. "Isn't that the million-dollar question."

Her brows hike toward her hairline. "What if that's why he wanted to fix your car?"

I shake my head, not trusting my voice. I never told my sister about Lorenzo and the dating app, and I don't intend to share our story now, especially not when she is this concerned about him liking me.

Imagine how she'd react if she learned I like him back.

Liked. You liked him back.

I bite down on my tongue.

Julian steps out of the station with a scowl directed straight at me. He stays rooted in place, giving Dahlia and me space to finish our conversation.

I look back at my sister. "Can you go calm your boyfriend down before he strains a neck muscle or something?"

She doesn't move from her spot. "He can wait."

Great.

"If you're interested in Lorenzo, you can tell me. I won't judge you."

Consider me surprised. "Really?"

"Of course. I want you to be happy."

"Even if I'm happy with Lorenzo?"

She doesn't look too excited when she nods, but maybe her strained expression has more to do with Julian drilling a hole into the sides of our faces.

"Don't worry." I spare her from answering my question. "I don't want anything to do with him."

She exhales. "Thank God. That would've been complicated." *Tell me about it.* "You know how Julian feels about him."

I force a laugh. "Isn't it kind of silly for Julian to still be upset with Lorenzo? All he wanted to do was buy a few properties your boyfriend was interested in."

"I think Lorenzo also beat him in an elementary school spelling bee once." She chuckles to herself.

"They weren't even in the same grade, so it wasn't a fair fight."

"Okay, you're right. That one is ridiculous."

"Thank you."

"But what about Lorenzo being involved in the mafia?"

"That's a dumb rumor the Ludlow family made up because they want to scare people into voting for Trevor instead of him."

My sister's mouth falls open.

"What?" I ask.

"For someone who claims they aren't interested, you are quick to defend Lorenzo."

"I dislike the Ludlows for lying. That's all."

"Fair enough."

"Are you done interrogating me now?"

She clears her throat. "Perhaps I came off a bit…strong before—"

I cut her off with a sharp look.

She laughs. "Okay, I gave you the third degree. But I was taken aback. Lorenzo isn't known for being sweet, so I was worried he had some ulterior motive or something."

"Oh, I'm sure he did." Lorenzo wouldn't help me unless it benefited him somehow.

"I only ask that you be careful. The last thing I want is for you to get hurt by someone like him."

"It's sweet of you to care, but your worries are unwarranted. I've got it all covered."

Lorenzo might've hurt me once, but I'll never give him an opportunity to do it twice.

I'm sure of it.

Julian drops me off at home before taking Dahlia out for dinner, so I switch into my PJs and heat up some leftovers. While the food is in the microwave, I finally work up the courage to text Lorenzo.

ME

Why did you take my car to the shop?

He doesn't answer me, so I distract myself with eating dinner. My mom isn't back from her Bible study group yet, so I keep myself occupied with my phone while I wait for his reply.

When he still doesn't reply after twenty minutes, I follow up with another message.

ME

> I was in the middle of
> filing a stolen car report
> when they found it.

I hit Send and instantly regret not adding more, so I type up another text.

ME

> The sheriff, his deputies, and
> Julian and Dahlia know what
> you did, so if people start
> assuming you like me or
> something, it's all your fault.

Despite him not showing any signs of answering me, I end up falling asleep to thoughts of him.

When I wake up the next morning, my phone is bombarded with new photos Rafa shared of him, Nico, and Ellie enjoying a sunset in Hawaii. My mom and Josefina, who raised Rafa like her own son, Julian, are losing their minds in the Lopez-Muñoz group chat over how cute Nico and Rafa look in their matching swim trunks, so I add a comment of my own.

ME

> You're practically
> unrecognizable with
> a smile on your face.

Rafa answers with an eye-roll emoji.

JULIAN

Wait. That's Rafa?

DAHLIA

I forgot what he looked
like without the beard.

Rafa sends a single middle-finger emoji to our Kids' Table group chat, most likely because my mom would pass out at the vulgar gesture.

I exit our chat and check my thread with Lorenzo, wondering if he answered, only to be disappointed when I find out he never replied.

Are you really surprised after he ghosted you?

No, but it still sucks.

I carry on with my morning routine, only for it to be derailed when my mom asks me about my car, which she saw outside. I'm shocked to find it parked in our driveway with a note tucked under the brand-new windshield wiper.

keys are hidden by your favorite place.
Ps: Like your car, it's in need of some repairs.

With how much he ignores me and our shared past, I'm surprised he referenced a conversation we had on the Eros app where I told him about my three favorite places in Lake Wisteria— one of which is in my own backyard. At the time, I thought I was so unbelievably clever, dropping a clue about my house in hopes of Lorenzo searching for me like some Dreamland prince.

Once upon a time, I wished our story would end with a happily-ever-after, only to realize Lorenzo is the villain in mine.

The handwritten note crumples underneath my fingers, and I toss it into the trash before walking over to the small fountain my dad installed. My mom has had it fixed a few times over the years, but she gave up on it a while back, so I took over the responsibility.

The fountain located in a corner of our yard was my dad's labor of love because it broke down more often than it worked. So much so, it became a running joke between our parents, with my mom threatening to get rid of it and my dad convincing her not to.

It was his happy place, and when he passed, it became mine—up until last fall when I ran out of the gold coins he gave me when I was little.

After spending years preserving the fountain and the garden surrounding it, I started neglecting the area. Spring came and went, and the rose bushes my father loved withered away until they stopped blooming altogether.

A chill spreads across my arms as I head down the winding path leading to my dad's garden. Dried leaves and pebbles crunch underneath my shoes as I walk below the trellis that once was covered with blooming bougainvillea. While the flowers are long gone, the hedge surrounding the entire garden has the opposite issue, growing wilder by the week.

I follow the winding path toward the fountain. The mostly dry basin is full of stagnant rainwater, disgusting muck, and an endless number of leaves. A few quarters sit at the bottom of the bowl too, but it's the gold coins that catch my attention.

"Make a wish." My dad offered me a golden coin from his satin drawstring bag after tossing his into the fountain.

I crossed my arms and raised my brows. "Those never come true."

He cracked a smile. "I used to think that way too."

"Really?" I asked, surprised.

"Yes." He nodded. "Then one day, I made a wish and then I met your mom, and I never stopped wishing ever since."

"Like what?"

"I can tell you now, but only because they came true." He knelt down so we could be eye level. "I wished for you." He bopped my nose. "I wished for Dahlia. I've wished for so many different things in my life because to wish is to hope, and that's the one thing no one can take away from you."

My eyes sting, and I turn away from the fountain until I'm no longer at risk of crying. Maybe my mom was right about getting rid of it, because its decrepit state is more depressing than comforting.

The fountain or you?

Desperate to leave this place, I search for my keys until I find them on the pedestal.

I go inside the house and get dressed. Once I'm done with my makeup, I head into the kitchen in search of coffee. My mom is leaning against the counter, watching her favorite morning talk show on her tablet while sipping coffee from a mug.

I'm surprised to see her already dressed for work when

she isn't on the schedule today. She only comes in a couple of times a week now that I'm a co-owner of Rose & Thorn, although she's always happy to help me with large orders or rush deliveries.

It was hard to convince her to take a step back, but after the doctor noted their concern about her heart and some unideal test results earlier this year, she finally listened to Dahlia and me.

"*Hola, Mami*." I kiss her cheek before making my own cup. "*¿Estás trabajando hoy?*"[1]

"Yes, I plan on stopping by this morning to check on some bookkeeping things, but I'm only going to be there for a few hours before my hair appointment."

"Want to grab lunch afterward?" I reluctantly offer, knowing I'll have to get the uncomfortable conversation out of the way sooner rather than later.

"Sure. I'd love that."

My pulse grows stronger with each heavy beat of my heart. "Great," I manage to say, the word fighting to make it past my tight throat.

She pats my cheek affectionately on her way to the sink. "You okay? You look tired."

I cringe. "I didn't sleep the best, to be honest."

"Did it have something to do with your car being stolen yesterday?"

"It wasn't *stolen*," I say.

---

1   **Estás trabajando hoy:** Are you working today?

"According to Julian, it was."

"Julian's only annoyed Lorenzo got involved."

She doesn't crack a smile. "Manny's mother texted me to tell me how sweet it was of Lorenzo to cover your repair bill."

This is news to me.

She continues, "Apparently Lorenzo asked Manny to give it a full workup."

"Maybe Manny should practice mechanic-client privilege."

My mom makes a face. "I don't know if that's a thing."

"Well, it should be with how much Manny and his mom like to talk," I grumble more to myself than her.

She toys with her crucifix pendant. "Sweet boy. It's a shame you don't like someone like him."

"Seeing as I grew up during his *eat dirt* phase, I'll politely pass on the opportunity."

"Better him than Lorenzo."

I swallow hard.

She continues, "*Perdóname, mijita[I].* I'm a little concerned, but do you blame me? Julian doesn't like him, which is what worries me most."

"Who is Julian to talk? Half the town still dislikes him for tearing down heirloom homes and turning them into gray boxes."

"Liliana!"

"What? You know it's true."

"He had good intentions."

I **Perdóname, mijita:** Forgive me, my daughter.

"Okay, so let me get this straight—if Julian does something wrong or unlikeable, it doesn't matter because he had good intentions, but if Lorenzo does something nice, he must have some secret motive?"

Perhaps deep, *deep* down, part of me feels protective over Lorenzo because once upon a time, I *did* like him, and people judging him makes me wonder what would've happened if we had become a real couple.

At least you'll never have to find out.

I decide to grab two sandwiches before meeting my mom in the Park Promenade for lunch. We sit at a bench underneath one of the structures, watching boats glide across the water and a group of summer campers prepare for a hike around part of the lake.

I'm so anxious to talk to her about the letter, I can only manage a few bites of my food. When my mom asks me if everything is okay, I decide to open up to her.

"I want to start with saying I have everything under control." I don't, but I *will*.

"Okay…what's going on?"

Her face leeches of color as I describe how the condemnation act works.

"So that's it? They buy us out, tear down the building, and repurpose it?"

I nod. "They are offering a lot of hush money to those who sign an NDA. That combined with the purchase price for the property would be hard for people to resist."

She clutches her chest, and I panic. "Are you feeling okay?"

My mom's heart condition is minor, but her doctor said any additional stress and high blood pressure can turn it into a much bigger issue.

She shuts her eyes and nods. "I'm a bit…overwhelmed."

"I'll figure it out, *Mami*. No one is going to take our shop away from us."

She cups my cheek. "I know you'll try your best."

Not exactly the vote of confidence I need, but I'll take it.

"But…" my mom starts, and now I'm the one who's suffering from cardiac issues.

"What?" I whisper.

"I don't know if there is anything we can do."

"Of course there is." I just haven't figured it out yet.

"How much money are they offering?"

I grab her letter from my purse and hand it over.

Her eyes go wide as she reads it. "That is a lot more than I thought."

"Yup." I scowl. The Ludlows are mega-millionaires who can afford it, which is why they wouldn't care if Julian offered them triple the fair market value to stay away from Lavender Lane.

My mom continues looking at the fancy piece of paper. "Liliana…"

"No," I immediately say.

Her gaze darts back to the paper. "I think we should sign the NDA."

"What?" I screech. "Are you joking?"

"We could split the money—"

"I don't want anything to do with it."

"But you can use your half to open the Pressed Petal somewhere else in town." I'm upset she would even suggest such an idea, seeing as I rejected Julian's, Dahlia's, and Rafa's offers to loan me money.

I shake my head. "Absolutely not."

"Why not? I'm getting closer to retirement, and then you'd be free to chase your own dream."

Angry tears spring to my eyes, coming in hot and heavy. "Rose & Thorn is a big part of that."

Can she not see how the two ideas go hand in hand? There wouldn't be a petal-pressing business without Rose & Thorn's customer base, and the main reason I enjoy creating the art pieces is because I am a part of the wedding bouquet-making process from the start.

I don't notice a tear slipped out until my mother wipes it away.

"No llores," she says softly while pulling me into a hug. Her embrace is tight, and the smell of her perfume is familiar, soothing the ache in my chest.

"I can't lose this place, Mami." It's Papi's and her legacy, and I desperately want to be a part of it. My sister always had dreams that were bigger than this town, but Rose & Thorn...it was the beginning of mine.

She brushes my hair out of my face before cupping my cheek. "Even if we lose Rose & Thorn, I want to say I'm so

---

I   **No llores:** Don't cry.

very proud of you, *mija*. You took our legacy and made it even better, and if your father was here, he would be just as proud of the successful woman you've become."

I frown. "Why does it sound like you're quitting?"

"Because…I don't know if I have the fight in me anymore. I'm tired, and hiring a lawyer sounds stressful. Way more stress than it's worth."

I know she doesn't mean to hurt me, but her giving up feels like she is turning her back on me.

This is her anxiety talking, Lily.

I put my feelings aside. "If the buyout wasn't an issue, would you keep Rose & Thorn?"

"Of course. I love that shop." Her voice cracks. "I know you've taken on more responsibility, but my heart will always belong there. Your father and I…we put our heart and soul into it, and it will always feel like home."

Which is why I'll save it one way or another. "Please. Give me a chance to figure this out before you throw in the towel."

My mom takes a few deep breaths. "Okay. How about this? I'll schedule a meeting with Mayor Ludlow to discuss the letter and voice my concerns while you think of some solutions."

I might not like it, but I think I know exactly where to start.

The enemy of my enemy is my friend, and his name happens to be Lorenzo Vittori.

Secret Garden Studio

WWS ???
Wildflower Washes Studio

Petal + Press

The Pressed Petal

CHAPTER FIVE

Lily

Before I reach out to Lorenzo's team to schedule a meeting to discuss the city council's buyout plan and ask for help, I want to consider all my other options.

After thirty minutes, I narrow my ideas down to two: my original one of meeting with Lorenzo, or starting a petition to abolish the amendment, which gives the mayor permission to buy up properties.

The Ludlows want discretion, so it makes sense to do the opposite, but what if it affects those who might have already signed the NDA? Would there be legal or financial consequences for them? Just thinking about the loopholes makes my head hurt, so I ditch that idea and go with my first one.

Maybe Lorenzo's campaign manager, Willow, can help

come up with a better solution to my problem. She's Ellie's best friend, and I was in the same running club as her before I graciously bowed out after a disastrous 5K, so I feel comfortable enough to talk to her about the issue.

My worries lessen when Willow answers me back and invites me over to her house for a wine night, only for them to reappear thirty minutes later when I'm dropped off by my mom at her front door.

What if she can't help me?

What if Lorenzo agrees with the Ludlow family because my part of the Historic District is run-down?

What if—

"Oh, it's you! Thank God." Willow opens the door and yanks me inside before closing it.

"Were you expecting someone else?"

"Hopefully not," she replies before shutting all the blinds and curtains in her living room.

"Is everything okay?"

"Yes!" She turns with a huff. "We might have to swap the wine for something a bit stronger though."

"What happened?"

"I'm having a bit of a campaign emergency."

"Who knew a small-town mayoral election could have such issues."

"You're telling me."

"Want to talk about it?"

"Sure, but first let me give you a quick tour." She shows me around her two-bedroom bungalow, which is nestled in front of Lake Wisteria. I love everything about the quaint space, but

I'm pretty sure my sister would have a meltdown at the clashing fabrics, bold paint colors, and interesting choice of green carpet in the sunken living room area.

Design choices aside, I'm surprised Willow hasn't sold the place because I'm sure her lakefront property is worth a million or two for the land itself.

Her phone rings in the distance.

"Do you want to answer?" I ask.

"Nope."

I follow her into the small kitchen, where her laptop was left open beside a half-empty bottle of wine.

"Got started without me?" I joke.

She laughs while pouring me a glass. "I only needed a minute to recover from the new poll numbers I got."

"Not what you wanted to see?"

"Nope." She tops off her glass and uncorks a new bottle. "Just in case," she says when I look at my full glass.

"I'm sorry about the polls."

She shuts her eyes. "Me too. Ten points... Ugh. Lorenzo's going to be so pissed."

"Ten points? That doesn't seem too bad, right?"

"It might not sound like a lot, but it might as well be thirty when we have less than five months left until election day."

I wince. "Oh. In that case..." I hold my glass up, and she clinks hers against mine.

"I've been trying to help us get ahead. With single-issue voters, Lorenzo's gained good ground, but now he's fallen behind with more complicated swing voters." Her computer makes a noise, and she quickly becomes distracted with something on the screen.

"Shit," she mutters under her breath, completely forgetting about me altogether as she scrolls through some PDF with charts and graphs. "He's going to go ballistic when he sees this."

I'm about to say something when her phone starts ringing.

"Called it." She grimaces. "Do you mind if I take this?"

"No. Not at all."

She leaves the kitchen, but her house is less than a thousand square feet, so despite her disappearing into one of the rooms, I can still hear her side of the conversation.

"You saw for yourself how people want someone with connections to the town, and your charity events aren't enough."

Safe to assume she's speaking to Lorenzo, then. I sip my wine and try not to eavesdrop, but that becomes impossible when I hear her say, "You're the one who refuses to find yourself a wife."

I choke on my wine.

A wife?!

Willow groans. "Fine. I meant a *fiancée*. Are you happy now?" There is a pause before she says, "I can only do so much. A ten-point lead is going to be difficult to overcome."

Silence follows, although my rising heart rate fills the quiet while I wait for whatever Willow says next.

"I didn't say impossible, just difficult. Whether we agree with them or not, people associate stability and values with family, so either you pick one of the women I vetted for the job or you can say goodbye to ever winning this election."

I stare at a wall and process what I overheard. I'm so stuck in my own head, I don't notice Willow walking back into the kitchen until she speaks.

"How much did you hear?"

I flinch.

"Shit. Can we…pretend you don't know anything?"

"Um…" I'm so stunned by the entire conversation that I can't even begin to formulate a response, and thankfully her phone vibrating saves me from doing so.

"Dammit," she says when she checks to see who's calling. "It's him again."

"Maybe you should let it go to voicemail?"

"Yes! Love that." She takes a few gulps of her wine.

I take another small sip before saying, "So…fake fiancée?"

She squeezes the bridge of her freckled nose. "I had hoped you didn't hear that part."

"I assumed as much, but your walls are kind of thin."

She rubs her forehead. "He's going to kill me."

"It's not your fault."

"I know, but…" She takes a deep breath. "Since you already overheard the conversation, will you let me vent for two minutes? I swear to shut up afterward so we can focus on whatever it is you came here to talk about, but I need to speak with someone. Ellie's out of town, and I don't want to burden her—"

I stop her from worrying any further. "Sure. What's up?" I play it cool in front of her, but I'm spiraling on the inside because what the hell does she mean by *fake fiancée*? Is that something people *do* in real life?

She takes another sip of her wine before beginning. "You'd be shocked to know how difficult it is to set two people up."

"Coming from someone who has spent years of her life navigating different dating apps, I believe you."

"At least you want a relationship. Lorenzo is the complete opposite, even if it's all fake."

"Hm." I can't say much more with the way my throat tightens.

"I've vetted a ton of options and interviewed a few candidates who I thought were real contenders, yet Lorenzo rejected them all."

"How long has he been looking?"

"It's been a more recent thing," she answers vaguely. "Although about a year back, he used a dating app to try to find a fake fiancée on his own—"

No. I don't realize I said the word aloud until Willow looks at me for clarification.

"He used an app?" The question comes out as a half squeak, half wheeze.

She nods.

Hell no, I say stronger this time, but the sharp pain lacing through my chest doesn't pay it any attention.

There is absolutely no way…

"What was it called?" Do I sound anxious? I can't tell with the way blood is pounding through my ears.

"Eris?" She taps her chin. "No. Wait. *Eros.* Like the Greek god of something."

"Love," I say. "He was the Greek god of love." My voice sounds so small.

"Yes! You're right." She is completely unaware of the damage she's inflicting as she carries on. "I never heard of the Eros app before, but based on how much Lorenzo hated it, I assume it sucked."

"He said that?" My heart feels like it was punctured with a thousand thorns.

"Yes." She nods with pinched brows, only for them to dart up toward her hairline. "Wait. You just said you used dating apps too, right?"

"Yeah." The word slides against my tongue painfully.

"Did you try Eros?"

"Briefly."

"What did you think?" she asks.

"Wouldn't recommend it."

"He said as much too." She laughs while I wish for a hole to open up underneath me.

"So he wasn't looking for a real relationship?" All that time I spent talking to him, imagining a future together...

God. You're so stupid.

"No, and the experience made him shy away from the idea until a month ago."

"Why?" I rasp.

"A focus group pointed out how he lacked any deep connections to the town, and someone said maybe if he had a family, they'd be more likely to take him seriously..."

I'm no longer paying attention. Willow continues talking, but I'm too lost in my own thoughts to reply.

He realized finding someone on an app was a bad idea.

Someone or *me*?

The pang in my chest becomes unbearable, the throb impossible to ignore.

After spending all this time wondering why I wasn't good enough to make him stay, I feel devastated. Deceived. And most of all rejected twice over, because for some reason, I wasn't an ideal choice for his plan.

My heart feels like it's being torn apart once more, and the dull throb in my chest whenever I think of Lorenzo transforms into a full-blown ache that can't be ignored.

"Lily?" Willow asks, yanking me out of my spiral.

"Yeah?" I ask, shaking my head to clear it.

"Do you want to take a seat? You look a little pale."

I take her up on the idea and have a seat on one of the counter stools beside her.

She shoots me a grimace. "I'm sorry for freaking you out. I didn't mean to throw all that at you."

I reach for my wine and take a long sip. "No worries."

"Speaking of worries, could we *please* keep the whole fake-fiancée scandal between us?" She picks at a random cuticle. "I don't want to get into any trouble, and if Lorenzo found out I told you…"

He'd what? Get mad at her? Try to silence me with a bribe or an NDA? I wouldn't put it past him to fire Willow either, and I like her too much to let that happen.

"Of course," I reassure her. "I have no interest in making your job any harder."

The stiffness in her spine lessens a bit. "Thank you."

I bump her shoulder with mine. "No worries. Your secret is safe with me."

"Okay, enough about me. Tell me what's up with you."

I open my mouth to share my concerns about Rose & Thorn's future, but then I slam it shut. After tonight's revelation, I'd rather stick to easy topics because my heart can't take any more.

It's easier to pretend the shop I love—the shop I've poured years of my life and personal savings into—isn't about to be torn down and rebuilt into some luxury commercial building. Just like it's easier to pretend Lorenzo didn't spend two months talking to me solely because he was looking for a fake fiancée.

It's not the right choice, but I want to continue pretending for a little while longer. Tomorrow I plan on talking to Willow about the shop, but tonight…

I'm choosing to forget.

I do my best to ignore all thoughts about Lorenzo, the dating app, and my daunting future. It takes a few glasses of wine, but now that I've got a good buzz going, I'm no longer worried about anything but what song Willow wants to play next.

Or I *wasn't* until someone knocks on Willow's front door.

"Who's that?" I ask, my brows rising at the sound of the heavy pounding.

She gets up from the couch and checks the peephole. "Shit!"

"What?" I ask.

"It's Lorenzo," she whisper-shouts.

I walk up to her side. "Tell him to go away."

"My car is parked outside, so he knows I'm here."

My sluggish brain forgot about that. "So? Establish some boundaries!"

"I know you're in there, Lily, and yes, I can hear you," Lorenzo says on the other side of the door.

"He's so annoying," I say.

"I heard that too." His voice is muffled by the door between us.

I roll my eyes.

Willow snorts.

"Open up," he commands.

"Say he needs to come back tomorrow," I push. "We're having a girls' night."

"And I'm having an emergency," he replies.

Willow grimaces at me while she slides the dead bolt. "Sorry."

"Is it too late to sneak out the back?" I ask before she turns the knob.

"With the amount of wine you drank, I'd feel responsible to stop you." Willow opens the door with a laugh. "Lorenzo! Fancy seeing you here."

"Lily," he says, his gaze instantly connecting with mine like we're the only two people in the room.

It does something funny to my stomach, and I welcome the warmth that comes with his attention, right until it turns to a boil when I remember I'm supposed to hate him right now.

My common sense must have disappeared along with my inhibitions because I stupidly ask, "Are we back to pretending we know each other tonight?"

Willow stares at me with wide eyes. "What?"

"You're drunk," Lorenzo replies.

"Not nearly enough to deal with you at this hour." I hold my glass up higher. The wine sloshes around, sending a few droplets down the side of the glass. I'm quick to lick them up, all while locking eyes with Lorenzo. He holds my stare for a second before his hot gaze drops to my mouth, and I soak up his desire with a smirk.

Who knew a thirty-dollar cabernet turned me into such a seductress?

"I'm taking you home." Lorenzo reaches for the glass, but I pull back.

"No. I'm not ready to go yet, but when I am—which I'm not—I'll request a rideshare." That sounded much clearer in my head than out loud.

His laugh has an edge to it. "That could take at least an hour."

"Better than suffering through ten minutes in your company."

"Um…" Willow's gaze flickers between us. "I take it you two don't get along?"

I turn to Willow and smile through the pain. "Remember that fake fiancée Lorenzo was looking for on the Eros app? You're looking at her."

Willow's eyes go wide with shock.

Shit. Did I say that?

One glance at Willow has me thinking, *Oh God, you totally did*.

Lorenzo's cold stare makes me shiver.

Willow crumbles from the pressure and throws her arms up. "It was an accident! I swear!"

He squeezes his eyes shut and mutters *"Cazzo"*[1] under his breath. The Italian curse word sounds undeniably sexy coming from him, and my stomach flutters.

Must be the alcohol.

"How do you accidentally admit something like that?" he asks.

Willow looks over at me with panicked eyes.

"I'll fix this," I whisper to her, but I'm not sure she believes me—or, more so, believes it's possible to rein in Lorenzo's anger.

"You know what? I think Lorenzo's right." She turns to him. "You should take Lily home because she's clearly had way too much to drink."

With a half smile, half flinch, she snatches the wineglass from my hand, hands me my purse, and pushes me outside before shutting the door behind me.

Damn.

The last person I want to drive me home is Lorenzo, but if it means fixing my slipup and saving Willow's job, I'll do it.

Here's to hoping I don't break down crying in the process.

---

[1] **Cazzo:** Fuck.

CHAPTER SIX

Lorenzo

ily, who seemed mighty confident only a minute ago when she brought up the Eros app, stares at the ground, looking unusually pale. The moonlight reflecting off her skin doesn't help matters, nor does the beige running outfit she has on.

The color doesn't suit her, and neither does black or white, which she seems to prefer as of late.

How is this the same woman who once told me her favorite neutral was pink? I can't make sense of what happened to the confident person I've watched from a distance since I first laid eyes on her.

What did she do with the pearl clips in her hair, or what made her no longer tuck flowers into her face-framing braids? And where did her range of pastel clothing go, or the collection of sneakers she wore with ribbons for shoelaces?

It's like she hit the Factory Reset button on her personality, and while I want to know why she turned into a blank slate of a human being, asking her would make her think I care.

Which I don't.

I can't.

She follows me to my truck, her steps slightly uncoordinated. I'm not sure what possesses me to open her door and make sure she gets into the truck's cab without cracking her head open on the driveway, but I don't shut it until she's buckled in.

Whatever drunken bravado she had during her outburst fades, all while the uncomfortable silence between us grows. It's hard to speak, let alone breathe, in her presence, given her addictive scent of flowers, wine, and something I can't place.

I'd spend the whole car ride trying to determine what it could be, but her speaking ruins the idea.

"Don't be angry at Willow," she says once the lakefront bungalow is in my rearview mirror.

"A little too late for that."

Her hands clench against her lap. "It wasn't her fault."

"Did you force her to talk about it?"

"No."

"Then she clearly didn't have a good enough reason to break her NDA." I keep my attention focused on the road ahead while ignoring the alternating lawn signs supporting either Ludlow or me. Trevor has more, which isn't a surprise, but I'm pleased by my growing number in Willow's neighborhood.

"You can't fire her." Lily turns to look at me.

I don't return her stare. "I can do whatever I please after she broke our agreement."

"No." She grabs my arm. Usually I find people's touch repulsive, yet whenever Lily lays a hand on me, my body doesn't shudder with revulsion. It craves more, and that kind of obsession is exactly why I stayed away from her once we met face-to-face after two months talking on Eros.

When I tense at the contact, she lets go and clasps her hands together instead. "If you fire her, I'll make you regret it."

I can't help laughing. "Are you threatening me?"

She lifts her chin. "Yes."

"And pray tell, what will you do if I fire her?"

"Make your life miserable."

Not a hard task given the state of it, but I'm curious enough to ask, "How so?"

Lily is the type of woman who will get upset over killing a bug, so I can't picture her doing much harm.

"I could ruin your campaign like that." She snaps her fingers.

An amused huff slips out of me. "I'd love to know how."

"You're not the only one who could run for mayor."

"Since when are you interested in local politics?"

"It's a relatively new discovery."

"How new are we talking?"

"Thirty seconds, give or take."

I'm more entertained than annoyed, right until she opens her mouth again.

"Imagine what would happen to the gap between you and Ludlow if I join the race."

I bite my tongue from sharing how I feel. "No one would take you seriously."

"Maybe not everyone, but I only need enough people to pick me over you to do some damage. And who knows. Maybe the town prefers me over you and that other asshole."

"Trevor?" I'm more surprised by Lily calling him an asshole than her flawed plan because I've never heard her speak ill toward anyone, let alone call someone an asshole. What does she have against the Ludlows, or better yet, what did they do to her?

Her nose twitches. "Yes. Him. It's not like he's a good candidate either, so I'd be doing everyone a favor by jumping into the race."

My hand chokes the steering wheel. "You're bluffing."

She smiles. "Do you want to risk it?"

I stew in silence for a minute before speaking up. "What has Willow ever done to deserve this kind of loyalty from you?"

"For starters, she didn't pretend to care about me when she only wanted a fake fiancée, so I automatically like her more than you."

"I..." I *what*? Yes, it's true I joined the app to find a fake fiancée, but I ended up liking her more than I should've, which is why I cut her out of my life.

I had ignored the warning signs—like the urge to constantly check my phone or the worst-case scenarios that played out in my head whenever she didn't answer my messages quick enough—until it was too late.

All it took was one meeting and I became paranoid about growing obsessed with her, like my father was with my mother. They both taught me obsessive thoughts only lead to an early grave, and I refuse to leave this world without stopping Trevor from becoming mayor.

"You *what*?" she asks, annoyed.

"Nothing," I reply.

"Classic Lorenzo, avoiding questions like a real politician."

"I'm *avoiding* hurting your feelings."

"You're a little too late." The way she slurs her words makes me think she wouldn't have admitted that under any other circumstance.

"You're drunk," I say instead.

"What I *am* is sick of all this and you." Her voice cracks. "Were you ever interested in a relationship? Or was it all a part of your bigger plan to become mayor?"

The way I press my lips together is answer enough.

She laughs to herself, the sad sound coming out soft yet no less powerful. "Got it."

I want to tell her that yes, there were fleeting moments where I wondered if I was capable of a relationship like the one she desired, but I wasn't in the mindset for one.

I'm still not in the right headspace. Not when I need to focus on my plan to protect the place my parents loved, and definitely not while I still struggle with being surrounded by memories of my father's obsessive need to make my mother's dream of living in Lake Wisteria come true.

With my right hand on the wheel, I tuck my other one into the front pocket of my pants and touch my father's dice to remind myself of what matters. Of whom I'm doing this all for, and why I can't allow myself to get distracted by a beautiful woman with the most alluring brown eyes I've ever seen.

Lily is quiet for a few minutes before she talks again.

"Why not ask Willow to pick a fiancée from the start? Why try finding one through an app?"

I keep my mouth sealed.

"I deserve the truth," she says when I don't answer. "At least give me that."

My stomach muscles spasm at the idea of hurting her—a weakness that only applies to her—but I take a deep breath and stroke the dice in my pocket to ground myself. "I was bored."

She sucks in a breath.

I continue, knowing my answer will destroy any positive feelings she might still have toward me. "You were the first person who messaged me, and I thought you were funny. I didn't expect anything more than a single conversation, but then you messaged me the next morning…and that night… and I don't know. It went on way longer than I expected."

She covers her mouth with the palm of her hand, and tears fill her eyes. I feel like shit—complete and utter shit at causing her any distress whatsoever.

"Why did you agree to meet up, then? You could've used it as an out."

But instead I met up with her on Halloween, not knowing at the time how that night would change everything. One incredible kiss was all it took to send me running, and I haven't stopped ever since.

I clear my throat. "I will admit that I was curious about what you looked like and why you'd use an anonymous app when you clearly have a decent personality."

The silence is suffocating.

"Then I met you, and it all made sense. You're too…"

She makes a choking sound, and it feels as if she wrapped her small hands around my heart.

"Too…" I struggle to think of something strong enough to deter her.

"*Too* what?" Her voice sounds so damn distant, and I realize it's because she's moved as far away from me as humanly possible by tucking her body against the door.

I deserve the sick feeling bubbling in my stomach and much more as I throw the final emotional punch. "You were too much for someone like me."

You wanted kids, a husband, and a dog, while I only cared about myself, I want to tell her.

You'd spend all your energy defending a man who your family doesn't like and never will, I nearly add.

I would've become obsessed with you. Completely, utterly, undeniably obsessed, and it would've killed me in the process.

"Pull over!"

My head whips in her direction. "What?"

She reaches for the handle.

Shit! Is she about to open the door to a moving vehicle?

"I'm going to be sick!" she shouts with misty eyes.

"Fuck! Hold on." I turn the wheel to the right, nearly swiping another car parked along Main Street in the process of parking in the emergency lane.

Lily jumps out of my truck before I can pull to a full stop. I'm not fast enough, so she is already bent over and retching in front of the fire hydrant by the time I get to her.

I reach for her hair and pull it back from her face.

"I hate you." She lets out a strangled sob that chips away at my icy heart.

"I know." I adjust my grip on her hair so I can capture a few loose strands that were hanging in her eyes.

"You taking care of me right now changes nothing."

I tighten my hold. "Wasn't expecting it to."

"I'm aiming for your precious little Ferragamos next."

"They're far from little, but be my guest. I deserve it and worse."

My comment seems to set her off in the worst possible way.

I'm surprised Lily has anything left in her system, but she manages to vomit again. She doesn't spin around and shoot for my shoes like promised, but a bit splatters against the handmade Italian loafers.

Obsessive thoughts about cleanliness rise to the forefront, waging a war against my better judgment.

My inner voice is loud and intrusive as it says, *She could pass that sickness along to you.*

She's drunk, not sick, I try to reason.

Are you absolutely sure, though? What if she passes something along and you're bedridden for weeks?

Weeks? That's ridiculous.

I'm ripped away from the conversation happening inside my head when Lily turns away from the hydrant and teeters before reaching for my thigh. Her touch is innocent, only meant to catch her balance, but heat courses through my body.

She sags against me. "I think I'm done."

I don't entirely believe her. "You sure?"

"I hope so, but there's only one way to find out."

See? She's still not feeling well, so it can't be the alcohol.

Oh, fuck off, I reply to myself.

I release the makeshift ponytail I made. I doubt she wants her hair in her face right now, so I gently remove the hair tie from her wrist and pull it back—something I've never done for another woman before.

I ignore why that is and say, "I'm going to run inside the bar and get you some water."

"Okay."

I pluck her hand from my thigh, ignoring the electricity shooting across my skin as I direct her toward a bench. "Stay."

"Wasn't planning on going anywhere."

I rush inside Last Call, ignoring the people gathered around the window who witnessed Lily's incident. Their attention is redirected to me as I head over to the bar for a cup of water.

The bartender tries to offer me the smallest plastic cup, so I toss a hundred-dollar bill on the counter and ask him to fill up a large plastic pitcher instead. Someone seated at the bar hands me a few sticks of gum, and I take them with a quick thanks before heading outside with Lily's water.

I pass it to her, and she retains her gracefulness as she rinses her mouth out before taking a few delicate sips from the pitcher. It doesn't take long for her arms to start shaking, so I hold it up for her until she says she's done and then offer her a stick of gum.

I'm placing the pitcher on the ground when she goes to stand. She seems to overestimate her sobriety, and she stumbles forward.

I jump to my feet and wrap an arm around her to stop her from falling over. "You good?"

She leans into me and shuts her eyes. "I'll answer once the world stops spinning."

I take the opportunity to get a good look at her. Even with tangled hair, a sickly tinge to her skin, and smeared eye makeup, I still can't take my eyes off her.

"I can feel you staring at me," she says without ever opening her eyes.

I deflect in an act of self-preservation. "Your mascara is running."

"Just when I thought tonight couldn't get any worse."

I grab my pocket square and wipe at her cheeks and underneath her eyes before cleaning the corners of her mouth.

Throw that infested rag away right now, the voice speaks up.

I'm about to when I look up from her mouth to find her staring back at me with wide eyes.

"What?"

She looks away. "Feeling a little dizzy."

My arm curled around her tightens.

You're supposed to let her go and walk away before she gets you sick. I breathe heavily through my nose.

And what are you still doing holding on to that disgusting pocket square? I drop it on the ground and kick it away right as someone calls Lily's name.

"I thought I recognized you, but I couldn't be sure," the woman says to my back.

Lily's gaze snaps toward the person, and her already wide eyes stretch to their limits.

"Jane," she squeaks out. "What are you doing here?"

"Uh…it's Trivia Night at Last Call." Jane, the Rose & Thorn employee Lily recently hired, comes up to stand in front of us.

Lily turns her head and finally notices where we are. I follow her stare and clock a few people standing in front of the bar's window. They're quick to turn their heads, but it's too late.

Lily and I seem to be collecting witnesses like some protection program.

"Lorenzo." Jane shoots me an indecipherable look before her attention is diverted to the fire hydrant. "Are you okay?"

Lily winces, and I absorb the recoil like it's my own. I'd remove my arm from around her waist, but Lily still looks shaky, so I keep my hand glued to her hip, pretending I don't notice the slight tingle in my fingertips at the close contact.

"I'm not feeling my best," Lily replies.

"What happened?"

"I think I got a bad case of food poisoning."

"Oh no!" Jane's gaze flickers over to me. "Good thing Lorenzo was here to help you." She sounds genuine.

"Yeah, he was giving me a ride home." Her eyes comically widen when she notices the mistake.

"From where?" Jane asks, giving me a second glance.

"Uh…" Lily scrambles, making our situation worse.

I step in. "I took her out to dinner to apologize for the incident with her car."

Jane nods. "Ah, yes. It's been the story of the week."

Of course it has.

Jane's gaze falls to the soiled sidewalk.

I intervene before she can ask any more questions. "We should get going…"

Jane smiles at Lily. "I'll bring you some of my mom's chicken noodle soup tomorrow. You look like you could use it." She heads back inside Last Call, leaving Lily and me alone.

Lily slips out of my hold and manages three whole steps in the wrong direction before I loop my arm around her and direct her back to my truck.

"I really hate you," she says as I help her inside.

After tonight's confession, I'm inclined to believe her.

CHAPTER SEVEN

Lily

The next morning, I wake up with the worst hangover, and no amount of greasy food or pain relievers can fully cure it. I haven't made myself sick from drinking in years, so I'm still shocked about what happened.

Part of me wishes I blacked out because I remember the conversation Lorenzo and I had right before I told him to pull over, and I've been suffering from an ache in my chest whenever I think of him since.

You were too much for me, Lorenzo said, driving a knife through my already-bleeding heart.

What utter bullshit.

I've heard a variation of those words before from past men I've dated, and while I wondered if Lorenzo felt similarly, it still hurts to have my worry confirmed.

I stare at the box of clothes hidden in my closet and question if I should show Lorenzo what it looks like to be *too much*, only for me to shake my head.

Don't reveal how much his words got to you, I tell myself before picking a simple black dress and driving to work.

Word travels fast here, so halfway through the sluggish workday, I've collected ten bottles of ginger ale, four Tupperware containers of chicken noodle soup, and the largest bottle of Pepto-Bismol I've ever seen.

Between people passing by and my sluggishness, I don't stop to check my phone until I lock up for the day and head to my car.

The Lopez-Muñoz chat is active, but I'm more interested in a new message from Willow.

WILLOW

> Whatever you did to convince Lorenzo not to fire or sue me, THANK YOU!

I blink twice at the message.
Did I say something? I don't remember—
Oh.

ME

> It's the least I could do after risking your job to begin with.

ME

> I'm SO sorry about mentioning the fiancée thing. You asked me not to say anything, and I broke my word.

WILLOW

No worries. All is forgiven!

ME

Really?

WILLOW

Yeah. I can't completely hold your drunk actions against you when I'm the one who suggested opening another bottle.

ME

I'm old enough to cut myself off before I ever let myself get to that point.

I was too down on my luck to stop, but I've learned my lesson.

WILLOW

Out of curiosity, how did you convince Lorenzo to keep working with me?

It takes me a few seconds to remember, and when I do, I groan.

ME

I may have threatened to run against him.

WILLOW

I had no idea you're interested in politics.

ME

I can get a little sassy when drunk.

Not that I think my attitude had any sway over Lorenzo's choice to keep working with Willow.

WILLOW

I'd say!

WILLOW

Thankfully whatever you said worked because he's pretending last night didn't happen.

WILLOW

But don't assume you're off the hook because I need to know everything about you, Lorenzo, and the Eros app.

So much for my plan to put last night behind me, and it's all thanks to my big mouth and hurt feelings.

Two days later, I'm scheduled to open the shop before our second-newest employee takes over for the afternoon. I'm not much of a morning person, so I treat myself to an iced coffee from the Angry Rooster Café.

A few people in the café stop me to chat, and I entertain their conversations before I have to drag myself back to my car and drive over to the Historic District.

My stomach sours when I find the mayor and his two sons standing in the middle of Lavender Lane, reviewing what looks to be architectural plans. I'm tempted to keep driving around until the Ludlows leave, but I still need to wrap up the flower-wall design before we open for the day, so I park my car in an empty spot and walk over to Rose & Thorn.

My shop is in the Ludlows' direct line of sight, so I brace myself for the inevitable.

"Lily!" the mayor calls out. I would love to ignore him, but I'd risk looking too immature in front of Richard, so I turn to face the three of them with an empty feeling in the pit of my stomach.

Mayor Ludlow has overseen Lake Wisteria for nearly three decades after taking over from his late father, and he recently celebrated his sixty-fifth birthday last year before announcing his upcoming retirement.

"Mayor Ludlow." I take advantage of our proximity and memorize the company logo on the corner of the plans.

The mayor keeps a smile in place while he rolls up the paper, but I don't return it before acknowledging his other son. "Trevor."

I ignore Richard altogether, earning a raised brow from Mayor Ludlow and a grin from Trevor. The eldest Ludlow son is thirty-five, while Richard was born five years later. They look similar with their matching blond hair and blue eyes, although Trevor stands out with his warm smile and friendly demeanor.

Of the two Ludlow sons, Trevor is the more approachable one, so I understand why Mayor Ludlow chose him as his predecessor over Richard, who usually looks like he is suffering from a chronic case of IBS.

Or maybe he only appears that way around me.

"Nice to see you, Lily," Trevor says.

"What are you all doing out here?" I ask.

Mayor Ludlow's smile returns. "We're going over some of the architect's plans for Lavender Lane."

My heart stutters. "A bit premature, don't you think?"

"I want to hit the ground running after I'm sworn in." Trevor winks.

"Assuming that even happens." I spare Richard a glance and wish I hadn't.

His icy-blue eyes are laser focused on me.

"We know the letter must've come as quite a shock," Mayor Ludlow speaks. "But Trevor is going to make sure everyone is taken care of and given first dibs on the new retail spaces."

"How thoughtful of him to offer us an opportunity to buy our own properties back for quadruple the price."

"We understand rent prices have gotten a bit out of hand…" the mayor says. "But we're partnering with the local bank to offer small business loans to those who are misplaced."

"You mean the bank you own?"

The mayor's smile falters. "Yes, but our rates are competitive, I assure you."

Richard, who probably suggested Lavender Lane for this plan to spite me, says, "For the price we're paying for the building, you should be grateful."

"I guess I'm too blinded by my rage to appreciate your generosity."

Richard shrugs.

Any lingering hope of convincing the mayor to change his mind goes up in flames because there is no way Richard will let that happen. He resents me far too much.

Mayor Ludlow intervenes. "What Richard means to say is that we want to take good care of your mother and everyone else on this street. That's why we're giving everyone six months to get their affairs in order because we know this will be difficult on everybody—"

I interrupt, "Which I'm sure Richard *loves*."

Mayor Ludlow looks at us curiously, most likely confused since no one in town knows that Richard and I had a short fling.

Whoever said the best way to get over someone is to get under someone else clearly left out a few important details, like don't assume it'll make you feel any better, and more importantly, do not pick a person who can make your life miserable should you break things off with them.

"A word, Lily?" The vein in Richard's jaw jumps.

I'm about to deny his request when he grabs my elbow and steers me away. Once we round a corner, he spins around.

"Have some class and stop making a scene in front of my family before they realize my lapse of judgment."

My mouth falls open. I don't want anyone to know what we did either, but damn, it still stings to be spoken to like that by someone I was once intimate with.

He continues, "Whether you like it or not, this project is happening."

"A project that is purely coincidental and has nothing to do with what happened between us a few months ago, right?" I reply sarcastically.

His smile is all types of wrong. "I have no idea what you're talking about."

I take a deep breath and push my feelings aside for the greater good of Lavender Lane. "Seriously. Can you act like an adult and put an end to this vendetta? Or at the very least, keep it between us and don't target innocent people."

He shrugs. "My father always had these plans. I just happened to suggest Lavender Lane over his other option."

I throw diplomacy out the window. "You're such an asshole."

"At least I own it. I can't say the same about you."

My face turns red. He might see me as one, but that doesn't make it true.

I *never* led Richard on, and I was vocal about only being interested in something casual, especially after the situation with Lorenzo. When I realized I still had unresolved feelings for him, I respectfully told Richard where my mind was at and ended things like a mature adult.

Even though Lorenzo ignored my existence, my heart was still invested in him, and Richard took it more personally than I originally thought. I can take a few guesses as to why he felt slighted, but I bet it stems from an inferiority complex that began when he was labeled the *spare* to his brother's *heir*.

"You know how many women would have been grateful to be in your shoes?" he asks.

I'm not sure how I keep from gagging. "Sounds like you shouldn't have a hard time finding someone else, then."

"I liked you. I really did, to the point where I was willing to look past your particular…quirks." His gaze is as demeaning as his words, but I act like they bounce off the white two-piece set I borrowed from my sister, even when that isn't the case.

Judgy gazes or comments like his are why I started dressing like I do now. Because my closet and the clothes I wear reflect who I am at my core, and I'm not interested in sharing that part of my heart with people who openly judge me or use it against me.

I'm too vulnerable at the moment, but I won't be like this forever.

Just for *now*.

Richard leans in, an air of vicious energy surrounding us as he whispers, "But I should've known you were too good to be true. That there had to be a reason most men stay away from you, including the one you still had feelings for, and it isn't because you're a prude like some people assume."

I flinch and instantly hate myself for showing a reaction. He said something similar after I told him I couldn't continue seeing him, so I should've been better prepared, but I'm sensitive, especially after the other night.

Instead of giving Richard an opportunity to tear me down some more, I walk away, exhibiting more maturity in ten seconds than he has in his entire life.

I was already motivated to save my business, but this conversation with Richard took the fire burning inside me and doused it with gasoline. I don't care what it takes, but I'm going to make sure Trevor and his entire family lose all their power over this town—even if it means putting my anger aside and teaming up with Lorenzo to make it happen.

My mom breaks down as soon as I walk inside her bedroom.

"I'm sorry, Liliana," she cries, her anguish etched into the fine lines of her face. "I tried to talk to the mayor, but then he showed me all the plans, and he tripled the money the city council is offering if I signed the NDA right there. I couldn't say no. Not when I knew there was nothing I could say or do to change his mind."

All my rage from earlier today is wiped away, replaced with worry.

"Mami." I help her take a seat at her vanity. "Take a few deep breaths."

I model a lungful, and we both breathe in and out until she is no longer hyperventilating. I've had lots of practice over the years, so I have a whole toolbox of techniques to help my mom through her anxiety attacks, along with a sixth sense I've developed to anticipate them before they happen.

Once she gains control over herself, she shows me the NDA, which requires her secrecy in exchange for a hefty sum of money. If she tells anyone about the plans, she will face a bunch of legal repercussions.

The mayor and his sons backed us into a corner because even if I wanted to tell the town about the Lavender Lane plans, I couldn't do so without putting my mother in financial and legal jeopardy—something they know I'd never risk.

Richard successfully trapped me, but I won't accept my fate without putting up a fight.

Un Muñoz nunca se rinde[I], I tell myself while accidently crumpling the pages of the NDA.

I   **Un Muñoz nunca se rinde:** A Muñoz never quits.

My mom's wide-eyed gaze flickers over my face. "Please don't be angry at me."

I smooth the paper out and get better control over my facial expression. "I'm not angry." Disappointed, yes, but how can I be angry when she is clearly struggling with her choice?

I reach for her hand and give it a squeeze. "I wish you had talked to me first since we're in this together," I say, exhaustion bleeding into every syllable. "But I understand he put you in a difficult position."

One that I'm partially to blame for, which is why it's up to me to find us a way out.

CHAPTER EIGHT

Lorenzo

Willow paces behind me while I watch the focus group through the one-way glass once again. Things between us are a bit tense, but hopefully she doesn't hold the Eros app situation against me for long.

"What are key traits you look for in a politician?" our campaign volunteer asks the group seated at the conference table.

I brace myself for their responses.

"Honesty," one man says.

"Kindness," another adds.

"A good sense of humor," the town's paid-by-the-hour party clown replies, earning a mixed reaction.

The volunteer allows a few more people to answer before asking, "When you hear the name *Lorenzo Vittori*, what's the first thing that comes to mind?"

The responses are mixed, ranging from *casinos* and *fancy cars* to *charity fundraisers* and *Julian Lopez's nemesis.*

"Lily." Nura, a woman I recognize from my time volunteering at the animal shelter, speaks up.

Someone goes *"Aw."*

"What do you mean?" a person near the head of the table asks.

"I was at Last Call the other night when Lily got sick and Lorenzo took care of her."

A few people nod and make confirmatory noises as if they know what Nura is referencing.

Someone raises their hand. "I was there too. It was sweet of Lorenzo to hold Lily's hair back."

"Talk about doing the bare minimum," a woman replies in a sarcastic tone.

"Actually, he wiped her tears, cleaned her mouth, and ran inside the bar to get her some water, so I'd say he did way more than that."

"Has anyone texted Lily to see how she is feeling?" a woman fidgeting with her pearl necklace asks.

An older woman with white hair says, "She's good. I brought her some soup after I heard what happened."

Someone asks, "Am I the only one who's confused? What was Lily doing with Lorenzo?"

The woman decked out in pearls replies, "I heard a rumor that they had dinner together before she got sick."

Multiple gasps fill the room. I imagine it must come as a shock to hear that I, an alleged mafioso, was hanging out with the people's princess. Based on their reaction, I bet someone might suggest locking Lily up in an ivory tower and throwing away the key.

Nura lifts her shoulders. "I don't know, but I'm not surprised to see them together."

"Why not?" the person at the back of the table asks.

"They both volunteer at the shelter, so they've crossed paths before."

Everyone speaks at once, and it's chaotic trying to absorb all their responses.

"Wait. Lorenzo volunteers at the shelter?"

"I didn't know he liked animals."

"Lily and Lorenzo? There's no way. Julian *hates* him."

My gaze flicks to the ceiling.

This is what you get for trying to be nice.

Willow halts her pacing and drops into the chair beside me. "I'm interested in seeing how this all plays out."

"In what sense?"

"It's Public Relations 101. If you—a man without any connections to the town—are seen with one of the most beloved residents, it's bound to have a positive effect on your approval rating."

"Are you suggesting I hang around Lily some more?"

She chews on the inside of her cheek. "I shouldn't after the stunt you pulled on her."

"But if it's good for the campaign…"

She releases a reluctant breath. "Then I suppose it's worth a try."

"How much influence could a few encounters have?"

"They brought her homemade soup, Lorenzo. You

know what happened to me when I got the stomach bug in January?"

"You got soup too?"

"No, I wish. I was stuck heating up a can of Campbell's while Lily, the people's princess, was given the royal treatment." She follows up with a laugh, so at least she isn't bitter about the favoritism. "It makes perfect sense why people would react so positively to you taking care of her. They adore her."

The other night, I was reacting out of pure instinct when Lily got sick, so I'm surprised people care more about that than all the good deeds I've done on purpose.

Throwing a charity softball game to raise funds for a park? People were happy, and the polls reflected that, but it didn't have a huge impact on my overall ratings.

Investing my personal time and injecting money into small businesses around town in exchange for company equity because I want them to flourish? Great for the town and venture capitalism, but no one talks about it because needing money is a sensitive topic.

But helping Lily Muñoz when she's sick? Now *that* interests people, and it cost me nothing more than a pair of thousand-dollar shoes, an extra dose of Vitamin C, and washing my hands until my skin was cracked and bleeding.

Great. I bite back a groan.

"I think we should do a little experiment," Willow says once the focus group moves on to answering another question.

"Based on the smile on your face, I'm good."

"What if I told you there's a chance it could impact your polling numbers?"

"In that case, I'm a huge fan of the scientific method."

When I call Nura the next morning to switch my time slot at the animal shelter, claiming I can't make it for my usual shift, she laughs and says it's no problem. After yesterday's focus group, I had a feeling she would give me the same volunteer block as Lily, and my intuition was right.

The only issue? I had no idea Lily's shift was taking place at the Park Promenade, where the shelter is hosting an event to encourage adoptions.

During the first hour of our shift, Lily hangs out with the dogs underneath the canine tent while I work the parking lot, encouraging people to stop by the shelter's pop-up adoption center. Thanks to the afternoon sun hanging over us, my volunteer shirt sticks to my back, and my nose and cheeks are getting progressively more burnt.

Despite volunteering at the shelter, I don't *interact* with any animals. I prefer it that way, and I have a childhood trauma of losing my own dog to blame.

But if I want to see an impact on my town approval rating, I need to step out of my comfort zone, and doing so means ditching the clipboard and heading toward the crowded tent full of people, dogs, and Lily.

It isn't fair for me to use her after I rejected her. I'm well aware of that, and honestly I'm ashamed by the idea, but not enough to stop myself. I have too much on the line and not enough time to come up with a better plan.

Lily catches me by surprise by waving at me. A few people turn to see who she's looking at, including myself, only for me to curse when I don't see anyone around.

After shaking off my foolishness, I dip my head underneath the tent and instantly notice the drop in temperature.

Lily walks over to me when my eyes are closed. "Here." She presses a cold water bottle against my chest.

"Look at you caring about my well-being."

"Well, unfortunately for me, you can't become mayor if you're dead," she replies with a toothy smile.

"Since when do you care whether I win the election?"

"Since I realized you're the best of two bad options."

I place a hand over my heart. "Can I use that quote on an ad?"

"If you want my endorsement, I'm sure there are better quotes you can use."

I consider that the green light to absolve my guilt and continue my experiment because I can't think of a better endorsement than her company.

Someone standing nearby shifts a few feet closer to us, and I grin.

Willow will be pleased.

Lily's gaze falls to my mouth. "What?"

"Nothing." I crack open the water bottle she gave me and drink half of it in a few gulps. Her eyes drop to my throat before she quickly looks away, her cheeks burning like she was standing in the sun.

Clearly affection may come and go, but attraction is a lot more difficult to shake.

I would know.

She doesn't look at me when she asks, "Don't you have a parking lot to work?"

"Eh. I think I'll hang out in here for a bit."

"Just my luck." She grimaces.

Nura walks over to us, a wide smile stretching across her face. "How's it going over here?"

"Good!" Lily clasps her hands together. "I was meaning to come find you. I thought I could switch places with Lorenzo and give him a break from the heat."

"That's so nice of you!" Nura cradles her clipboard against her chest.

"It's not necessary," I interject.

Lily ignores me and stares straight at Nura. "Really. I don't mind. I could use a little sun, and he's been working the lot for an hour already."

Nura sends Lily off with a new clipboard, ruining my plan to be seen together for longer than a few minutes.

Lily might've outsmarted me, but I won't stop until I prove Willow's theory correct. But first I need to make sure Lily can't escape me so easily next time.

X secret garden studio

wws ???
wildflower botanics studio

petal + press

The Pressed Petal

CHAPTER NINE

Lily

After my embarrassing incident, I want to avoid Last Call, but I couldn't turn down Dahlia and Julian when they invited me out for drinks. It's hard enough to share some quality time with my sister, so I'd rather take advantage of the opportunities I do have.

I haven't had a chance to talk to her about Lavender Lane or the NDA yet since she's been busy and out of town, and because I can't exactly open up about it in the middle of a crowded bar, I'll have to pretend nothing is wrong.

How very on-brand for me lately.

Once Julian returns with our mocktails and takes a seat next to Dahlia, she starts talking about the gallery idea for the Pressed Petal.

"I'm thinking sleek, modern frames with some good

backlighting to showcase the art." She pulls out her phone so Julian can see the mock-up.

"Looks easy enough," he replies before taking a pull from his beer bottle. "Although I think the art should be suspended from the ceiling rather than hung on the wall. That way people will have a three-sixty view of the piece."

Her face lights up. "Good idea! But wouldn't it weigh too much?"

He scratches his jaw while considering it. "We can add some extra support beams and drill into them."

I hear the faint sound of a cash register in the distance, getting louder with every one of Dahlia and Julian's expensive ideas.

"Maybe we should stick to hanging them from the walls," I offer.

"Do you not like Julian's suggestion?" she asks without any judgment.

"Depends on if it fits within my budget."

Julian leans back in his chair with a smile. "We told you not to worry about that."

"And I told you that I wanted to do this on my own."

To some, it might seem silly to reject a billionaire's offer, but I've spent my life watching Julian, Rafa, Dahlia, and my mom become successful, self-made entrepreneurs. I've witnessed firsthand how much time and energy they put into achieving their goals, and I want to do the same, even if it takes me longer to accomplish mine.

Dahlia swallows a sip of her drink. "We'll run the numbers and make sure to stick to the budget you gave us." She turns to look at Julian. "How long would it take you to do all the lighting?"

He is cut off by the last person I expect to show up. "Julian."

No.

Julian twists his torso in the direction of the smooth voice I'd recognize anywhere. "Lorenzo."

"Dahlia." Lorenzo dips his head before tilting it in my direction. "Lily." He says my name with a hint of a sexy rasp.

I nod before taking a sip of my water. When I look up from the table, I find a few people glancing in our direction.

Great.

Julian gets right to the point. "What do you want?"

"I was hoping we could talk about the endorsement you promised."

"I'm a little busy right now," he replies.

"What endorsement is he talking about?" Dahlia asks with a furrow between her brows.

"An unimportant one," Julian mutters under his breath.

"Don't sell yourself short," Lorenzo taunts before looking over at Dahlia. "Julian is speaking at a fundraiser event for my charity."

"I wasn't aware you had one," Dahlia replies.

Lorenzo steps closer to my chair, so his arm ends up brushing against mine. "It's still pretty new. I started Healing Hearts over two years ago."

"What's it for?"

"Supporting families affected by drunk drivers."

My sister's eyes soften. "That's a great cause."

Our town hasn't faced many tragedies, so everyone knows

about how Lorenzo's parents died in a hit-and-run accident. While the other driver was never found, could they have been drinking? If so, how did they get away?

Lorenzo's next comment snaps me out of the thought. "I'm surprised Julian didn't mention anything since he's a guest of honor."

A few days ago, Julian was giving me a hard time about Lorenzo fixing my car, only to become his *guest of honor*?

"Since when do you support Lorenzo?" My tone reeks of annoyance. I should be happy because a Lopez endorsement could go a long way for Lorenzo's campaign, but I'm too irritated to think about the bigger picture right now.

Especially after Lorenzo's confession the other night about the Eros app.

"Rafa asked me for a favor, so I had no choice but to agree to Lorenzo's endorsement request," Julian answers.

I pause at his phrasing. "Must've been one hell of a favor since you're deathly afraid of public speaking."

Julian sinks deeper into his chair, giving me nothing but anxiety to go off.

Lorenzo takes a seat on the empty barstool next to mine and casually wraps his arm around the back of my chair like we do this all the time—a move Julian takes note of immediately.

Before anyone can comment on it, Lorenzo states, "Rafa came to me for help, and I delivered, so that's all that matters."

"Couldn't you have helped him for free?" I ask, somewhat snippy.

"That would require a conscience, and Lorenzo was born without one." Julian smirks.

"I'm sure Lily would disagree with you." Lorenzo turns to hit me with an incriminating smile. "Especially after what happened the other night?" He teases the end of my ponytail as he winds a strand around his finger.

What is going on here? Speaking at the adoption event is one thing, but touching me like this in front of everyone?

Did he get abducted by aliens? If so, how do I convince them to take him back?

Julian's brows crinkle as his dark gaze swings toward me. "What's he talking about?"

"What happened while we were gone?" Dahlia asks at the same time.

I could strangle Lorenzo for the chaos he is causing, but my expression doesn't reflect my innermost thoughts. "Nothing important."

"On the contrary, I take Lily's health *very* seriously." He pushes my cup of water closer to me.

I respond by kicking my foot out. I aim for the leg of his chair, but I accidentally hit his shin instead. *Oops.*

"One kind act doesn't make you a hero," I reply with a tight smile.

"So you admit I'm kind."

"Only on rare occasions when it benefits you."

"In what way did you puking all over my Ferragamos benefit me?"

My sister's mouth falls open. "Wait. She *what*?"

"There's a reason Lily skipped out on her regular passion-fruit vodka seltzer tonight." Lorenzo has the audacity to look concerned over my health.

My head is reeling from this conversation and Lorenzo's proximity. If I wasn't stone-cold sober, I'd question how much I had to drink.

Not enough to make it through whatever he has planned.

For the life of me, I can't make sense of what changed since the Last Call incident, but I need to think fast, and I need to do it right now before Lorenzo gets too bold.

"I had too much to drink, and Lorenzo offered to drive me home. I ended up feeling sick during the car ride, and the rest is too embarrassing to talk about."

Julian makes a noise of discontent. "I'm not sure what disappoints me more: you getting drunk enough to think Lorenzo driving you home was a good idea, or you not getting sick *inside* his car."

Lorenzo's smile drops. "I'd *never* take advantage of her or any other woman, if that's what you're suggesting."

Something in my stomach flutters, and I wish I could crush the butterflies with my fist.

Julian shrugs. "*You* said it, not me."

Dahlia crosses her arms. "Am I the only one confused about what's going on here?"

I'm about to add my two cents when Lorenzo speaks up. "Now that everyone knows about Lily's and my relationship, I thought there was no point in hiding it anymore."

Dahlia's mouth falls open. "Your *what*?"

"Friendship," I correct, although it kills me to suggest such a thing.

My sister doesn't look happy at the word. "You two are... friends? Since when?"

Great question I'd love to know the answer to.

Lorenzo doesn't look too pleased at my save, but too freaking bad.

"I don't believe it," Julian scoffs.

I'm relieved once Lorenzo turns his attention away from my face and looks over at Julian. "Well, you didn't want to believe me when I told you Santa wasn't real either, so I'm not surprised."

I blink twice, and Julian's face turns red in an impressive five seconds flat.

Dahlia bursts out laughing. "Hold on. Is that the real reason why you hate Lorenzo?"

"No. It's one of many." Julian's posture turns rigid.

"What happened?" she asks. "I thought this was all because he wanted to buy a house you liked."

"*Houses,*" Julian grumbles. "He tried multiple times."

"Only because you made it impossible to get a single one of my offers accepted," Lorenzo replies.

Their dislike for one another stems deeper than just one misunderstanding, right? It has to, or else I'll never let Julian live this grudge down.

"You could've paid more for a house," Julian snaps back.

"I wasn't interested in participating in your billionaire pissing contest."

"From what I heard on the news, you aren't one anyway."

Lorenzo smirks. "Keeping tabs on me?"

"More like I'm invested in your downfall."

"You are aware I'm still worth a quarter of a billion, right?"

I choke on my drink because no, I didn't. Obviously,

Lorenzo still has money despite quitting his job at Vittori Holdings and selling his shares, but I didn't realize he had that much.

"Did you selling your shares have something to do with the company's value tanking from your poor decisions as the director of operations, or was it because you were jealous that your cousin replaced you?" Julian's chair creaks as he leans forward.

Lorenzo laughs. "Me jealous of my cousin? He is the one who wishes he was me because unlike him, I had the courage to walk away from everything."

Acid churns in my belly at Lorenzo's candidness.

Julian raises his brow. "You couldn't keep your emotions out of business decisions? That doesn't sound like a trait we need in our future mayor."

"Julian," I reply with a hiss, directing my frustration at him. "Enough."

"*¿Dije algo mal?*"[I] He tries to look apologetic, but it fails to work on me.

"*¿Puedes tratar de comportarte bien?*"[II]

"*Él empezó.*"[III] He huffs.

"*Tienes treinta y un años, por el amor de Dios. No te comportes así.*"[IV]

I   **Dije algo mal:** Did I say something wrong?

II   **Puedes tratar de comportarte bien:** Can you try to behave?

III **Él empezó:** He started it.

IV   **Tienes treinta y un años, por el amor de Dios. No te comportes así:** You're 31 years old, for the love of God. Act like it.

Lorenzo smirks as he replies in Spanish, *"Treinta y uno y todavía molesto conmigo por lo de Papá Noel."*[1]

Lorenzo speaking Spanish was not on tonight's bingo card—that's for sure.

"You speak Spanish?" Dahlia's mouth remains wide open.

"Surprise." Lorenzo arches a brow at my sister. "And yes, I've heard you and Julian talk shit about me before."

Julian grumbles something under his breath.

Dahlia glances between them both. "So, can we get back to the important subject here?"

"Yes," I add. "Who's going to explain the Santa thing?"

"It's stupid," Julian mutters.

Lorenzo shakes his head. "Is it? Because you're still holding it against me to this day."

Dahlia and I both wait for one of them to explain.

Julian takes the initiative. "Lorenzo thought it would be a great idea to ruin Christmas for our soccer team when we were little."

On the Eros app, Lorenzo mentioned playing soccer when he was in elementary school, but I didn't connect him playing on the same team as Julian until now.

"You two played soccer together?" I ask.

"Not for long. Lorenzo got booted after the whole Santa scandal. Apparently selfish assholes shouldn't be allowed to participate in team sports."

Lorenzo shrugs. "With how much you all sucked, it was a blessing in disguise."

I **Treinta y uno y todavía molesto conmigo por lo de Papá Noel:** 31 years old and still bothered with me about Santa Claus.

"We were *eight*."

"Excuses, excuses."

"Will you two ever get bored of antagonizing each other?" my sister asks.

"No," they both say at the same time.

Dahlia laughs. "Right. Just checking."

"But for Lily's sake, I'm willing to put our past aside." Lorenzo looks over at me, his dark eyes full of mischief.

"Can we have a quick chat in private?"

Lorenzo slides off the barstool before making a show of pulling mine out. "Lead the way."

CHAPTER TEN

Lorenzo

The crowd on the dance floor parts to give Lily and me enough room to walk across it without issue. I get an array of looks in return, ranging from a couple of winks and a slap on the back to a scowl or two from men and women alike.

Lily doesn't stop to check if I'm following her down the hall until she opens the emergency exit, which leads to an empty alley behind the bar. We both have been here before, although the last time she was wearing a pink bedazzled outfit and I was hiding behind a mask.

"Well, isn't this a trip down memory lane?" I ask with a dry tone.

She slams the door shut and whirls around, her hair whipping me in the face in the process.

"What the hell was that back there?" She pokes me in the chest. "You spent the last several months ignoring me, only to have a complete personality transplant?"

"There's a good reason."

"I'm waiting to hear it."

I stroke my chin. "I have a theory, but you'd need to sign an NDA first."

She scowls. "I'm not signing an NDA, so either you trust me to keep whatever private information you share tonight between us or I head inside and go back to ignoring your existence like you've done for nearly a year."

"You can't." I rush to get the words out.

"Why not?"

"Because I need you."

She laughs, but it's hollow. "Let me guess—this has something to do with the campaign."

"Yes."

"You seriously think I'm going to let you use me for political gain when you don't even *like* me?"

I blink twice. "I never said I disliked you."

"Your actions say otherwise." She looks away with a dismissive scoff.

I'm driven by some unknown force when I reach for her chin and direct her head back to me.

"If my actions said anything, it was that I liked you too damn much, Lily. *That* was my problem. Never *you*."

I don't know what I expected, but her shoving my hand away isn't it. Neither is her jabbing me in the chest with an impressive amount of strength.

"Is that supposed to make me feel better? Or *special*?" Her upper lip curls. "Because the way you ghosted me isn't how you treat someone you *like too much*."

I deserve her anger and worse, so I take it without interrupting, even when it kills me to see the pain in her eyes.

"We spent two months talking, Lorenzo. Two months of you being the first person I texted in the morning, and two months of you being the last person I spoke to before I went to sleep. It was nearly impossible to get you to share anything personal, but when you did—like that story about when your uncle broke your nose—it felt like we were finally getting somewhere."

She holds my stare and forces me to look into her glassy eyes. "During that time, I thought what we had was unique. That it was *real*." Her voice doesn't waver, doesn't so much as crack while she bares her heart to me once again.

A heart I took for granted, and a heart someone else will show better appreciation for one day.

The idea sends an ache through my chest, strong enough to bleed the air from my lungs.

She points at herself. "I was honest about what I wanted, and you made me believe you were looking for the same. You made me wish for more, and then you took that hope and destroyed it like I didn't matter. So no, I don't believe you liked me too much. On the contrary, I don't think you like me *enough*."

I can't let her continue with that narrative, so I reveal a secret I've kept hidden in the darkest depth of my mind, never meant to be uncovered.

Until now.

"I wasn't looking for anything real when I joined the app, but meeting you made me consider it."

Her eyes widen.

I continue before my anxiety talks me out of it. "I'd never expect you to forgive me for what I did, and I hope you don't because I don't deserve it. But I *am* sorry for how I treated you after we met, and I'm sorry for leading you on before that. I had every intention of ending things after you told me about your thirty-year plan, but then I made up excuses for why I wasn't ready to let you go. Reasons like I was bored or entertained or lonely.

"I wanted you to tell me why you loved bees enough to create a garden for them or what made you want to buy a cottage versus some big house. I wanted to know *you*, and in the process I realized I could never ask you to play the part of my fake fiancée. You deserved someone who could give you that thirty-year plan, and he wasn't *me*."

She glances away, the sheen in her eyes visible from the light above us.

After a few breaths, she says, "Okay."

I take a step back. "Okay?"

She nods. "Now tell me why you're acting like we're friends in front of everyone."

"It's stupid." I scrub a hand down my face. "And I won't do it again."

I *can't*. I'll figure out a different way to boost the public's opinion of me without dragging Lily into it.

She crosses her arms. "That's not an explanation, Lorenzo."

I have no choice but to answer her, even if it makes me

look like an ass. "I was seeing if you helped improve my image. I'm falling behind in the polls, and if I don't fix it, I'll lose the election."

It's a bitter pill to swallow after spending two years planning my revenge for my parents' deaths, but I'm willing to drink poison if it means saving my campaign.

She takes a step back, as if to distance herself from my words. "And how am I supposed to do that?"

"Everyone in town likes you. All it took was one public sighting of me holding your hair back and a focus group is already using it as an example of why I'm not so bad, so I wanted to test out a theory and see if hanging around you has a positive effect on my reputation."

She blinks once. Twice. Three times, and I still have no response.

"What do you think?" I ask.

"You want my honest opinion?"

"Do your worst."

"That's a terrible idea. I'm sorry, but there's no way it'll work, and even if it did have some impact on your polling numbers, they wouldn't be long-lasting."

"Are you a political expert now?"

Her laugh puts me on edge. "Not at all, but I've spent my whole life here, so I know a thing or two about the people."

My teeth grind. "And?"

"No one would choose to vote for you because I'm your *friend*."

"Not exclusively, of course, but it can cast me in a more positive light."

"Maybe, maybe not, but I have a feeling it wouldn't have much of an impact."

"For someone so invested in me winning, I don't hear you making suggestions."

She takes a deep breath. "Just…give me a few minutes." She walks down the alley and stops beside a mural someone painted to look like a Lake Wisteria postcard.

Her eyes shut, and I focus on the hypnotic motions of her mouth. She was born with lips meant to be kissed, and for one weak moment, I allow myself to remember what it felt like to have them pressing against mine.

I don't even know why I agreed to let her kiss me. Maybe after spending two months talking to *Ana* online, I wanted to prove to myself she didn't hold this power over me. To show I was still very much in control, even if she has this strange ability to make me question my stance on relationships.

She savored our kiss like one does water after a drought. It was as if she sensed my discomfort, so she took her time, teasing me with the faintest pecks until I was the one slanting my mouth over hers and deepening the kiss.

It's ironic how I demanded to be in control of how far we took things, yet I was completely at her mercy as she turned a lifelong aversion for kissing into a newfound addiction.

I knew then that I had to let her go. That I couldn't keep going or pursuing a fake relationship—not when everything about us felt so very *real*.

I give Lily my back, slide my hand into my pocket, and touch the dice I always keep on me, noting how they feel in my hand: cool to the touch, rough around one edge, and smooth besides the random nicks in the glass.

Focusing on my father's lucky dice always soothes my racing thoughts, and I need the extra help as I wait for Lily to wrap up her conversation, where she has spent the last three minutes listing my pros and cons *aloud*.

"I can hear you," I say when she mentions my annoying personality.

"I'm only getting started."

"Let me know if you need any help identifying my more… positive traits."

"Actually, do you have a few more negatives? I feel like twenty isn't enough."

I quit teasing her after that comment.

After what feels like forever, Lily walks back over to where I stand and stops in front of me.

She tilts her head back, and I'm temporarily stunned by the way she looks up at me. The high points of her cheekbones look sharp while the shadows draw my attention toward the subtle curve of her lips.

There you go again.

I force a harsh breath through my nose.

She shifts her weight. "I don't think us being friends is going to cut it."

And even if it did, I'm no longer interested.

"I agree," I say.

Her reply shocks me. "We need to do better than that."

"We?"

"I have an idea, but you're not going to like it."

"Why not?"

"You wanted a fake fiancée?" She jabs me hard in the chest with a manicured finger. "Now you've got one."

CHAPTER ELEVEN

Lorenzo

Lily volunteering to be my fake fiancée was never an option, and it isn't about to become one now, so I shut down the idea fast.

"No."

Lily's brows hike toward her hairline. "No, you don't want a fiancée? Or no, you're still against me stepping in for the job?"

"Both."

"It's not like I want to do this either after everything you've done, but if it means helping you win the election, then I'll do it."

"Why?" I ask.

She keeps her face emotionless. "I don't like the Ludlows."

"You don't like me either, so that can't be the only reason."

"It's personal."

I wasn't expecting that, or the reply that follows it.

"I don't want to talk about it, but trust me. I want you to absolutely decimate them in the election."

I can't get a word in because she keeps speaking. "You're not going to see some massive jump in the polls because you were seen with me."

My ironclad will is crumbling because I know she is right. I need *more*, and I need it now before the gap between Trevor and me becomes insurmountable.

She continues, "Our backstory would make sense. We're two star-crossed lovers who hid our relationship because my family doesn't like you. Plus we have..." She flicks her hand between us like I'm supposed to understand her version of sign language. "You know."

I don't. "Spell it out for me."

"I'd rather demonstrate." She brushes her hand over the front of my shirt instead, sending a blazing path of warmth down my body.

I bite my tongue. "Was something supposed to happen?"

To torment me some more, she runs a single finger back up my chest, and I fail to suppress my shiver.

"I can tell we're going to have fun together." Her voice has a husky rasp to it.

"This isn't supposed to be fun," I hiss, thinking of why I'm doing all of this to begin with.

My parents' lives were cut short by Trevor Ludlow, so I need to focus on winning. If she can put personal feelings aside, why am I struggling with her logic?

My eyes drop to her mouth and the tiny beauty mark she has—

That's why.

I glance away, hating myself for being so damn...*enamored* with her. "I can find another fiancée."

She unleashes a noise of frustration. "You can't come out of nowhere and announce you're suddenly engaged—at least not to a random someone. People here are smart. There's a huge chance they'll see through the lie and lose whatever trust they had in you."

I hate to admit it, but she has a valid point.

"In fact..." She pauses. "I bet that's why you haven't picked someone to play the part yet. You think it could backfire, so you're not willing to take the risk."

I'm impressed *and* annoyed, which are two feelings that muddle my brain, along with the entrancing way the corner of her lip pulls up in the sexiest smirk I've ever seen.

I force myself to look into her eyes instead. "I'm confused why you're offering to be my fiancée when you think my plan is stupid."

"I never said it was stupid. Is it poorly thought-out and risky? Yeah, but stupid...eh. I think there's merit to you being in a fake relationship with someone. It makes you seem... likeable."

"Didn't realize I wasn't."

Her nose scrunches. "Moving on... Unlike some woman you'd pay to be your fiancée, I'm a sure thing. People here know me, and even better, *I know them*, which makes me an asset. As you said earlier, they *like* me, to the point of being invested in who I'm dating and why, and best of all, they trust me." Her eyes sparkle with a confidence I find irresistible.

"Of course they do." She has had twenty-eight years to establish herself as a trustworthy person, and it shows.

"And most importantly, I want you to win."

"Because you don't like the Ludlows," I reply, my tone riddled with skepticism.

She keeps her emotions in check, making it hard to get a clear read on her, which only verifies my doubts.

What did the Ludlows do that made Lily switch to my side, and how do I get her to tell me?

So long as you two have the same goal, who cares?

I hesitate—a rarity in itself—before speaking. "If I agree..."

"Which you will, because my plan is the best." The way she beams at her own idea should be off-putting, but I like her confidence.

Her strong sense of self drew me into her orbit the first time, and it's the same trait that could threaten the protective barrier I placed around myself after she blew a hole through it months ago.

Reluctantly, I reply, "In theory, yes, your plan is better."

"There are already some whisperings about us, especially after the sheriff's station visit and my drunken episode, so planting additional clues won't be difficult. They'll have no choice *but* to believe it because the signs have been there all along."

It's alarming how perfect this all sounds.

Dare I say *too* perfect.

"So the official storyline is that we've secretly been in love this whole time but we hid it?"

She nods. "Ever since we met on a dating app last year."

"And we kept quiet all because your family doesn't like me?" Disbelief bleeds into the question. "Doesn't that seem extreme to you?"

"Anyone who has met my family will understand."

"So all of Lake Wisteria?"

"You got it."

"And what changed for us?" I ask. "Why did we decide to go public now versus months ago?"

"I couldn't stand the idea of keeping our love a secret anymore," she says dramatically. "But I think to sell our engagement, we should give everyone at least two months to adjust to the idea of us being a couple before we hit them with a proposal. Because if we come on too strong, too fast, it could be suspicious."

"Why bother getting engaged at all? We could fake a relationship and save ourselves from a future headache."

She pauses to think it out before shaking her head. "No. We need something more...permanent. Something that tells the town you're all-in."

I stroke my stubbled chin. "Couples call off engagements all the time."

"Then we'd better do a good job of convincing people that we won't."

Her idea *does* sound far superior to mine, and it could help revitalize my campaign. But the voice of reason questions what will become of me if I agree to work closely with the one person I swore to avoid.

You can't become obsessed with someone if you stay away, the voice I fight daily speaks up.

Well, I can't become mayor if I'm ten points behind my competitor, so there's that.

I can take careful measures to prevent becoming emotionally attached. It'll require effort on my end to remind Lily of our arrangement, but I've never been afraid of a little hard work.

So, without further delay, I decide to take fate into my own hands.

"Fine. Let's do this."

She's about to open her mouth, but a fire alarm goes off inside the bar, drowning out the noise.

"How do you feel about starting right now?" She fists the loose material of my T-shirt and tugs until my mouth is within striking distance.

It happens so fast, I don't fully process what Lily is doing until her mouth is pressing against mine, making me forget about the chaos ensuing around us.

All I can think about is how this kiss, along with everything else we do from this point on, will be nothing but a *lie*.

X secret garden studio

NWS ???
wildflower whishes studio

petal + press

the Pressed Petal

CHAPTER TWELVE

Lily

It took me five minutes to process Lorenzo's apology and accept that while I'm still angry at him for the choices he made and the heartache he caused me, I need to put our history aside if I want to save Rose & Thorn. Doing so won't be easy, but it'll be way easier than watching the Ludlows destroy me along with my parents' legacy.

If that requires me to fake that I'm "in love" with Lorenzo, so be it.

Except nothing about our kiss right now feels like *pretend*.

I have done my best to erase the memory of how Lorenzo's lips felt—of how they *kissed*—but all my efforts go to waste because one kiss ruins everything.

The world around us ceases to exist. I'm in no hurry, so I

take my time, setting a languid pace he matches, right before he turns the heat up.

I lean against the brick wall behind me because I don't trust my legs, and Lorenzo follows, his hands finding the curves of my hips. He presses his body into mine, and I gasp at how right it feels to be underneath him.

He grins against my lips, and I kiss it away to spare myself from craving *more*.

More smiles. More fleeting touches. More of his hard length pressing into my—

Rusty hinges creak, and a burst of cold air hits the side of my face. Lorenzo ignores it, deepening the kiss until I forget about the original plan.

It is hard to multitask with Lorenzo's teeth tugging on my bottom lip—

Someone gasps, followed by a squeaky, "Lily!"

Lorenzo tenses ever so slightly. I doubt I would've noticed his rigid posture if it weren't for how closely our bodies are pressed together.

More people pour out of the emergency exit, and a tingle spreads from the back of my neck straight toward my face.

I tuck my head against Lorenzo's chest—a genuine reaction that makes his hold on my hips tighten.

Reluctantly, I lift my head, and Lorenzo's gaze connects with mine. It's the heat in his eyes that has me questioning how much of this is real, but then I remind myself how I made that mistake before and where it got me.

Ignoring the crowd forming in the alley, I grab Lorenzo's hand and tug him toward the lights on Main Street. People's stares drill into the back of my neck as he slides his fingers through mine.

The main road in town is hectic, with two fire trucks parked in the emergency lane, casting a red-and-white glow on the larger crowd waiting outside Last Call. My sister is standing on the edge of it, looking panicked as she searches the group of people.

Julian's gaze lands on me first, and he whispers something into Dahlia's ear. She turns to look over at us with wide eyes. Her mouth falls open, and Julian's lips press firmly together as he takes us in.

Lorenzo's grip tightens, and Dahlia's and Julian's eyes drop toward our clasped hands.

Talk about a hard launch.

I let out a nervous laugh. "Hey."

"Hey?" She stares at me like she doesn't recognize the person standing before her. "I've been looking all over for you! Did you not hear the fire alarm?"

"Um...I was a bit busy." I lean into Lorenzo's side, and thankfully he doesn't step away.

Dahlia focuses her attention back on me. "I can see."

Earth, please swallow me whole.

I can't take the awkwardness anymore, so I look around, noting the twenty people all huddled by the fire trucks. Some whisper in our direction, while a majority talk among themselves.

"Can we go home and talk? *Please?*" I ask while fighting the compulsion to flee in the opposite direction.

Dahlia's eyes flick over to Lorenzo one last time before she nods. "Yeah. Let's go."

"Call me later." Lorenzo gives my hand a reassuring squeeze. The comforting gesture must be part of his act. It *has* to be.

"Okay, Romeo." Julian claps a hand around his shoulder and tugs him back. "I think I've seen enough."

"Then you're in for a rude awakening because we're only getting started." Lorenzo pushes him away.

The sirens pick an impeccable time to stop wailing, so everyone gets to hear Julian speak. "Never thought I'd see the day where you cared about someone other than yourself."

"The secret's out now."

"I'm sure you'll move on soon enough."

Julian's comment hits *way* too close to home, and my lungs malfunction. I end up choking on dry air, making Lorenzo spin around to face me.

His stormy gaze sweeps over me before he turns to look at Julian. I can't make out Lorenzo's expression, but the way Julian pulls back suddenly makes me wonder how unhinged he must look.

"If you have a problem with us, you talk to *me*. Got it?" Lorenzo asks, too low for anyone but us three to hear.

To prevent them from throwing punches, I step in and place my hand on Lorenzo's shoulder. "By the way, this right here"—I motion between Julian and Lorenzo—"is why I kept everything a secret. You can't have one normal conversation, and it hurts me to see two people I care about dislike each other so strongly."

Julian looks like I've slapped him. "Lily—"

I hold up my hand. "I think you've said enough tonight."

I take a deep breath and fight through the discomfort, knowing I need to put my morals aside to save my shop, including lying to my loved ones.

"All right. I think it's time we go home." Dahlia grabs my hand and starts to pull me away from Julian and Lorenzo, but she only manages a step before Lorenzo speaks.

"Text me when you get there," he says, loud enough for the crowd of people around us to hear. "I want to know that you got there safely."

We're doing this now? All right. "You don't need to remind me every time, baby."

Someone giggles, while another shouts, "She calls him *baby*!"

Baby, he mouths before he subtly shakes his head. *No.*

I'd laugh if it weren't for Dahlia dragging me away from the bar, reminding me how much trouble I'm in.

"I'm so upset with you right now," Dahlia whispers as we walk down Main Street.

The ache in my stomach travels toward my heart and stays there as we head to her car. Dahlia is awfully quiet as we climb inside her fancy sedan, and I'm about to curl into a ball of anxiety when she looks over at me.

"How could you have kept this all a secret from me?" Her voice breaks toward the end.

I'm hit with the full brunt of her hurt, and it makes me feel like shit. Dahlia is my best friend, and here I am, making her upset.

One day I hope we can laugh about this, but tonight I need to focus on the plan. She will forgive me eventually, but

I don't know if I can give myself the same grace if I lose the shop.

She continues when I don't speak. "I asked you about him the other day, and you lied to me."

I wince.

"I knew it was weird when he randomly fixed your car, but I took your word for it when you said it wasn't a big deal. And then when you told us about him driving you home and taking care of you, I ignored my gut because there's no way you wouldn't tell me about a guy you were dating, right? Because we tell each other everything."

"You didn't tell me about Julian right away." In fact, I only found out about them because I caught them kissing.

"At least you didn't have to wait very long to find out, and even if you hadn't seen us that day, I would've told you once I knew what was happening." Her words puncture my heart from ten different angles.

"You're right," I say earnestly. "I'm sorry."

She can't even look at me anymore. "I thought we were close—"

"We are." My voice shakes.

"Then tell me why you didn't talk to me about the city council letter."

I flinch. "Mom told you about it?"

"Yes."

"She could get in trouble," I grumble.

"Which is why I plan on keeping it a secret. Something you should be familiar with."

My stomach sours. "If you knew, then why did you bring up the Pressed Petal tonight?"

"Because it's happening, whether it be on Lavender Lane or somewhere else in town."

Emotion clogs my throat.

She continues, "But that's not important right now. Your relationship with Lorenzo is."

If only she knew the two issues go hand in hand. I'm tempted to admit the truth, especially now that our mom told her about the letter, but I can't until I speak to Lorenzo. Our situation requires some level of trust, and this is an opportunity for me not to betray his.

Even though he totally deserves it.

She rubs her temple. "I'm still having a hard time believing it."

Same. "I wanted to tell you. I really did." I'd been dying to talk to Dahlia about the Eros app and who I met, but I always found the perfect excuse not to.

First she was dealing with her own breakup, so it felt selfish to talk about a guy I was interested in. Part of me was nervous too, which was clearly justified given how Lorenzo broke things off. And then there was Richard, who made everything ten times worse.

After all that, I was too ashamed to talk about any of it, including how much I disliked myself.

"How long has this been going on?" she asks.

"Almost a year." I sink deeper into the seat.

"A year?" She groans. "God, Lily."

"I'm sorry." *For not telling you the truth then and for lying to you now.*

"I—" Dahlia shakes her head. She looks like she's about to

say something else, but she remains quiet as she pulls out of the parking spot instead.

Neither of us plays any music, so I'm left to stew in my unpleasant thoughts during the ride home. I knew Dahlia would be upset, because if the roles were reversed, I'd be just as hurt, if not more, but witnessing her pain gives me a whole new type of sister guilt.

Halfway through the quiet drive, I think about coming clean. I don't want Dahlia to be upset with me, but when I open my mouth, I slam it shut.

Wait until you speak to Lorenzo.

After she pulls into the driveway of our house and parks the car, she turns to face me. "Tomorrow morning you need to tell Mom about Lorenzo. It's not right to make her find out the news from someone else."

I clench my hands into fists. "I know."

All I can hope is that she doesn't connect the buyout letter to my relationship with Lorenzo. And even if she questions it, she'd write it off as a coincidence, choosing to believe the more plausible story.

Because who in their right mind agrees to a fake relationship?

Oh, right.

Me.

CHAPTER THIRTEEN

Lorenzo

Once Lily disappears inside Dahlia's car, Julian stalks me back to tonight's ride—a vintage Jaguar two-seater like the one my dad was always repairing for the Hawthorne family. While my mom managed their wealthy lakefront estate, my father worked odd jobs around town to provide for us.

Mechanic. Italian tutor. Firearms instructor, travel agent, and occasional bartender.

The life he had in Lake Wisteria was a far cry from his extravagant upbringing, but my mom—a military brat who believed in law and order—didn't want to expose a child to the Vittori lifestyle. Around the world, our surname is feared as much as it is loathed, so she moved back to the only place that ever felt safe.

Still to this day, I don't understand how my father managed

to go from a billionaire casino heir to a small-town nobody who was fixing luxury cars instead of driving them, but I suppose his hyperfixation with making my mother happy had a way of manipulating his mind.

Then again, I'm running for public office because of my fixation with avenging my parents, so it's not like I can judge.

"Lorenzo," Julian says to my back.

I turn and lean against the car. "Yes?"

He retains a few feet of distance. "How much will it cost me?"

"I'm not interested in selling my car," I say with a detached voice.

"I'm not talking about that, and you know it." His body is riddled with tension.

I can make an educated guess about what he's insinuating, but I want to hear him say it aloud so he has to face his own bad idea.

"I'd rather you clarify so I don't get pissed for no reason."

He holds my cold stare without looking away. "I want you to leave Lily alone."

"And you think money is going to do the trick?" I laugh.

"That's not what I'm offering."

I tilt my head. "Then what do you possibly have that I could ever want?"

"You wanted my endorsement, right?"

His question makes me pause. "Don't tell me you're going to back out of our deal now."

He shakes his head. "No, but what if I could get you more?"

Okay, I'll bite for curiosity's sake. "Like who?"

"A lot of people around here owe me favors. I'm talking about influential, well-connected people who probably have more in common with you than they realize."

"And you'd call in those favors for me? I'm touched."

His jaw ticks. "I'm doing this for Lily."

"Because you want me to stay away."

He nods.

"In that case, I don't think she'd be too happy to hear about this conversation."

If he keeps clenching his jaw, he won't have any teeth left to grind. "She doesn't need to find out."

"Ah. Well, that's a problem, then, because we don't keep secrets from one another."

"But you have no problem keeping them from us?" he snaps.

"Seeing as I'm not in love with you, no, I don't." My calculated reply only makes him twitchier.

"You can't expect me to believe you two fell in love."

"I mean, whether you choose to believe it or not doesn't make it any less true."

His forehead creases with concern. "I know if I loved a woman, I wouldn't be so quick to hide it from the world."

My lips curl at the corners. "What if I told you it was all her idea?"

Pushing Julian's buttons has become one of my favorite pastimes. I bet it eats him up inside to know the pseudo-sister he puts on a pedestal would lie to him because of *me*.

"There's no way she would suggest it." Julian shakes his head.

"Hm." I give him a quick once-over, noting his rigid body

language. "Think about it. What would I stand to gain by keeping our relationship a secret? If anything, I'd get to piss you off in a whole new way."

His lips press together, their color turning white.

I can practically hear the gears in his head turning as he considers who benefited most from keeping the relationship a secret.

I thought I was done, but I can't help myself as I say, "And Julian?"

He lifts his chin in silent acknowledgment.

"There is absolutely nothing you can offer me that would convince me to leave Lily—whether it be money, endorsements, or a guaranteed election victory. So bring up the idea again and I'll show you what it's like to be my enemy." I get into my car and drive away, ignoring Julian glowering in my rearview mirror as I head home.

It takes Manny precisely twenty minutes to find out about my "relationship."

MANNY

You and Lily are a thing?!

MANNY

WTF man. How could you not tell me? I thought we were close.

MANNY

And she calls you BABY?

MANNY

I'm kind of jealous.

Since I feel *slightly* bad for keeping my fake secret to myself after he helped me fix Lily's car the other night, I reply right away instead of leaving him on read.

ME

It was a secret.

MANNY

No shit. I understand why, but to find out the news from my mom?

MANNY

That's cruel. Even for you.

It's good to know word is already spreading, but I don't know how it's being received, so I throw Manny an invitation in exchange for information.

ME

Come over tomorrow and I'll explain.

MANNY

Will you make up for the betrayal and let me take the Gullwing out for a ride?

He could mess with your car, the whispering voice replies, my obsession with safety always rearing its ugly head at the most inconvenient times.

You don't have to worry if you're inside of it with him, I reply, fighting off the intrusive thought.

But what if he crashes with you in the passenger seat?

A cold, uncomfortable feeling spreads through me.

ME

Only if you're okay being a passenger.

MANNY

I'll convince you to let me take it out for a spin one day. Mark my words.

I'm sure he'll try his best, but my controlling thoughts are stronger than any negotiation skills he has.

ME

Best of luck.

MANNY

See you tomorrow, lover boy.

With Manny placated, I lock my phone and walk inside my house. It's funny living in one that Julian designed given how much he detests me.

Julian made it nearly impossible to buy a house, either by outbidding me or using his connections to convince the buyer to sell to him instead. He was motivated to make sure I didn't own a property within the town's limits so I'd be ineligible to run for mayor, but I was fueled by more than the need to avenge my parents.

If Lily's the people's princess, then I'm the petty prince, living in a house I dislike strictly because it pisses the designer off.

It was so much more satisfying to outsmart him by purchasing the lakefront property through a trust before transferring the title over to myself—even if I loathe everything about the mid-century modern mansion.

All the clean lines, warm wood tones, and floor-to-ceiling windows remind me too much of my uncle's home in Vegas, but I didn't have the luxury of being picky. If I did, I would've chosen my parents' older but modest home.

But oh, wait, Julian tore it down before I had a chance.

I'm annoyed when Lily doesn't text me when she gets home. I don't have a real reason to be, other than her not listening to me, so I try to rationalize what could've happened.

She probably thought I was joking or putting on a show for the crowd, which technically is true.

Or maybe something bad happened to her. That same oily voice comes back, although this time it's concerned about Lily's safety, not my own.

Fuck. No.

This is your OCD talking. Lily is fine.

I screw my eyes shut and push the image of her being crushed to death inside Dahlia's car out of my mind, but once it pops up, I can't get it out.

Text her to check in. It's a common courtesy after tonight's events.

ME

Are you home?

There. Was that so hard?

When she doesn't answer immediately, the image of her being injured returns, the details far sharper than before. Blood oozes from a head wound, and her breathing is labored, as if her lung has collapsed.

I nearly rip my hair from the roots with how hard I tug on the strands, but no amount of pain will block me from sending Lily another message.

ME

If this is going to work between us, I expect you to answer me when I text you.

Shit. I sound way too controlling, but I can't send a third text without looking like I care too much, so I sit around and wait for her to answer.

Time passes by slowly, like I'm standing in the middle of an hourglass, counting each individual grain of sand.

Two minutes feel like ten by the time a new text pops up.

LILY

Yes. I'm home.

I want to throw my phone across the room because how can three words have the same effect over me as an emergency Xanax?

ME

Next time do what I say and text me when you get home.

LILY

Sure, baby.

ME

I hate the nickname, by the way.

Only because my heart does this little jolt every damn time she uses it.

LILY

Good. Now I love it even more.

I don't get ten minutes to myself the next morning before my doorbell goes off. A quick glance at the security app makes me consider ignoring the visitor, but then Willow yells, "Open up, or else I quit!"

I open the door to a red-faced Willow.

"What the hell, Lorenzo?!" she shouts.

I shut the door before any of my neighbors can hear us. "I can explain."

She barrels into my home like a hellhound, banging into the entryway table and nearly tipping over the vase with one of Lily's bouquets. The pink clashes with all the earthy tones in my house, but it reminds me of my mom and all the fond memories I have of my father surprising her with weekly bouquets.

The memory makes my chest tight, and I slip my hand into my front pocket and start counting the numbers on the dice to calm my racing mind.

"Lorenzo?" Willow waves her hands. "Are you even paying attention to me?"

I'm dragged out of the mental fog. "What?"

"How did you ever get Lily to agree to being your fiancée?"

"Girlfriend," I correct. "At least for the next two months before we begin Phase Two."

"There are phases now?"

"Apparently so."

Her lips purse. "You know what? I don't care what you label it. Just tell me how it all went down and why she would ever agree to being your fiancée after the Eros app incident."

"I don't know."

"You don't know?" She sounds as surprised as she looks. "What do you mean?"

Willow isn't going to let this go easily, so I lead her to my living room, where we both take a seat on chairs across from each other.

I tap my fingers against my thigh. "She mentioned not liking the Ludlows, but we were interrupted before I had a chance to push for more information."

"That's it?"

"Yes."

Willow's lips thin. "I don't know if I believe that."

What if she's doing this to get revenge? The worry grows like a virus, making me feel sick in the head.

I can't think of a better way for her to get back at you about the Eros app.

She's like a Trojan horse, destined to be the downfall of your campaign. Don't trust her.

I'm aware there are some pitfalls to having Lily play the role of my fake fiancée, but I will fight to always stay one step ahead of her.

Willow asks the same question I've had since I left Last

Call: "What else could you have that she possibly wants? It's obviously not money."

"No. She didn't even bring it up."

"Power?"

I laugh at the idea. "She doesn't care about politics."

"Revenge? Because you totally deserve it for the Eros app stuff."

I sigh.

"What if she's angry enough to tank your entire campaign?" Willow voices my exact concern.

When I spoke to *Ana*, she did mention loving spy movies and true crime podcasts, but I highly doubt she's some mastermind doing this all for revenge.

She isn't like me, which is something I appreciate about her. Lily always sees the good in people, to the point of it being a liability, while I seek every opportunity to assume the worst.

"I don't know her reason, but I'll stop at nothing until I find out," I say.

She nods. "Okay. So now that you've completely gone off the rails, what's the plan?"

I repeat Lily's idea back to Willow, and she quietly listens, only interrupting me to ask for further clarification on certain parts, like our two-month waiting period before I propose.

"I mean…" She pauses her pacing to look over at me. "I hate to say it, but this could work."

I exhale. "That's the only reason I agreed."

"But…"

I screw my eyes shut. "What?"

"You both have to be strategic about this. You need to be

seen everywhere but also not too much because we don't want people to be suspicious either. We can plan public outings, plus we have the Healing Hearts fundraiser dinner coming up." Her face lights up. "Oh! And imagine going on double dates with her sister and Julian—"

"Don't hold your breath."

"There's no other option but for you to play nice with Julian, so beg for his and everyone else's forgiveness if you have to."

My reply is nothing but a blank look.

She continues, "The best part about this plan *is* Lily's family, so do whatever it takes to get them on your side. Julian's endorsement speech will be a perfect full-circle moment for your relationship."

"If he doesn't use the opportunity to publicly roast me, that is."

She shakes her head. "He cares too much about Lily to embarrass her like that."

"He didn't seem to have a problem reaming into me last night. He even tried to offer his connections in exchange for me ending my relationship with Lily."

"Okay, clearly he's going to be angry, but I'm sure he'll come around in no time."

"Lily won't give him a choice."

"Exactly. And while we're on the topic of Lily, I think it's important to keep her in the loop."

"And how do you suggest we do that?"

"Let's invite her over for lunch and get to work."

Great. More time with Lily. Exactly what the psychiatrist ordered.

X Secret Garden Studio

WWS ???
Wildflower Wishes Studio

Petal + Press

The Pressed Petal

CHAPTER FOURTEEN

Lily

Telling my mom about my secret relationship with Lorenzo first thing the next morning goes worse than I expected. Her simple but significant "I'm disappointed in you" feels like I took a dagger to the heart, so I call Lorenzo in a panic once I'm locked away in my bedroom.

"I don't think I can do this," I blurt out as soon as he answers the phone.

"Can't do *what*?"

"Lie to my family. My mom is upset, and my sister is pissed."

The speaker crackles with his loud exhale. "Isn't that something you should've considered last night?"

My chest puffs with my restrained breath. "Of course I did, but it isn't so easy."

"And how will telling them about our fake relationship help matters?"

"They won't have a reason to be angry at me anymore."

"Are you sure about that? Your mom doesn't seem too fond of liars, and your sister would probably be upset you turned to me for help instead of her."

"They'd understand." I don't sound confident, and I blame Lorenzo for planting those valid concerns in my head.

"But what if they don't?" he asks.

"I…" *Don't know.*

Lorenzo continues when I go silent. "And if you told Dahlia, would you be okay with asking her to keep it a secret from Julian? Because there is no way in hell I'm trusting him."

I can't ask Dahlia to hide the truth from Julian. "If he understood the circumstance—"

Lorenzo doesn't let me finish the thought. "Am I going to hedge my entire campaign on Julian Lopez—a man who can't stand me? Because if word gets out, whether it be on purpose or by accident, it could ruin the entire campaign and make both of us look terrible."

The pit in my stomach grows. "I…I get it."

He exhales loudly. "You volunteered knowing the stakes. If you want to risk everything because you can't handle your choice, then so be it, but give me a warning before you destroy everything I've worked toward."

I fall back on my bed with an unceremonious *oomph*. "You're still giving me the option? Why?"

"Because we're a team, whether we like it or not. That

means I have to trust that you'll make the best choice for us, even if it feels like the wrong one for you right now."

I hate him for making sense—but not nearly as much as I hate myself for the flutter in my stomach at him using the word *we*.

Despite my conversation with Lorenzo, I still question everything when my mom leaves the house without giving me a hug goodbye. I didn't even find out she went to Mass until Josefina sent us a text in the Lopez-Muñoz group chat letting us know that it went on longer than usual, so Sunday lunch is going to be pushed back an hour.

I've never felt more disconnected from my family, and the recent Kids' Table texts I missed adds to the growing emotional divide between us.

RAFA

I come back home and less than 24 hours later there's already drama?

JULIAN

If you're referring to Lily's secret relationship with Lorenzo, then yes, it's true.

RAFA

Shit.

RAFA

Does that mean we're supposed to be nice to him now?

JULIAN

Nope. Carry on like usual.

DAHLIA

Julian. We talked about this.

Okay, at least my sister is trying to help me out.

JULIAN

No. You talked about it. I only listened and decided I'm not being nice just because Lily likes him.

RAFA

It could be a good test.

JULIAN

Exactly. Let's see if he has what it takes to fit in with us.

RAFA

I meant for you, not him.

JULIAN

And what am I being tested on exactly?

RAFA

I'm curious how long it takes before you throw the first punch.

JULIAN

I'd never lay a hand on another person.

RAFA

Wanna bet?

Dahlia responds with a face-palm emoji.

Since everyone is ragging on Lorenzo, I decide the most girlfriend thing I can do is jump to his defense.

ME

Don't you dare punch my boyfriend. You hear me?

JULIAN

I'd only be doing you a favor since that broken nose of his could use some realignment.

And my mom thinks *I'm* disappointing?

Filled with instant rage, I become a keyboard warrior, rapid-fire texting without thinking twice about divulging something *Laurence* once told me during one of our midnight conversations.

ME

Oh, you mean the fracture he got after his uncle punched him in the face and never got him proper medical attention?

Lorenzo would kill me if he knew I told Julian, Rafa, and Dahlia about that story, but I rarely get this angry, so I don't know how to process the feeling before acting on instinct.

My phone vibrates, so I check what else my family has to say.

RAFA

Well. I don't know about Julian, but I feel like a dick, and I didn't even comment on his nose.

JULIAN

Of course I feel like a dick.

JULIAN

I had no idea his uncle hit him.

ME

For the record, next time you question why I kept our entire relationship a secret, refer to this chat.

Everyone might still be upset with me for my *lies*, and their emotions are valid, but I'm putting my foot down. Either they can accept that this relationship is happening or they can learn to live with my absence.

I exit the Kids' Table group chat and open up a new message from Willow.

WILLOW

Hey, hey! How do you feel about Italian food?

ME

If I ever say no to wanting some, please alert the authorities because I must've been kidnapped.

WILLOW

HAHA. Will do!!

WILLOW

Do you want to meet up at Lorenzo's for a
late lunch and strategize?

I never skip a Sunday lunch, in part because I have nothing
better to do, but the idea of sitting at a table with my family
after everything feels like too much.

ME

Sure. Tell me the time
and I'll be there.

Lorenzo's house reminds me of Julian's, most likely because
it was built by Lopez Luxury prior to Julian restoring older
homes with Dahlia. I won't deny that the mid-century modern
mansion is a work of art, full of sharp lines and glass windows
that showcase design elements inspired by the 1950s.

It's stunning, grandiose, and lacking in personality given
the limited desert landscaping, but it's still breathtaking to
those who appreciate this kind of aesthetic. I'd much rather
have a little bungalow like Willow's any day of the week, with
painted siding, a wraparound porch, a bee sanctuary, and a
garden with unlimited access to flowers, but hey, if Lorenzo
enjoys a house to match his cold heart, then it's his money. He
should do whatever he wants with it.

Speaking of the devil, Lorenzo opens the door in nothing

but a black T-shirt and jeans. It's rare to see him looking so casual, and the sight of his thick arms and the faintest hint of abs test my heart rate.

"Ran out of clean suits to wear?" I say coolly as I step inside, only to lose my footing when I glance at his entry table.

I've never had the nerve to ask Lorenzo what he does with the flowers he orders, and I've spent way too many hours wondering why he bothered if he clearly wasn't dating anyone. Or at least that's what I told myself to feel better about making his bouquets because there is no way I would've fulfilled the order any other way.

To see one of them in his home, located right by the stairs so he walks by them every day...

Who's to say he didn't put them there this morning to look like a good boyfriend?

The thought sours whatever little happiness I felt.

I ignore the emotion clogging my throat. "Never expected you to be the kind of guy who likes fresh flowers in his house."

He shuts the door behind me without answering.

"Where's the other one?" I ask because I can't resist.

"Somewhere."

I roll my eyes at his vague response and step toward the table to remove a few dead leaves, only to stop when he asks, "Do you mind taking off your shoes?"

I look down at my sandaled feet and grimace.

"Floors were cleaned this morning," he says when I don't move right away.

With the way it gleams, I'm inclined to believe him, but that's not my issue. "But my feet get cold."

"Let me get you some socks." He heads upstairs and disappears without waiting for me to deny his request.

"Hey!" Willow pops out of a room and heads over to greet me. "Happy you made it." She pulls me into a hug.

"Anything sounded better than hanging out with my family today."

She winces. "How's that going?"

"About as good as expected."

"Should I bring out the wine?"

"Uh…"

Willow laughs.

"No wine," Lorenzo grunts from the staircase landing. I look up to see his bare feet slapping against the stairs.

"Catch." He tosses a pair of black ankle socks my way.

I look at them with a scrunched nose.

He frowns. "What's that look for?"

"Nothing." I kick off my first sandal and slip a sock on.

"Is there something wrong with them?" he asks.

"Do I need another reason besides them being yours?"

He crosses his arms.

Tough crowd today.

I place my sandals neatly beside a new pair of male running shoes and Willow's flats. "I'm more of a ruffled-sock kind of girl."

"A what?"

"You know, cute little socks with ruffles? I'll show you a photo later."

"Ruffles…on socks?"

"Bonus if they have bows or something fun embroidered on them." The comment slips out before I remember myself.

"Noted for next time."

Something flutters in my stomach at his use of *next time*.

You're going to have a hard time adjusting to this whole fake relationship if you get all hot and bothered at the mere idea of spending more time with him.

Willow is about to say something before all our noses twitch from the scent of something burning.

"The bread!" She takes off toward what I assume is the kitchen.

Lorenzo plugs his nose. "I swear that woman would burn water if it was possible."

I rub my rumbling stomach. "Now I'm wishing I had eaten before."

"I'd never let her cook me a meal." He turns and heads down the same walkway as Willow, silently ordering me to follow.

The extravagant interior is everything I'd expect from a Lopez Luxury build. From the conversation pit and stone fireplace to the imported marble floors, I can't help noting all the little details that make Julian's homes so popular among the rich.

I follow Lorenzo through a hallway. There are large photo frames hanging on both walls, all featuring different cars.

I stop to check out one of them. "I don't know what I expected when I first saw your house, but the lonely bachelor aesthetic isn't it." I motion toward all twenty frames.

"Who said I was lonely?"

"An educated guess based on how you don't have a single photo of you with someone else." I drag my finger across the bottom of the frame. I don't find a single speck of dust, much like the rest of this place.

We continue walking, and I only stop one more time to point at a car I've seen around town with the doors that swing up toward the sky. "I didn't realize this one was yours too."

"Most of the cool ones around here are."

I laugh without meaning to. "How many do you have now?"

He tucks his hand into his pocket—a habit I notice but never comment on. "Twenty."

I turn back to the photos to stop myself from staring at his sharp jawline. "Are you on the hunt for number twenty-one?"

He nods, his lips twitching like he wants to smile. "I'm currently searching for a Dawn Drophead."

I stare at him blankly.

"A Rolls-Royce. Preferably either from 1951 or 1953," he adds.

I let out a whistle. "Fancy."

"There's only a few in the US, but I'm in contact with someone in Europe who might be interested in trading cars." He sounds...excited, and it knocks at least five years off him in that moment.

"Is the person a fellow car collector?"

"He's known for it."

My brows rise. "I wasn't aware that was something one could become famous for."

"Only when their name is Santiago Alatorre."

I think I've heard Nico mention that name before, but I don't remember in what context.

A fire alarm goes off in the distance, and Lorenzo and I rush toward the sound. We run into a chef's dream kitchen, where Willow is jumping up and down underneath the fire alarm, waving a towel around to stop the noise.

While Lorenzo helps her, I take in the space. There are two massive islands—one for prepping food and one for eating—a walk-in wine cellar, integrated appliances my sister always gushes over, and a picturesque view of Lake Wisteria sparkling in the distance.

The kitchen, like the rest of the house, is beautiful in a showroom, *no one actually cooks here* kind of way. I'm afraid to touch anything because every surface sparkles and all the appliances look expensive as hell.

Every counter is spotless, void of typical clutter like spice jars and oil bottles, and all the small appliances are concealed. The only room that looks slightly lived-in is the butler's pantry, and that isn't saying much because the smaller room is fancier than most people's kitchens, with ingredients stored in apothecary-style glass jars and snacks hidden inside labeled baskets.

After Willow and Lorenzo get the fire alarm to stop blaring, she starts cutting some fresh, non-burnt bread. "This will take a few minutes to heat up."

I step up beside her. "Any way I can help?"

"Lorenzo and you can set the table?"

I assume she is referencing the breakfast nook that faces the lake and forest beyond, but Lorenzo chooses to put the placemats down at the second island before showing me where the silverware drawer is.

We both reach inside it at the same time, sending sparks scattering up my arm from a quick brush of his pinky finger against mine. The sensation startles me, and I suck in a breath.

It's not fair to be this...*imbalanced* around someone. It throws me off, turning me into a bumbling fool who can't seem to handle his presence. I blame the fact that I see bits of Laurence peeking through, like when he talks about his car collection or how he automatically serves me water without any ice because I once told him I preferred it that way.

I also see the man who threw me away like I didn't matter. Like the connection we had wasn't worth it, which sent me running straight into Richard's arms because I wanted to feel desired.

All I ended up doing was hurting myself.

Remember: You're doing all this to save your shop, so stop thinking about this as anything but an arrangement.

Yes. That's it. This is a mutually beneficial, strictly logical, no-strings-attached *arrangement* that will end once Lorenzo becomes mayor.

I only need to make it through the five longest months of my life first.

"What happened to Sunday lunch?" Lorenzo asks.

"What about it?" I don't answer until I finish my bite of the branzino.

I'd never admit such a thing to Lorenzo, but his skills in the kitchen deserve high praise.

"Since when do you skip them?" he follows up.

"Why do you care?" I reply, more guarded than before.

Willow leans back in her chair and sips her wine. "I assume your family is still upset by the news?"

"Yes," I say with a heavy breath. "It's been less than twenty-four hours, so they need time to adjust."

Lorenzo puts his fork down. "I'm still curious why you agreed to date me when you knew they wouldn't approve."

"*Fake* date," I emphasize. "And I have my own reasons for wanting you to become mayor, none of which are your business."

"But what if we could help you?" Willow is making this meal feel more like an interrogation than a strategy meeting.

"You can by making sure Lorenzo wins." I soften the words with a smile.

Telling Lorenzo about the mayor's plans will only help our cause and strengthen his campaign platform, but I refuse to share anything about it until I feel like I can trust that my mom and everyone else on Lavender Lane won't be put in legal jeopardy.

My mom's health can't take it, and I care too much about our neighbors to cause them more distress.

So until Lorenzo proves himself worthy, I'll keep quiet on the matter and enjoy the way it eats him up inside to not know all my secrets.

X secret garden studio

wws ???
wildflower touches studio

petal + press

the Pressed Petal

CHAPTER FIFTEEN

Lily

By the time Willow, Lorenzo, and I finish discussing the Operation Fake Fiancée plan, it is already half past nine, so I head home with more hope than I had left with.

The house is dark when I unlock the front door, so I'm startled when I don't notice my mom sitting in the living room until she says, "You were out late."

"*¡Dios!*" I press a hand against my racing heart. "*Mami, me asustaste.*"[I]

She shuts off the TV and stands. "Where were you?"

"With Lorenzo."

"Is he the reason why you skipped lunch?"

I   **Me asustaste:** You scared me.

"No, everyone else is."

Her eyes are downcast. "We're…worried about you."

"I'm fine. Better than fine, actually." Technically that *is* true. My personal life might be a mess right now, but I can rest easier tonight knowing Lorenzo and I have a solid plan in place and a common goal to reach.

"We missed you." She hits me with a wobbly smile. "You weren't there to overcook the pasta."

There's a small pinch in my chest. "I'm sure that was a nice change for once."

She laughs to herself. "Actually, I've come to enjoy my *espagueti verde* that way."

I can't stop myself from laughing. "I can only hope Lorenzo will pretend to feel the same way when he tries it next week."

She makes a face, and I instantly know I made the wrong assumption.

My amusement dies. "What?"

Her eyes fall to her plastic *chancletas*. "I don't know if him coming is a good idea yet."

Whatever hope I had earlier withers away. "Oh…I see."

She holds up her hands, panic written clear across her face. "I want to meet him—officially, that is—as your…as your…" She stumbles to finish her thought.

I help her out by saying, "Boyfriend."

She wrings her hands in front of her robe. "Right. But I think we should do so in a smaller setting. Maybe us three first, if that's okay with you?"

I'm kicking myself for not thinking about that idea first. When she said she didn't want Lorenzo to come to next week's lunch, I assumed the worst, not taking into account my mom's anxiety.

Julian made her believe he's some kind of mafioso, I reprimand myself. *Of course she's anxious about you dating him.*

"You want to get to know him?"

"You've never insisted on bringing a…boyfriend to Sunday lunch before, so yes, I'd like to get to know him in a more casual setting."

"I thought…" My voice wavers.

With Dahlia still not talking to me and the Kids' Table group chat going radio silent, I believed my mom harbored the same negative feelings toward Lorenzo and me, but I should've known hers were caused by anxiety rather than anger.

"You thought what?" she asks with that soft voice that always got me to admit to everything when I was younger.

"That you were mad at me."

She shakes her head. "I am. It's hard not to be after you kept this secret from me. Between that and the shop, I feel like I'm failing you if you can't trust me with something so important."

My vision is obscured from unshed tears.

You're doing this to help her. My mom protected me for twenty-eight years of my life, so the least I can do is save her shop and one of the last living memories we have of my father.

She walks over and pulls me into a hug. "I'm still angry with you, but I'm less so now."

"What changed?"

"I went to go visit your father at the cemetery."

You will not cry, I chant repeatedly, but my eyes won't cooperate.

"Spending time with him always calms me down."

I sniffle. My mom might be anxious, but at least she's brave enough to stop by his grave, unlike me, who hasn't since his wake.

She continues, "If he were still here, he'd tell me to give Lorenzo a chance. He'd say that your happiness is more important than my anxiety about you dating someone like him."

My mouth falls open, but words never make it out. Guilt threatens to consume me whole, and I'm hit with the strongest urge to confess my sin.

She cups my cheek. "I want you to be happy, and if Lorenzo is the man who makes you feel that way, then it's my job as your mother to support you."

"But—"

She pats my face. "No *but*s."

You're going to hell, my guilty conscience speaks out.

At least Lorenzo will keep you company.

After the conversation I had with my mom, I decide that I'd rather get awkward introductions done between her and Lorenzo sooner rather than later. That way I can ease some of her worries and assuage some of my guilt.

I've had boyfriends in the past who I've introduced to my mom, but I'm still nervous as we drive over to our favorite farm located on the outskirts of town. I don't even *like* picking berries, but Lorenzo was the one who suggested the activity. He thought it would buy him some points with my mom since she planned on coming out here anyway after she volunteered to make strawberry-flavored *agua fresca* for next week's Strawberry Festival.

A lot of people are at the farm today, picking berries for their own festival dishes and desserts, so we'll be seen by plenty of possible voters over the next couple of hours.

Lorenzo is already parked when we arrive, so he walks over and opens my mom's door first before helping me out of the car. He pulls me into a short but intimate hug, and I'm hit with the scent of his cologne. It isn't overpowering but rather nearly undetectable unless I press my nose right up to his skin.

I have enough self-control to resist doing so, but barely.

When he lets go of me, I see a group of people standing in the parking lot, looking over at us like we're their favorite couple on a dating show.

"¿Estás listo para recoger fresas?"[I] Lorenzo ignores them and turns to my mom.

Her lips curl. *"Lo que Dahlia dijo es verdad. Tú hablas español."*[II]

"Sí. Aprendí eso y el italiano cuando era pequeño."[III]

[I]   **Estás listo para recoger fresas:** Are you ready to pick strawberries?

[II]   **Lo que Dahlia dijo es verdad. Tú hablas español:** What Dahlia said is true. You speak Spanish.

[III]   **Sí. Aprendí eso y el italiano cuando era pequeño:** Yes. I learned that and Italian when I was little.

My mom gives him a confirmatory nod, and I throw him a thumbs-up behind her back that earns me an eye roll.

My mom, Lorenzo, and I head toward the wooden stand, where we are each given a basket. At first, she is quiet and will only speak when directly spoken to. Lorenzo takes her shyness in stride, actively making bids for her attention.

I appreciate how he never gives up, and finally after ten minutes of picking strawberries, my mom starts asking him questions. She's particularly interested in learning about his aunt, whose family moved to America from Cuba during the fifties, but she clams up again when he mentions his life in Vegas.

When my mom excuses herself to go use the restroom located on the other side of the farm, Lorenzo takes advantage of her absence to amp up the showmance for our nearby audience.

I should've known he was up to something when he accidently tipped my basket over, but I didn't expect him to smack my ass as soon as I bend down.

But that isn't nearly as bad as me liking it.

My lower half pulses when his palm connects with my ass, and if it weren't for the group of women standing a few rows away, I'd press my legs together to ease the ache that comes out of nowhere.

Don't you dare embarrass yourself like that.

Frustrated by my lack of control, I remind myself of how Lorenzo hurt me and why I can't get caught up in the moment. Not even for a single second.

I look over my shoulder to check out the group of

women. Josefina has invited them over to her house a few times for a romance reading club, so I recognize them, although they look different without their eyes glued to their paperbacks.

"Sorry. I couldn't resist," Lorenzo says loudly, making them giggle.

I stand up and turn so our chests are touching.

"No need to apologize, baby." My voice has a huskiness to it that I don't recognize.

Based on the way his nostrils flare, Lorenzo either loves or hates the sexy rasp as much as his nickname.

I brush my hand down his chest. "But next time don't hold back. I promise I can take it."

And that right there is how I helped Lorenzo secure the Smut Club readers' vote.

Little by little, as our pile of strawberries in the back of Lorenzo's truck grows, my mom gets more comfortable in his presence, to the point of inviting him back to our house to make some *agua fresca* once she is too hot to continue.

Her invitation was not part of the plan, and I'm instantly anxious at the prospect of Lorenzo hanging out in our home. It has nothing to do with the house itself but rather how I feel having him in my space.

Going out on dates with Lorenzo is one thing, but having him in my chaotic little sanctuary feels like a step too far.

"Oh, I'm sure Lorenzo is busy," I answer for him.

"I took the day off, *remember*?" he says aloud, acting like we memorize each other's schedules.

"That settles it, then," my mom says with a smile, and we head back to the house in separate cars.

My mom spends the first five minutes of the house tour in the garage, showing off my latest pressed-petal art. Lorenzo keeps a straight face while my mom tells him about how proud he must be of me wanting to pursue my own business venture with the Pressed Petal, all while shooting me looks.

"Any new updates on that since last week?" He is so damn smooth with his delivery that my mom doesn't think anything of the question.

"Nope. Everything's still on hold." I keep my answer vague, and thankfully my mom doesn't bring up Lavender Lane and the mayor's plan, although she is quick to shuffle us into the kitchen after.

She and Lorenzo work in comfortable silence while I pull out my sketchbook and get to work on a design I've fallen behind on. My mom's favorite telenovela plays in the background, and Lorenzo—who seemed completely uninterested at the start of the episode—has been equally invested in finding out who the bad guy is.

My mom has taken a liking to him, although I can't expect her to be as comfortable around him as she is with Julian or Rafa, whom she has known since they were little. The way she is with Lorenzo is different, but then again, so is he.

He's patient, polite, and intent on helping my mom with whatever she needs in the kitchen. My mom gives him a few tasks, including washing the buckets' worth of strawberries, and Lorenzo does it without a single complaint, following every request with a *"Sì, signora"* that makes me giggle.

"Your dad used to say that too."

I gape. Lorenzo blinks.

"You knew Lorenzo's dad?" I ask my mom because Lorenzo looks incapable of speaking.

My mom looks cautious all of a sudden. "I didn't know him too well, but I never forgot his flower order."

I can't resist asking, "What was it?"

"Whatever's in season—"

"So long as it's pink," I say at the same time as her, my eyes wide from recognition.

My mom laughs. "How'd you know?"

Because I've heard that phrase before, back when Lorenzo first started ordering bouquets from Rose & Thorn.

Lorenzo reaches inside his pocket and leans against the counter, looking unbothered if it weren't for the small twitch in his jaw.

Now the bouquet in his house makes so much more sense, although I can't say the same about the twinge in my chest at seeing his sentimental side.

His parents might not be here anymore, but he finds the smallest ways to acknowledge them, unlike me, who can't visit my father's garden without crying.

My mom's eyes crinkle at the corners. "Your father never missed a single Friday."

Lorenzo dips his head in silent acknowledgment, and I'm overwhelmed by the urge to pull him into a hug, although I hesitate after everything he has done and said to me.

Comforting someone else comes naturally to me, but comforting him…it feels like an instinct I hate to ignore.

Lorenzo and my mom carry on like the conversation never happened, but I obsess over it for the next five minutes, wondering what Lorenzo does with that second bouquet.

When Lorenzo finishes everything my mom asked of him, he starts to wipe the counter, but my mom pulls the rag from his hands and tells him to take a seat and relax.

"*Sì, signora,*" he says.

When my mom finishes rinsing the sink, she excuses herself to go use the restroom, but not before she reminds him not to help.

I bump him with my shoulder. "Who knew you could be such a gentleman?"

"I know it must come as quite a shock given our past, but I *do* have manners."

"Yet I haven't experienced them firsthand."

He tucks his hand underneath my chin and lifts it. "Don't tell me you're jealous."

"Imagine if you heard me telling another man *yes, sir* over and over again?" My face flushes at the wide smile on his face.

"In this particular scenario, is this man old enough to be a grandparent?"

"No!" I pull away with a laugh, and Lorenzo's hold on my chin slips. He stares at his hand, which is still hanging in the air, as if he too was wondering how it ended up anywhere near my face.

I shouldn't miss him touching me.

Shouldn't so much as think twice about why he even bothered to do so since we don't have an audience present.

And I most definitely should not, under absolutely any circumstance, think about when he will do it again.

CHAPTER SIXTEEN

Lorenzo

Phase One of Operation Fake Fiancée, a subtle title Willow came up with, is officially a go. I still haven't pushed Lily on the subject of why she dislikes the Ludlows enough to help me win the election, but I plan on figuring it out tonight during our first official date.

Since I was too busy working with one of my clients—a man who needs an investor for his water-containment system that helps farmers save water—to plan a date tonight, Willow took it upon herself to fit Lily and me into a fully-booked cooking class in town.

It's the perfect kind of setting for a date. A staged dinner would've been too awkward, so a cooking class gives us something to do while remaining in the public eye.

Tonight's meal is one I could easily make in my sleep

thanks to growing up with an Italian father who hated store-bought ravioli, but Lily looks excited about it.

Maria, an older Italian woman I've spent time getting to know, and her American husband pull Lily and me aside to say hello.

"Lorenzo!" The chef throws her arms around me. "What a nice surprise. I had no idea you'd be attending tonight's class."

I freeze up, only to be further physically tested when her husband claps a hand around my shoulder.

"Good to see you."

I'm about to shake him off, but Lily's hand wrapping around my bicep puts a temporary stop to that idea.

Careful now, the same black fog slithers through my mind, sucking some of my life force away.

"I love what you've done with the place," Lily says while looking at me out of the corner of her eye.

"Thank you! Lorenzo helped us with the rebranding project." She beams. "Without him, it wouldn't have been possible to turn the restaurant into a cooking school."

Maria's husband, who looks extremely uncomfortable at the reminder of my help, is proof why. Most people, especially men, hate asking for money, so I'm typically brought on as a silent investor when people are out of options and need capital.

I provide funds in exchange for a small percentage of annual profits, and based on the way Maria's cooking class is thriving, I made the right decision investing in the remodel. Although he'd never say it, I'm sure her proud husband agrees given how packed the room is.

He and Maria politely excuse themselves from the

conversation so they can welcome the other guests. The attendees' ages range, and our group is full of newlywed couples and retirees who are looking for something entertaining to do on a weekday.

"Who else have you helped in town?" Lily whispers to me while Maria hands out plastic aprons to the group.

I press my mouth against her ear. "Wouldn't be much of a secret if I told you, would it?"

She is a little slow when pulling away. "I'm surprised you're not flaunting it for everyone to see."

"Unlike the Lopez cousins, some of us don't need to have a street or soccer field dedicated in our honor."

She sticks out her tongue as Maria stops by our station to hand us our aprons. "For my favorite student."

Lily grabs both. "Better not let your other ones hear that."

"They'll understand once they see this man cook."

Lily waits until Maria takes off before teasing, "Sounds like I'm in the presence of a professional."

"Hardly." I'd rather downplay my skills than be praised for them.

"How'd you get into cooking?" She speaks low so no one hears us.

"My parents." Hopefully my short answer wards her away from asking more questions about it.

Cooking is more about control than enjoying the art. My first and last therapist told me as much, along with how control was one of the reasons I most likely developed OCD.

Sometimes when a child is ripped away from their life like I had been, they feel the need to establish control over every aspect of their environment.

Which is why tonight is that much more difficult for me. In my own kitchen, I know exactly where and when the food was bought. I can double- and triple-check expiration dates without anyone noticing the compulsion, and I'm able to wash my fruits and veggies until it feels *just right* without anyone judging me.

It isn't healthy. My brief stint in therapy taught me that, but my compulsive behaviors can be difficult to stop, and me staying in my comfort zone where I have full control over everything doesn't help. So instead of learning how to better manage them, I've built quite a repertoire of recipes since I rarely order takeout or eat at restaurants.

Lily slips her plastic apron over her head, making her dark hair stand up in all different directions. Before I think twice about it, I reach behind her head and fix her hair so it's no longer catching on the plastic.

She blinks up at me, her eyes slightly wider than before.

"What?" I ask.

She rips her gaze away. "Nothing."

We both know she's lying, but I don't push, instead holding out the permanent marker so she can write my name across the front of the apron. When it's my turn to do the same, I'm questioning if I can make it through the four letters of her name without making a fool of myself.

In the middle of writing the letter *y*, her body goes rigid.

"What?" I look around for what threatened her happiness and easily locate the source.

Cazzo.

Richard, Trevor Ludlow's younger, less charismatic

brother, walks into the room with a blonde woman on his arm. She hangs on to him and bats her lashes at everyone in the vicinity.

He immediately zones in on us.

"Ignore him." I step in front of her, blocking his view of Lily as Maria starts talking about the history of pasta and the basic instructions of tonight's class before assigning us to our tables.

Lily and I are sent to one in a corner nearest the window. It gives us privacy from the other couples while simultaneously allowing people walking by the class to see us.

The location is perfect…right up until Richard and his date get set up at a station parallel to ours. I can feel his attention focused on us, and I don't like it one bit, but I do my best to forget about him.

My issues are with his brother, not him, although I'm starting to have a problem with the youngest Ludlow, who keeps glancing over at Lily.

I check our ingredients for tonight's dinner and dessert before Lily and I start working on our dough.

"How often do you make fresh pasta?" she asks as I crack an egg over my well of flour.

"Never."

She lets out a fake gasp of outrage. "I thought you were Italian."

I grab a pinch of flour and flick it at her face.

With a giggle, she wipes her flour-speckled cheek. She ends up missing a spot, so I brush it away. A camera flash startles us both, and we look over to see Maria winking. She checks the photo before scurrying away with a promise to send me a copy.

Lily eyes me rolling the dough into a ball while her flour-egg combo remains untouched. "When's the last time you did this?"

I need a second to think of a response. "Sometime after I moved to Vegas. One of the nannies wanted me to"—*stop crying*—"feel comfortable."

Although all it did was make me miss *home*.

Her eyes soften, and I wonder if she can read between the lines of my answer.

"Did your parents teach you?" she asks, her gentle voice soothing the scratchiness in my throat at the mention of them.

I look at my ball of dough. "Yes, and once I learned, I helped them make pasta every Friday afterward."

She gives my bicep a squeeze, leaving a dusty handprint on my skin. "Sounds like a tradition I can get behind."

"Don't get me started on traditions," I tease, surprised by my own lightheartedness. Usually I avoid talking about my parents, but with Lily, I don't even notice, most likely because the typical heaviness I feel whenever I think about them is dormant.

Which is probably why I tell her about their yearly sauce-day tradition.

"As a little kid, I hated every second of it," I say after explaining the concept, my throat thick with emotion. If I could go back, I would've spent my time enjoying my parents' company rather than complaining.

I close my eyes and picture my mom and dad working

outside, their backs hunched as they took turns stirring the pot full of tomatoes. Back then, life was simple, and I didn't have the same contamination worries or concerns about food prep.

"Do you have their recipe somewhere? I'd love to try it," she asks.

No, because my uncle donated or discarded most of my father's possessions—another unforgivable act to add to his never-ending list.

"Before…you know…my parents had this recipe book." I have no idea why I am sharing so much about myself, but I can't seem to stop myself as I continue. "They'd always try new ones, and if they liked it enough, they'd write it down."

I regret sharing such a small detail about myself, especially when she looks at me with an expression I've learned to recognize.

Pity.

It's gone as soon as I blink, and for that, I'm grateful.

She smiles instead. "Seems like they were a lot of fun."

The conversation seems to die after that, and I miss the curious sparkle in Lily's eyes once she resumes her task of shaping the dough into a ball.

With each pass of the rolling pin we have to share, energy crackles and the air thickens around us, and it all comes to a crescendo when Lily struggles to flatten her dough. She sucks in a breath when I step behind her, only for her breathing to stop altogether when I place my hands over hers and create a cage with my arms.

"What are you doing?" she whispers low enough for only us to hear.

"At this rate, you and I will be stuck here all night," I say louder.

"Don't threaten me with a good time, baby." She winks, and Richard looks ready to keel over his table nearby.

"But I have plans for us later." I drop a kiss on the spot where her shoulder meets the curve of her neck. Her flesh pebbles from the brief contact, and I smile against her skin that smells of flowers, vanilla, and a note of something else I can't identify.

"Fine." She sighs dramatically. "Help me."

I resume our task of rolling the dough, each press of my body against hers drawing a different physical reaction.

"Why do you enjoy antagonizing me?" she whispers.

"I'm showing my girlfriend how much I want her."

"In that case…" She shimmies her hips, rubbing her ass against my crotch until some of my blood rushes south.

I bite down on my cheek hard enough to taste blood.

"You good?" She looks over her shoulder with a smirk.

"Peachy." My gaze drops to her incriminating ass and the bulge forming beneath my jeans.

Think about anything else. Manny kicking your ass in poker. Willow saying you'll never win the election. The CDC announcing that an emerging virus is turning everyone into flesh-eating zombies.

Lily glances over her shoulder and smiles in a way that makes me wish it were real. A dangerous thought given our situation, and a reminder of why I can't get caught up in the ruse.

The side of my face prickles with awareness, and I turn

my head toward Richard, who is staring at Lily. His obvious interest in her doesn't surprise me because most men react the same way, but something about him screams *wrong*.

My intuition hasn't led me astray before, so I listen to it and goad Richard into showing me his cards.

I cover Lily's hands and help her with the last few rolls, earning an eye twitch from Richard.

Hm.

I never doubted her when she claimed to dislike the Ludlows, but I also never got around to pressing her on the subject. All that will change tonight because I'm going to get the truth out of her.

One way or another.

CHAPTER SEVENTEEN

Lily

Maria, who is like our very own *nonna*, miraculously turns us average—or in my case, *fire hazard*—cooks into decent chefs for the night. When she collects everyone's raviolis in a large bowl and tosses them into a boiling pot of water together, we wait patiently, sipping wine and mingling by the portable stove Maria works at.

Hopefully everyone took hygiene as seriously as Lorenzo, who was diligent with cleaning his hands and prep station.

Eventually Maria and her husband shuffle everyone over to the long, family-style table set up at the back of the room and ask us to take a seat. The steaming raviolis on my plate look like they could've been served at a restaurant, but I can't say the same about everyone else's dinner. Lorenzo's plate looks like a mix of ill-prepared ones, with a few leaking from the corners.

Everyone starts to dig into their food. One taste of mine has me shutting my eyes with a quiet groan, while Lorenzo clutches his fork like it might break free from his hand and make a run for it.

I expected him to socialize with everyone in a setting like this since it's the perfect natural opportunity, but he seems uncharacteristically quiet.

Underneath the table, I nudge him with my thigh. "You good?"

His Adam's apple bobs from his swallow. "Yup."

I take another bite of my food while he watches me out of the corner of his eye.

"What?" I ask when he doesn't break his stare.

"You feeling okay?"

"Me?" I forget my manners and laugh in the middle of chewing. "Yes. Thankfully it's not poisoned."

Between breaks in the conversation with other couples, he shifts some of his dinner around on the porcelain plate without taking a single bite. I've spent enough time around Rafa to recognize unique eating habits, although Rafa's compulsory need to finish everything on Nico's and his plates is completely different compared to Lorenzo's inability to touch his food.

I want to ask him more about it, but I've experienced enough of Rafa's embarrassment to understand now isn't the time nor place.

At one unfortunate point, I accidentally lock eyes with Richard in the process and immediately wish I hadn't. Lorenzo's gaze might be cool and detached most of the time, but I'd choose that any day of the week over Richard's unwanted leer.

Lorenzo seems to sense my discomfort, and his hand reaches for mine underneath the table. After spending the better half of our *date* reminding myself that this is all a show for the town, all it takes is him holding my hand to have my stomach swooping again.

"I don't like the way he looks at you." His eyes glance at something over my shoulder, and I turn to find him staring at Richard.

"Ignore him."

Lorenzo readjusts his hold on my hand and slides his fingers between mine. "Why is he so interested in you?"

I swallow a panicked laugh.

Lorenzo presses his mouth to my ear. "Is he someone you dated?"

I can't help the incriminating flush that blooms across my cheeks.

A small, hardly noticeable vein appears in his jaw. "When?"

"After the Eros situation."

He releases my hand and plays with a strand of my hair, teasing my shoulder with the tips of his fingers in the process. "I see."

My answer appears to spur on Lorenzo, and he packs as much PDA into our date as humanly possible.

He even makes a show of feeding me a bite of panna cotta, and a woman from down the table gushes about it. My taste buds are overwhelmed by the flavors of strawberry and cream, and the custard-like texture practically melts in my mouth as Lorenzo drags the spoon away.

I'm still recuperating from the way he stares at my mouth

like he wants to kiss it, only to be tested yet again when he reaches for the linen napkin and wipes the corner of my mouth with it. My bottom lip tingles when his thumb accidentally brushes over it instead of the napkin, but the feeling fades when I catch Lorenzo winking in the direction of the swooning group of women at the other side of the table.

They're not the only ones.

We're only one date into our arrangement and I'm already struggling, so I can't imagine how I'll feel once we're months into fake dating.

I can only hope I escape with my heart still intact.

When Lorenzo doesn't return from the bathroom after a few minutes, I excuse myself and seek him out. I want to make sure he is okay since he has been tense all night, but all my worries come to a screeching halt when I find Richard and him in a standoff.

The only reason they're eye level is because Lorenzo is holding Richard up against the wall by the material of his T-shirt. His feet dangle beneath him, the toes of his fancy shoes scraping the tiled surface beneath.

My heart beats wildly in my chest as two people from my past collide. "What's going on here?"

Lorenzo's jaw ticks. "Dick and I were having a chat."

I keep my eyes trained on Lorenzo's face rather than the one currently glaring at me. "Looks like a friendly one."

Lorenzo releases Richard without giving him a chance to

brace for the landing, so the youngest Ludlow's knees nearly give out in the process of finding his footing.

"I think you have something to say, Dick," he spits out with a curled upper lip.

Richard's eye twitches. "I'm—"

Lorenzo holds up his hand. "The next word out of your mouth better be *sorry*, or else."

What the hell is going on?

Richard's eyes glint with malice. "I'm *sorry* for your loss, Lorenzo."

Lorenzo seems more stunned than pissed off, while Richard appears extremely pleased with himself.

His loss? I thought Richard might've said something about me that upset Lorenzo, but maybe he's goading him about the election? Because what other loss could he be talking about?

Richard moves to walk around me, but he leans in at the last second so he can whisper, "He's the guy who dumped you, isn't he?"

The words get stuck in my throat.

"Does he know about us, or does he just not care because he doesn't expect any better of you?" His cutting words might as well have been carved into my chest. "Because if I were him, I'd run far away from a woman like you."

I know Richard is wrong, and even if he was right, then screw any man who judges my choices, whether it be who I sleep with or what clothes I decide to wear.

Richard gives me a parting glance before disappearing around the corner. I expected Lorenzo to jump in and do *something*—anything will suffice after the way Dick insulted me—but he's got this faraway look in his eyes that makes me realize he wasn't listening.

"Are you okay?" I reach for Lorenzo's arm, but he takes a step back and crosses them against his chest, adding a physical barrier between us. Someone without any context might interpret it as a brush-off, but it seems more like a self-soothing hug than a defensive maneuver, and it makes my heart hurt *for* him.

After everything he has put me through, it shouldn't. But then again, my feelings for Lorenzo have always been... complicated.

And that was before I notice how his hands are slightly trembling.

So, I give in to the impulse to comfort him, wrap my arms around his waist, and squeeze. At first he bristles, his body hard as stone, but eventually his muscles loosen and he exhales loudly, his body loosening automatically.

It's strange to comfort someone who causes me so much sadness, anger, and self-doubt, but when I see Lorenzo like this—lost, lonely, and paralyzed by some invisible adversary I know nothing about—I can't leave him to drown in his own demons.

I wasn't raised to be heartless, even if that's all he's known for most of his life.

So, despite my better judgment, I hug him, and I hug him *hard*. I even rub his back like my mom always does whenever Dahlia and I are upset.

I don't stop or release him until the tension bleeds from his body, and even then, I struggle because I don't *want* to let go.

And that right there is a problem.

CHAPTER EIGHTEEN

Lorenzo

I can't stop replaying the conversation I had with Richard despite Lily's best attempts to lighten the mood.

Thankfully the cooking class ends soon after the bathroom encounter, and Lily and I leave the space without speaking to one another.

She stays quiet as she climbs into my Ferrari, and I'm grateful for the silence.

I'm sorry for your loss, Richard said with a smile.

If I didn't have a mayoral race to win, I would've punched him hard enough in the face to cause permanent damage. It's the least he deserves after bringing up my parents.

I thought Trevor kept his dirty little DUI a secret between him and his father, but the Ludlows are a tight-knit family, so I'm not surprised that Richard knows all about what his brother did the night he decided to get behind the wheel and kill my parents in the process.

Hell, they probably used it as a learning lesson for Richard, reminding him why he shouldn't drink and drive.

At least Richard didn't comment on Lily, and for that I'm grateful because I'm not sure I would've taken that well. She had every right to get with whomever she wanted after what I did to her, but I don't want to think about it ever again.

I don't notice I'm fiddling with my father's dice until one of them slips from my hand and falls in the narrow gap between my driver's seat and the center console.

"Shit!"

Lily jumps in her seat and looks out the windshield. "What's wrong?"

With one hand on the steering wheel, I reach into the gap but struggle to fit my fingers past the first knuckle.

"Do you need help?"

"No." I grunt as I pull over to the side of the road. With my phone's flashlight, I locate the die, but I can't reach it with the size of my hands. I even get out of the car to try from a different angle, but the narrow space and lack of room behind the seat makes the task of retrieving the die impossible.

"Let me try." Lily unbuckles her seat belt and walks around the car.

"I've got it." I don't want Lily to ask me questions about the dice or why I was fidgeting with them.

After another minute of watching me struggle, she places her hand on my shoulder. "Lorenzo?"

My jaw clenches as I pull myself out of the car.

"What am I looking for?" she asks before softly pushing me out of the way.

I help her with the flashlight. "See that die?"

"Oh yeah. Hold on." She shimmies her body and lets out a grunt before she makes an excited noise.

"Did you get it?"

"Almost, but I dropped it." Her voice is strained, but with one last push, she squeals. "Yes! Got it!"

She pulls her arm out from underneath the seat and stares at the die like she discovered an artifact. "*Moirai*? What does it mean?"

"None of your business."

"Not the translation I was expecting for such a pretty word," she replies dryly.

If you want her to trust you enough to open up about her reason for loathing the Ludlows, you're off to a strong start.

I pluck the die from her palm and reunite it with the matching one in my pocket. I check to make sure they're both there three times before I can exhale without feeling a weight pressing against my chest.

"Thank you," I say before ushering her back to the passenger side.

"Are those from one of your family's casinos?" she asks once I return to my spot behind the wheel.

My lack of a response pushes her to take matters into her own hands, and she pulls out her phone. There is no way to stop her from being curious, so I drive quietly while Lily searches the internet for the answer.

After a minute, my stomach drops when she asks, "Your father helped run the Moirai?"

I keep my eyes glued to the road. "Yes."

Better.

"Is that why you had it torn down?"

"No." I itch to touch the dice, but I stop myself. While I like to use them as a grounding tool and a coping mechanism, I don't want it to become a compulsion. I already have enough of those to keep me busy.

"According to an article—"

"I wouldn't trust everything you read because that particular journalist owed my uncle a lot of money in gambling debts." The truth slips out easier than expected.

Her lips part twice before she speaks. "He asked them to write this story?"

I nod.

"Why would he do that?"

I take a deep, centering breath to prepare myself for her never-ending curiosity. "Because he knew everyone would assume I'm an asshole."

Out of the corner of my eye, I catch the way her lips press firmly together. Seeing how she was quick to believe the worst only a few seconds ago, she knows I'm right.

The Moirai being torn down was the final straw for me, but at least something good came out of it—if you can even call him divulging the truth about my parents' deaths that.

After that, I dug into the hit-and-run accident, and once I discovered what really happened, I sold my shares and got the hell out of Vegas. I had no plan outside of wanting to visit my parents' graves.

When I learned about Trevor's plan to run for mayor,

I joined the race too. My uncle was spiteful about it, and he knew hurting my reputation would do wonders for my competition.

"I'm sorry," Lily says quietly after a couple of minutes.

"What are you apologizing for?"

"For assuming the worst without thinking twice about it."

I shrug. "It happens more often than you think."

"That's so sad."

"I better not be hearing pity in your voice." I don't deserve it after all I've done and said to her.

She fakes a gasp. "Me? Pitying *you*? I could never."

My lips curl at the corners.

"But if I *were* to feel that way—"

I'd shoot her a sharp look if I wasn't driving.

She continues, "It's because at some point in your life, you learned to protect yourself by letting people think the worst of you. It was probably too easy to play the part of a villain, and I bet you became so comfortable with the role, you never expected anyone to question it."

I pause at what she says and wonder how she got to that conclusion. People are quick to write me off as an uncaring asshole, and I've embraced the incorrect assumption. It was safer, because then no one—especially not my uncle—could exploit me.

"If you're expecting me to agree with your psychological analysis, you'll be waiting a long time."

She shakes her head. "I don't expect someone as defensive as you to come out and admit anything."

"I'm not defensive."

"Sure you're not." She laughs in a condescending way that grates on my nerves. "Do you ever get tired?"

I lean away despite not having anywhere to go. "Of what?"

"Pushing everyone away to keep up this false pretense. It must get pretty lonely."

Her assessment of my life couldn't be more wrong, but I don't correct her. I don't feel lonely because I prefer my company over others. It's safer that way. More *controlled*.

Which is exactly her point.

I'm not lonely. I may have felt that way for a short while before I joined the Eros app and met Lily, but after that situation blew up in my face, I learned to prefer isolation again.

Learned? Or tricked yourself into believing you were better off without Lily?

I tap my fingers against the wheel. "I'll answer that question when you tell me why you really agreed to this fake relationship."

Her mouth opens, and she looks like she's about to speak, only to press her lips together.

I shake my head. "You expect me to trust you, but you can't do the same?"

"I didn't have a problem trusting you *before*."

I realize that if I want an answer to my question, I'm going to have to give one in return. It's not like Lily hasn't figured me out already, so I might as well get something out of this conversation.

"I don't get lonely."

She rolls her eyes. "You liar."

"Just because you don't agree doesn't mean it's not true."

"Because there's no way that's possible. *Everyone* gets lonely."

Not when you have endless worries to keep you company.

"I've learned to appreciate the quiet." If you can even call it that.

"Then why would you join a dating app because you were bored?" She smirks.

"Boredom doesn't equate to loneliness."

"I beg to differ."

"Why did *you* join the app?"

"The same reason that most people do." She glances out the window, making it impossible to get a read on her expression without taking my eyes off the road.

"To fall in love?"

"That was the goal." Her voice is tinged with sadness, making my chest uncomfortably burn.

"Then why waste your time on a fake relationship?"

She takes so long to answer me, I assume she won't, but then she starts talking about the condemnation notice she received from the mayor's office, Richard's involvement in swaying the mayor toward Lavender Lane, and the NDA her mother signed.

By the end of her explanation, she is winded and looking over at me with eyes shiny from unshed tears. "They can't take Rose & Thorn away. I don't care what people say about reopening it somewhere else—nothing can replace the emotional attachment I have to the shop and the memories I shared with my dad there."

I relate to that more than she will ever know. And while I may not have been able to save the Moirai, I can do this.

I *have* to.

I ignore the burning sensation. "We won't let them."

"You promise?" She sounds surprised, hopeful, and scared all at once.

I nod. "If I become mayor—"

"*When*," she corrects.

I catch myself smiling. "When I become mayor, there's no way I'd ever let something like that go through."

She exhales loudly, and the tension in her shoulders bleeds out. "Thank you." She reaches for my bicep and gives it a squeeze. "You have no idea how badly I needed to hear that."

I miss her touch as soon as she pulls back.

"Why didn't you tell me about this from the start?"

She chews on her bottom lip.

"What?" I ask when she doesn't answer me.

"I didn't trust you. I still don't, but if this is going to work, we need to start learning to."

"Right," I reply, my throat constricted.

She peers over at me, and I can tell by the look on her face that I won't like her next question. "Why are you running for mayor?"

The cabin of the car closes in around me. "I care about the town."

"Okay, sure. I assumed as much with all the small businesses you help, but can't you do that without going up against Ludlow?"

"I can do a lot more for everyone if I'm in charge." I hope my answer pacifies her.

She shrugs. "Maybe. It just seems like you're putting in a lot of effort for a town you just moved to."

Panic grips me, but I breathe through my nose until I'm no longer at risk of revealing my motives.

Before our first meeting at Last Call, I trusted Lily with a few stories about my life, like when my uncle broke my nose, but I can't tell her about my parents or the Ludlows. I *won't*, even if the idea of sharing the burden with someone else is tempting.

Someone, or Lily?

Instead of exploring the thought, I deflect. "I think I can do a better job than Trevor, so why not run against him? And now that I know about his Lavender Lane plan, we can use that to our advantage. Once people find out about their plan for the Historic District, they'll have no choice but to switch sides."

She latches onto my arm, her fingernails digging into my skin hard enough to leave a temporary mark. "No. You can't tell people about it without affecting my mom and anyone else who signed the NDA."

Shit. I comb through all the information she shared. "You mentioned something before about architect plans?"

"Yeah. What about them?"

"Do you remember who drew them up?"

She taps her chin. "I don't remember the name exactly. It was something like Morris and Holmes?"

"I'll look into it."

She pulls in a deep lungful of air. "Please don't make me regret trusting you with this. The last thing my mom needs with her heart condition is a stressful legal battle."

"Okay."

Her relief is palpable. "Thank you."

It's quiet in the car for the duration of the drive to Lily's house, and I'm relieved when I pull into her driveway. There is something about the silence that feels oppressive, and I have a strange urge to fill it with sound.

Particularly the sound of Lily's voice.

When I first met her, I knew she could ruin everything I've worked toward up until this point. She had this way of quieting obsessive thoughts—of making me forget that I hate kissing or that I rarely like to drink because I don't like losing even the slightest bit of control over myself. She had me thinking, at least for a few seconds, about a future that wasn't only about me.

A future that seemed promising, right up until I remembered that I wouldn't only be worrying about myself but about her too—something that didn't end well with my parents.

I already have enough to worry about when it comes to myself, so becoming obsessed with Lily is the last thing I need.

Even if she's everything I want.

CHAPTER NINETEEN

Lily

Over the next week, Lorenzo and I increase our public outings. I pop into his campaign headquarters for a very public lunch, we hang out together at Last Call, and I join him at the Park Promenade one afternoon—and by *join*, I mean sat on a bench and gawked at Lorenzo while he used the park's outdoor fitness equipment.

Shirtless, I might add.

And *dripping*.

By the time he was halfway through his workout, he had formed a fan club of nannies and dog walkers, which was slightly annoying. The only way I got rid of them was by throwing my arms around Lorenzo's half-naked, glistening body and staking my claim.

Word spreads all over town about our relationship. I'm not

the only one everyone is talking about because it turns out Rafa is dating Ellie, who gave her two weeks' notice because she likes her boss as more than a friend.

I've been meaning to talk to Rafa about it, so when he asks me to help him take his new family of kittens to the vet, I agree to tag along. I'm the second-biggest animal lover in the family, so there's nothing I'd love more.

Rafa didn't outright admit he adopted them because of Ellie, but I connected the dots when he retold the adoption story during our drive into town. He even *smiles* at one point when talking about her, and I'm overwhelmed by his happiness.

But I'm also a teeny, tiny bit sad—not for him, but for myself. Because how many years have I spent longing for a person who talks about me the same way?

I've been on dates. I've joined every matchmaking app. I've given men multiple chances because I wanted to be sure they weren't the person I could see myself spending the rest of my life with.

Then I met Lorenzo, and I thought he was that person for me. I was so confident about it that I *wished* for him to be.

Just like my dad said to.

I shove the painful memory away and focus on Rafa telling me another story about his trip. By the time we arrive at the animal clinic, the kittens are meowing like crazy, so the secretary shows us to a private room where we can let them loose while we wait for the vet.

"So, you and Lorenzo..." Rafa says as he plucks the one with the pink collar off the floor.

I reach for the kitten and place her back with her brother and sisters. "What about it?"

"How's it going?"

I laugh. "I mean, as good as can be expected after hiding our relationship for nearly a year."

His eyes turn to slits. I brace myself for a judgmental comment, but he surprises me by saying, "I'm sure that was hard on you."

"Yeah…but I feel so much better now that people know."

"I'm curious—how did you both keep it a secret for so long?" He stares at me instead of the kitten currently destroying his shoelaces with its tiny claws.

"Why are you asking?"

"Because you're the last person anyone tells anything to."

My mouth falls open. "That's so uncalled for."

He shrugs. "But true."

"I *can* keep a secret."

"So can I." He looks so smug after saying it, and I instantly know something is wrong.

The vet then walks into the room, cutting our conversation short. At first I'm grateful for the interruption, but the longer I have to wait to ask Rafa what he meant, the larger my concerns grow.

Relax, I chant, trying to find my inner yoga voice and failing miserably.

When the vet leaves the exam room after promising to return with some results, I can't take Rafa's smugness anymore.

"What did you mean?"

He pauses in the middle of stroking one of the kitten's bellies to look over at me. "What?"

"When you said you can keep a secret. What were you referring to?"

"*Oh.* That." He goes back to playing with the kitten.

"Rafa," I say with a groan. "Come on."

He stands to his full height and crosses his arms. "I know the truth."

My whole world tilts as I come to terms with Rafa knowing about my big, bad secret.

"How?" I ask, although I'm certain Ellie is the one who said something.

And people think *I* can't keep a secret?

I can't believe Lorenzo gave me a whole speech about not telling my sister and Julian about us when he should've been worrying about Willow talking to Ellie.

But I'll deal with that issue later.

Rafa rubs his stubbled cheek. "I don't get how you landed yourself in this…situation."

I can't look at him head-on, so I pick up a kitten and cradle it against my chest. "It's a long, uninteresting story."

"I'd rather be the judge of that myself, if you don't mind."

I'm the one grimacing now.

"Come on, Lily. How can you go from wanting to find the love of your life to faking a relationship with Lorenzo?"

I drop my gaze. "I have my reasons."

"I'm sure, and I'm not trying to judge them." He exhales loudly. "I just want you to know I'm here if you need any help. Anything at all. You know that, right?"

My bottom lip quivers. "Thank you."

"I hope you're at least talking to Dahlia about all this."

"No."

He pulls back, appearing stunned. "You're not going to tell your own sister? She's your best friend."

I bite down on the inside of my cheek. "Lorenzo and I decided against it."

"Why?"

I explain Lorenzo's reasoning, including his reservations about Julian, before saying, "One day I'll tell her the truth."

"But not soon."

"No." I shift my weight while trying to hold eye contact. I do my best, but when he doesn't stop staring at me, I cave and look away.

"Ellie mentioned you're getting engaged. Is that still true?"

"Uh...yes."

"Fuck." He spears his hands through his hair, and the shorter strands stick up. "A fake relationship is one thing, but an engagement? What are you thinking?"

Words evade me.

Rafa's eyes follow the flush toward my neckline. "I'm going to come out and ask: do you like him?"

"No!" I say too loudly, startling the kittens playing by my feet.

"You sure about that?" he asks, my face turning redder.

"Okay." I sigh. "Listen. I did like him once. Past tense. But that was nearly a year ago."

"And you think those kinds of feelings go away?"

Before the cooking class, I would've said maybe, depending on the circumstance, but now...

"I thought so," he says.

"I can't like him, Rafa." I shake my head, wishing I could turn back the clock so this conversation never happened.

Rafa carefully walks around the kittens and pulls me into his arms. "Why not?"

"Because he's never going to feel the same way."

Rafa is in the middle of paying the bill when a dog is rushed into the clinic, being carried like a baby in an assistant's arms. We both pause our conversation, too distracted by the swarm of vet techs scurrying about, trying to find an empty exam room for the pit bull mix.

The pit bull's brown eyes find mine, and my chest aches at the heartbreaking whine it lets out. There is something about the sound combined with the overall deteriorating state of the dog that makes me want to cry on its behalf. It is clearly malnourished to the point of having protruding bones, and its fur is in a state of disarray, the neglect evident to anyone who has eyes or a nose.

I've seen my fair share of abused animals thanks to all of Rafa's rescue efforts and my time volunteering at the shelter, but this… This one hits me hardest, and I'm not sure why, but I want to walk over and pull the dog into my arms.

It's hard not to feel attached when it looks at me and lets out this piercing sound that drills a hole through my heart.

"Where did they find the dog?" Rafa asks the person working the front desk.

"A junkyard not too far from here. The owner skipped town and left her tied to a pole for who knows how long."

"Is she going to be okay?" My voice trembles.

"Daisy's in critical condition thanks to some infection she got from another dog bite. The doc is going to do a full evaluation and blood panel now to see how bad it is, but he's hopeful."

"Her name is Daisy?"

"According to her collar, yes." The secretary gasps. "Wait. You're both named after flowers. How cute."

I shoot her a soft smile. "Love it." Before I can stop myself, I ask, "Will you call me once you have an update on her condition?"

The secretary hands Rafa's card back. "Sure."

Rafa looks at me, his eyes roving over my face before he turns to hand the secretary his card again. "I'll cover the treatment costs."

I give his bicep a squeeze and smile. "You didn't have to do that, but thank you."

"Consider it an adoption present."

I jerk back. "I can't get a dog. Mom's allergic."

"What about Lorenzo?" He smirks, and the secretary *beams*.

I shake my head with a laugh, not thinking much of his comment. I'm not going to adopt a dog with someone who plans on breaking off our fake engagement in a few months. That would be reckless, and while I have made some interesting decisions lately, I need to draw the line at adopting a dog.

Right?

CHAPTER TWENTY

Lorenzo

For the last couple of weeks, Lily and I have found a comfortable rhythm with our fake relationship. When I'm not meeting with constituents or preparing for the mayoral debate with Willow, Lily and I go on a few dates each week.

We have a picnic in the park and rent a rowboat so she can take photos of bouquets for her shop's social media page, and we also attend the Strawberry Festival together.

I also make it a point to stop by Rose & Thorn multiple times throughout the week, and the four employees Lily hired have started to take a liking to me, especially when I arrive with coffee from the Angry Rooster Café or baked goods from Sweets and Treats.

Despite our strong public presence, I still haven't been invited over for Sunday lunch, and I haven't asked any more questions about it after Lily got visibly upset when I checked in to see if everything was okay with her sister, who has been out of town working on a project and skipped the Strawberry Festival.

Despite telling myself Lily was the one who got herself into this mess, I still feel bad about causing any kind of division between Dahlia and her. Or more so, I'm unhappy that Lily is upset, which is a cause for concern.

Like usual, I stop by Lily's shop in the afternoon with her go-to coffee order. She is busy on the phone, so I take a lap around the shop while pretending not to eavesdrop.

"How much longer does she have to stay there?" Lily asks.

I don't hear the other person's reply, but Lily seems happy with it. "When do you think she will be transferred?"

Lily listens to the answer before letting out a huff. "Oh. That soon?" Another pause. "No, no! I'm happy she's recovering well. I just need a little more time to sort out a few things."

I'm itching to know more about this conversation, but Lily choosing not to use her speakerphone isn't helping matters.

"Do you think you can give me another week please?" Her reply is followed by tense silence before she says, "Thank you! I hope I can figure out a plan by then."

I stop in front of the counter, and she holds up her finger before spinning on her heels and giving me her back.

"Yes, I know." Her shoulders slump. "Thanks again." She hangs up. Instead of turning to greet me right away, she takes a deep breath first.

"Who was that?"

Tension ripples down her back as she finally faces me. "The vet's office."

My head tilts. "I thought you didn't have a pet."

"I don't, but I went to help Rafa with his kittens the other week."

"Are they okay?"

Her brows scrunch together. "The cats are good. All healthy and back at his barn."

"So who's recovering well, then?" I pass her the to-go cup.

She takes a sip while glaring at me. "Eavesdropping is rude."

"So is talking on the phone when you have a customer waiting around, but you don't hear me complaining."

She puts her cup down. "Do you mind watching the store while I go grab your bouquets in the back?"

I don't call her out on wanting to escape the conversation. "Go ahead."

She disappears through the swinging door, leaving me alone with the sketch she must have been working on before her call. With modern technology, I'm surprised Lily still uses pencil and paper to design her bouquets, but given her talent, I understand why.

I start flipping the pages, only to stop at one sketch of the garden she talked about a few times. It looks different from the one I saw recently when I hid her keys. The fountain, which was deteriorating when I saw it, looks to be functioning in the drawing, with water cascading down the sides. The luscious landscaping is completely different in the drawing too, no longer appearing abandoned but with flowers blossoming and hedges neatly trimmed.

This drawing is what I imagined her special place to look like, but for some reason the garden currently lacks that charm.

Lily rips the sketchbook out from underneath my hand and slams it shut.

"Here you go." She all but tosses the flowers at me. If I didn't have quick reflexes, they would've fallen to the floor and been crushed.

"Pretty drawing you have there."

Her jaw works itself. "Goodbye, Lorenzo."

I'm surprised by her snippiness, so I poke around for answers because I can't help myself. "Did that phone call put you in a mood?"

"You snooping around did."

She fans the flames of curiosity burning inside me, but with the way her mouth pulls tight with barely restrained irritation, I'll seek answers elsewhere.

I should leave, but I loiter instead by the counter like my feet are glued to the floor.

Lily ignores me. She doesn't return to drawing, instead choosing a task she thinks I'd find boring.

Truth is I could watch her complete the most menial tasks, like trimming flowers or reviewing invoices, and never get bored. There's too much about her that interests me, from the delicate way she curls ribbons or organizes wrapping paper to the amusing furrow she gets between her brows whenever she has to do inventory counts.

That's the only plausible explanation for why I'm lingering, wanting to ask Lily more questions. That and my curiosity about why she was talking to the vet's office when Rafa's kittens are all accounted for.

A curiosity that I shouldn't feel, but one I plan on satisfying regardless.

With or without her help.

An overwhelming sense of sadness hits me when I stop in front of the vet's office. I'm assaulted by the memory of my parents and me visiting this same clinic with our family dog, and the stabbing sensation in my chest worsens when I think about how they never made it here on the night of their accident.

With a few steady breaths and a reminder of why I'm here, I walk inside, looking like I don't have a single care in the world outside of finding out what Lily is hiding.

Turns out the woman working the front desk was more than happy to give me all the answers I needed. All I had to do was flash a smile and share how much Lily raves about the clinic, and *ecco qua*, everyone was ready to talk all about Daisy, the dog Lily loves to visit every day, and how Rafa is paying all the pricey medical bills.

Him covering the bills annoys me, but not nearly as much as Lily keeping secrets from me.

But why does that matter to you?

It shouldn't, but I'm a bit peeved at how she never even talked to me about Daisy, who clearly is important since she is so invested in her rehabilitation. It's not like she hasn't had plenty of opportunities to bring it up.

Yet she didn't want to.

I'm not a fan of the little pinch in my chest when I think of her keeping secrets. Not a fan at all.

I'm still thinking about Daisy when I pick up Lily from her house that evening in a vintage 1956 Cadillac Eldorado. The convertible felt like a fitting pick for tonight's drive-in movie date, but she doesn't comment on it like I expected.

Lily is rather quiet during the drive to the lot near the edge of town, and I find her checking her phone more than once for new messages.

"You good?" I ask once we arrive at the drive-in theater, where rows of cars are lined up for tonight's film. We are directed toward an empty area, but with how popular the spot is for couples and families, it's only a matter of time before we are surrounded on all sides.

"I'm fine," she replies without an ounce of emotion.

"You sure?" I ask, knowing an answer like that deserves a follow-up.

"Yes." She glances over at me. "Why are you asking?"

"Because you're unusually quiet tonight."

Talk to me about Daisy, I say in my head.

Tell me why she matters to you so much, I add.

Any iteration of the question makes me sound like I care too much. Like I'm snubbed because she chose to lean on Rafa for help instead of me.

Nothing about our agreement requires us to share

everything about ourselves, so I have no right to private information.

Yet I want to know anyway, and I hate myself for it.

Her lips go from pursing to flattening into a thin line. "You know, I *am* capable of being silent sometimes."

"Doesn't mean I want you to be." My comment is followed by a pause full of crackling tension.

Lily's gaze is hot on my face. "Why not?"

"I've come to enjoy your rambling."

"Is this your discreet way of telling me you like the sound of my voice?"

"Depends. Is this *your* discreet way of asking if I do?"

She cracks a smile. It's the first one I've seen all day from her, and it fills me with a relief I have no business feeling in the first place. "Maybe."

I tip her head back so I can get a clear look at her eyes. "If you want an answer, then ask the question." An interesting piece of advice coming from the man who won't bring up Daisy, but I'm nothing if not consistent when it comes to not revealing my cards.

It takes Lily a moment to reply, and I should've known it was because I wouldn't appreciate her next line of questioning.

"Why do you care if I'm quiet?" she asks.

I walked myself into this trap, so I need to deal with the consequences of my honesty. "Because that means you're upset, and I've come to realize I don't like that."

She smiles to herself, like she is in on a joke I'm not privy to.

"What?" I ask, somewhat affronted by her amusement.

"Nothing." Her eyes fall to her lap again and that damn phone.

I tangle my fingers in her hair and force her to look at me. "Tell me."

"So you can run away when shit gets too real? I think not."

"I don't run away. I…"

"Flee?" she teases, and I'm motivated to do something about that smirk on her face.

I turn her ponytail into a rope, winding it around my hand until her head tilts in my direction. She tries to pull away, but she can't go anywhere.

"Look who's fleeing now." I smile.

Her eyes darken, and I want to drown in their inky depths, only to have that thought interrupted by a car pulling up next to us.

Lily slides a dazzling smile onto her face like our conversation never happened, and I have no choice but to let our conversation—and her hair—go.

Regardless of my personal desires, we have a show to put on, and I excel at my role as I offer to grab us milkshakes and popcorn from the concession stand.

"You're the best, baby." Lily waves me off, and the young couple parked beside us snickers.

"Will you grab me some popcorn too, *baby*?" A man I've seen working at Manny's shop taunts with a kissy face.

I roll my eyes at him before heading to the concession stand. The line of twenty people wraps around the booth, but it seems to be quickly moving thanks to the four employees working behind the counter.

I'm about to get in line when I find my living nightmare standing near the end, looking casual with his hands tucked into his pockets.

I stumble back a step and bump into someone in the process, gaining the attention of a few people around me.

The person I ran into claps me on the shoulder. "You okay, Lorenzo?"

"I forgot my wallet."

Trevor Ludlow turns at the sound of my voice, but I bolt before he can get a look at me. I've done my best to avoid him, and for the most part I've been successful, but tonight was a close call.

Too close.

My heart is racing by the time I make it back to the car.

"What happened to the snacks?" Lily asks when she sees me return empty-handed.

"Line was too long, and I didn't want to miss the beginning of the movie."

If Lily senses a lie, she doesn't call me out on it, and I'm grateful. I can only handle so much tonight, and seeing Trevor pushed me to my absolute limit.

I can't avoid him forever. Sooner or later, my past and future are going to collide.

And I have a feeling that when that time comes, it's going to eat me alive.

CHAPTER TWENTY-ONE

Lorenzo

'm in the middle of wrapping up a phone call with the head architect at Morrison and Holmes—the architecture firm Lily mentioned being involved with the Lavender Lane project—when Manny strolls into the empty office space that I turned into my campaign headquarters. He takes a seat near the front entrance and pulls out his phone after I hold up a finger and tell him to wait.

"Are you still there, Mr. Vittori?" the architect asks.

"Yes. Sorry about that. I just wanted to say I appreciate how forthcoming you've been during this call." I can't find it in me to smile. Despite the huge win for my campaign and the upcoming mayoral debate, my stomach is in knots from this conversation, and it has nothing to do with lying to get information out of the Ludlows' architects.

I hate to admit it, but my uncle was correct when he said if the price is right, people will always talk, and turns out the architects at Morrison and Holmes are loyal to a paycheck rather than a person.

Their lack of integrity absolves me of any guilt I'd feel from lying to them about my Vittori Holdings connections or the made-up project they'll get to bid on.

"We look forward to working together," the woman says.

"We'll keep in touch." I hang up and wave Manny into my office.

My campaign volunteers are used to Manny stopping by unannounced, so they ignore him as he walks past their desks and heads straight toward mine located in the back of the office space. The little chip on his front tooth is on full display, and his brown eyes crinkle at the corners from how wide he smiles at me.

He holds a bouquet of flowers out for me to grab. "Here."

"Don't tell me these are for me," I deadpan before assessing his choice of flowers like he's a contestant on some show.

"You owe me seventy-five bucks."

"What for?"

"Your girlfriend's flowers aren't cheap."

"She should've charged you double for bothering her."

He laughs as he takes a seat beside my desk. "I didn't bother her."

I shoot him a look. He's been hounding me about her for the last few weeks, and I've avoided planning any kind of outing together.

"At least I hope I didn't. But I needed to take matters into my own hands since you haven't introduced us yet."

"Have you forgotten that you two already know each other from school?"

"Yeah, but she doesn't know me as Manny, your best friend."

"I prefer to call you Manny, the pain in my ass."

"Well, at least you always have stand-up comedy if the political stuff doesn't work out."

I glare.

He grins. "Kidding!"

I lean back in my desk chair and cross my arms. "So how did it go?"

"Great! She suggested we all go out for drinks tomorrow."

"We?"

"You, me, Lily, and that sweet employee of hers, *Jane*." He says her name in a wistful way.

I pull out my phone and text Lily, who unfortunately confirms Manny is telling the truth. To avoid him for a little longer, I reply to her message.

ME

Isn't it a bad idea to invite your employee on a double date?

LILY

I can tell you didn't grow up in a small town.

ME

What does that have to do with anything?

LILY

When you see two people hit it off, you do everything possible to make it happen.

> **ME**
> By "it," you mean...?

> **LILY**
> Love, Lorenzo. Do try to keep up with me here.

> **ME**
> Florist. True-crime junkie. Matchmaker. What's next?

I don't catch myself smiling at my phone until Manny punches me in the shoulder.

"What was that for?" I rub the sore spot.

"Being rude and ignoring my company."

I exhale, relieved he didn't see her latest text. "Now that I have a date planned tomorrow, I should get back to work before I fall behind."

"Can't you take a break?"

I motion toward the stack of earnings reports I have to review from a dentist who would like to sell her office in town and retire. "Only if you want me to cancel."

"In that case, stop being lazy and get to it! My soulmate waits for no one."

Manny decided to park his car at my house so I could drive us both to the Historic District, where Lily and Jane are meeting us at a new speakeasy bar. They're making a big deal out of celebrating the end of strawberry season with special drinks and a live band who also played last weekend at the festival.

The drive is a short one, especially when Manny spent the entirety of it going over answers to possible questions Jane might ask him. I've never seen him this nervous before, and I have no idea how to calm his fraying nerves.

"How do I look?" Manny asks as I park in a lot not too far from the bar.

I have a hard time responding to his question because his short-sleeve, button-down shirt is one I'd never be caught wearing. The tiny strawberry pattern might be on-brand with the rest of the town's favorite fruit, but that doesn't make it a fashionable choice, so I stick with a basic "You look fine."

He gapes at me. "Fine? Might as well tell me to go change while you're at it."

I squint at the busy pattern. "I mean, I wouldn't be against it."

His eyes turn to slits. "Can we swap?"

"Swap what?"

"Shirts." He motions toward my white button-down with the sleeves rolled up.

I shut my car off to end the conversation. "No."

He holds his hands up like he's praying. "Please, Lorenzo? You have a girlfriend already, so it's not like you need to impress anyone, but me…"

He stares at his shirt like he can't believe he ever thought it was a good idea.

"I can't go in there and embarrass myself."

"It's not that bad."

He pops open the mirror and checks himself out. "God. Why did I ever let my mom talk me into wearing this?"

"A little word of advice? Hold off on admitting your mom still helps pick out your clothes."

"How else can I explain this fashion choice?"

"Town spirit?"

He claps his hands together. "Yes! Town spirit! Which is why you have to wear it as the man who's running for mayor."

I choke on a laugh. "Good try, but no."

"Okay. Forget about town spirit. Do it because I'm your best friend and you don't want to see me blow my chance with one of the prettiest girls around. Because I don't want to be single anymore, Lorenzo. It's lonely as hell, and I'm ready for the next phase in my life. I've been ready for a while, but dating here is hard."

I stare at him without blinking. "You're serious."

"Of course I'm serious, but it's not like you'd understand since you have Lily."

Except you don't have her, do you?

"Maybe we could head back to my house so I can change?" He checks his watch and curses. "No. Being late is even worse." His groan fills the car.

I shouldn't say yes. If I were anything like my uncle or cousins, I would stick to my original answer and tell him no, but then I think about what that would look like for him should I refuse to help him out.

Manny is a good guy. He goes out of his way to check on me even when I don't do the same, and he's decent at blackjack and poker after I taught him a few tricks. Even though we are complete opposites, I like his company, and the thought of upsetting him enough to risk losing it makes my throat tighten.

Maybe Lily was right, because the thought of being alone is more than tiring.

It's *unsettling*.

When I first moved to Lake Wisteria, I never cared about making friends, but now I'm thinking about what could happen should I upset the only real one I have.

Not a risk I'm willing to take.

Selfishness has always been my default setting, but tonight I am choosing to put someone else first while receiving nothing but their company in return. All because Lily is right and I *am* tired of being alone.

And I have no idea what to do with that new piece of information about myself.

secret garden studio

wws ???
wildflower wishes studio

petal + press

the pressed petal

CHAPTER TWENTY-TWO

Lily

When Lorenzo walks into Night Cap wearing a shirt that surely can't be his, I burst out laughing, earning the attention from other tables nearby. I can't help my reaction, but his bold outfit is too much to bear.

I look over at Manny to find him dressed in one that looks a little too tight on his bulkier frame. Jane seems to appreciate it because I find her ogling his arms, which look more defined thanks to what I assume must be Lorenzo's shirt.

Part of me wants to bring up the suspected shirt swap in conversation, but I'm not sure if Jane is aware of it, so I keep quiet.

Instead I jump out of my seat and throw my arms around him. "Love the outfit, baby."

His hands find the curve of my ass and stay there,

claiming me in front of the entire bar full of twenty- and thirtysomethings. "Make another comment about it and I'll find a better way to keep your mouth busy."

A pleasant warmth rolls through me at the unspoken promise.

For the love of God, can you control yourself?

Nope.

"What if I like the sound of that?" I brush my thumb across his bottom lip.

"You're trouble." His lashes flutter as his eyes start to close.

Fake. Fake. Fake, I chant, like that can stop me from feeling all warm at the obvious sign of his arousal.

At least his reaction to my touch makes me feel slightly less guilty about mine.

When I pull my hand away from his face, his eyes snap open, and like that, we're back to playing our roles.

Manny takes the empty chair beside Jane, and Lorenzo picks the one to my left.

I give them a little privacy as I look over at my *boyfriend*, whose gaze is already focused solely on me. "So…strawberries?"

"Lily," he warns in a voice that should be reserved for the bedroom, because the indecent things it does to my body are not meant for public consumption.

"What? I'm commenting on the pattern."

"I warned you." He reaches across the wood table, laces our fingers together, and gives me a squeeze.

Regardless of how many times he holds my hand, it always feels like the very first time—with my heart skipping and my skin prickling with awareness.

"I'm pretty sure I have a dress with a similar pattern somewhere in my closet."

"You should look for it tonight so we can match for our next date."

"Since when are we the kind of couple who coordinates outfits?"

"Since you forgot what the colors of the rainbow looked like." His gaze flickers down to my plain white lace dress.

My heart comes to a complete stop—a full, achy pause before it picks back up, the pace much faster than before.

I never thought Lorenzo paid close enough attention to notice the change, let alone care enough to bring it up. I'm not sure how to feel about it or the way he looks at me like I'm a mystery he wants to solve; his comment and my lack of a response adding to his collection of clues about why I changed.

"I told you the shirt would be a hit," Manny says, breaking up our moment.

"I couldn't agree more." I rub my hand over Lorenzo's bicep, drawing goose bumps.

"It was a birthday present." Manny smiles, and I instantly like him even more.

"You're about four months early, but thanks," Lorenzo replies.

"I couldn't wait." Manny winks. "As soon as I saw it, I knew you had to have it."

I laugh while Lorenzo grimaces.

Lorenzo waits until Manny becomes distracted with Jane again to rope his leg around the foot of my chair and drag it until there is no gap of space between us.

My heart beats harder in my chest as I'm hit with the full force of his cologne, and I'm not given any time to recuperate as he leans in and asks, "Do you think this is funny?"

"Hilarious."

"I look ridiculous."

I pat his chest. "I think it's a nice change."

He shoots me a look. "You can't be serious."

"No, I am." I do a better job of keeping the amusement out of my voice. "You look less…"

"What?"

"How do I put this nicely without sounding mean?"

He leans back and crosses his arms. "I doubt you know how to be mean."

"Dahlia would disagree with you, especially when we play Monopoly."

He laughs. It's strong and hearty, leaving no room for me to question whether it's genuine or not, and it makes my heart sing.

Danger, my brain blares out, but I'm too busy smiling at Lorenzo to notice it.

My nose scrunches.

He tracks the move. "Tell me what you were thinking and don't bother censoring yourself. I'm a big boy. I can take it."

My gaze falls to his muscular arms because *yes, he is*.

"Lily?"

I look up to find Lorenzo's lips curling with amusement.

"All right." I take a deep breath. "You tend to look a little… stuffy? Or perhaps that's not the right word."

"Out of place?" Manny intervenes.

Jane makes a face, and Lorenzo notices it immediately.

"You agree?" he asks her.

Jane lifts her shoulders. "I mean, I'm not from here, so who am I to comment?"

"You're the most unbiased person here, so that's good enough," Lorenzo replies.

"Well, I mean, I think mixing it up every now and then would make you seem a little more approachable."

"What about this says approachable?" Lorenzo motions to his shirt.

"I think you look like you don't take yourself too seriously," she says.

"Ah, yes. A trait everyone wants to see in the person running for mayor."

I jump in. "People here only wear suits for weddings and funerals."

"But the Ludlows—"

Manny interrupts, "Are known to be a bit…"

"Uptight?" I offer. Snooty. Condescending. Born with a *holier than thou* pretentiousness that I once mistook as confidence.

Manny nods. "Exactly."

Lorenzo's petulant frown makes me laugh.

"I'm *not* uptight." His voice is riddled with tension.

"You're a billionaire, man—"

"Was. I *was* a billionaire." Lorenzo's body is getting progressively stiffer, so I decide to help him in the best way I know how.

"You know," I say, "we can go shopping this weekend and see what we find."

Manny hoots. "Yes! My mom knows—"

"No," Lorenzo and I both say at the same time, making Manny and Jane laugh.

We look over at each other, our eyes both wide.

Manny places his elbows on the table, clasps his hands underneath his chin, and bats his thick lashes. "Look at them finishing each other's sentences. Isn't that cute?"

Nope, I lie to myself. *Not even a little bit.*

I stare longingly at the crowd on the dance floor. Manny and Jane were swallowed up by the large group of people two songs ago, and I haven't seen them since.

Lorenzo surprises me by asking, "Do you want to dance?"

I arch a brow at him. "Together?"

"No, I was thinking you should go ask the guys who keep staring at you from across the bar."

I lean into him so I can get a better look at the men he pointed out. It doesn't take me long to notice the group hanging around the end of the bar, who quickly look away from our table.

I can't help myself when I ask, "Does it bother you?"

"If they look? No."

I didn't expect his answer to bother me so much.

"What did I say now?" he asks, reading me yet again tonight.

"Nothing important." Which is exactly my problem because part of me *wants* Lorenzo to give a damn.

I try to scoot my chair farther away, but he drags it right back before possessively wrapping his hand around the back of my neck.

"Look at me."

I don't dare take my eyes away from the dance floor.

Lorenzo squeezes the back of my neck again, silently willing me to listen, and because I'm a glutton for his rejection, I follow his command.

"I can't get angry at them for something I've been guilty of. So let them look. Let them *stare*. Let them wish they were going home with the most beautiful woman in this bar—in this *town*—for all I care. I've been there. Many times, in fact, when it comes to you. So if anything, I sympathize with them because they can want you, but they'll never truly *have* you."

My stomach, which finally settled down post-Lorenzo last touched me, turns into a giant knot because oh my God. I never expected that kind of response to pour out of his mouth.

Not wanting him to see how much his words affected me, I blurt out the first thing that comes to mind.

"I don't know... The blond one is kind of hot."

A dark look passes over his face. "I'm starting to wonder if you have a thing for blonds."

"Is that a problem?"

"Only because I'm not one."

I laugh, and he smiles, and for a second I forget about our goal and live in the moment.

I crack a smile. "You can always bleach it."

"Would doing so when we're this close to the mayoral debate be cause for alarm?"

"Absolutely. People only dye their hair or change their clothes if something drastic happens."

His brows scrunch together. "Drastic?"

Shit. "I mean, I'm talking like from lace to leather or—"

"Color to monochrome?"

Somehow I refrain from flinching. "That's normal."

"How about no longer wearing bows or flowers in their hair?" He tucks a loose strand of my hair behind my ear before teasing my cheek with the tip of his index finger.

"That could be a sign of maturing."

"Maybe…but I don't think that's what happened."

My hands clench against my lap—something Lorenzo notices since he refuses to let me have a single inch of distance.

I brush him off with "You're reaching."

"And you're hiding something."

I glance away, unable to stand the weight of his stare.

"Why'd you change?" he asks softly, talking like I do to scared animals in the shelter. Fitting because I feel like a cornered one.

I stand up. "You know what? I am in the mood to dance." I pause before adding, "*Alone.*"

I join a circle of women on the dance floor who I recognize from the running club I was a part of. Lorenzo's eyes burn a hole into my back as I sway to the music, and I allow myself one single glance over my shoulder to confirm what I already know.

I catch him staring at me while sipping his drink, and I return his burning gaze with a smile before looking away.

With every song, I make more of an effort to push all thoughts of Lorenzo away, only for a pair of familiar hands to find the curve of my waist and pull me backward until I'm separated from the group.

"You're a tease," Lorenzo whispers, his voice thick with arousal.

"I'm just dancing," I say innocently.

"Then go ahead and *dance*." He spins me around, his grip punishing as he closes the little gap between our bodies. His thick erection presses into my belly, and my eyes go round.

"I'm waiting," he taunts, his tongue darting out to wet his bottom lip.

One glance into his cloudy eyes full of promise has me shutting my own, and I lose myself in the music—in the feel of Lorenzo's hands on my hips, matching my rhythm with his own.

His ability to dance was one of the initial things that caught me by surprise on the night we first met. He never mentioned it before, so when he found me on the dance floor, I was shocked to learn that the man behind the neon blue mask managed to find the beat to any song and dance in a way that captivated me.

When his mouth starts to follow a path down my throat, I tremble in his arms.

It's an uncontrollable response, and one I don't want him reading into, so before he can see the emotions written across my face, I twist around and press my back against his front.

None of this is real.

Our bodies mold together, moving in perfect synchronicity. One of his hands splays across my stomach and secures me to his front while the other brushes my hair away from my shoulder so he can drop another kiss.

Let them wish they were going home with the most beautiful woman in this bar—in this town—for all I care. I've been there. Many times, in fact, when it comes to you.

Is that what he's doing right now? Or is he simply putting on a show for everyone else around us?

It's unfair, the way my body reacts to his, so I decide to fight fire with fire and spin around, returning his searing kisses and warm touches with my own until we're both staring up at each other with our hearts beating in perfect, erratic harmony.

His gaze drops to my mouth, and my lips tingle in anticipation.

It hits me that I *want* Lorenzo to kiss me—not for appearance's sake but because I crave to have his mouth pressed to mine again.

And that right there is why I can't go through with it. Not when the line between real and fake is so blurred, I can't tell reality apart from fiction.

When he dips his head forward and shuts his eyes, I turn mine at the last second so he ends up kissing my cheek instead.

His eyes snap open, and for once the unwavering control he has over his emotions drops long enough for me to see the sting of rejection in his gaze.

I hope he spends the entire drive home wishing I let him kiss me.

I hope he thinks of me when he gets home, especially when

he climbs into bed all alone tonight with nothing but his hand to keep him company.

I hope his decision to push me away haunts him and that his regret grows with every fake date we have, until he resents every choice he's made which led us here.

CHAPTER TWENTY-THREE

Lily

I've given my sister plenty of time to stew in her emotions before I decide to approach her and get this awkward conversation out of the way. Giving her space was a given since she spent most of our time apart out of town for a few work projects and filming some content for her show, but I've had enough.

I miss Dahlia, and I don't want a guy to get between us ever again.

So today, during my lunch break, I seek her out at the office she shares with Julian. Compared to the rest of the modern office, my sister's private one fits her personality to a T, with warm wood tones, bookshelves full of design samples, and a trendy wallpaper that adds a touch of personality to the space.

Dahlia looks up from her tablet when I knock on the door.

"Hey. Isn't this a surprise."

"Brought you some lunch." I hold up a paper bag from her favorite sushi place in town. It's nothing fancy like Julian's imported rolls from Aomi, but Dahlia will never turn down a food-related peace offering.

She waves at the chair across from her desk. "To what do I owe this visit?"

I pull out one container and pass it to her. "I miss my sister."

"We live together, dork."

"Yeah, well, if it weren't for the lack of hot water at night, I would've forgotten you moved back in."

She snorts as she pops the lid off, and I grab my box and place it on top of her desk.

"Tell me how to fix this," I say before stuffing a roll into my mouth.

"For a while there, I was mad at you." She snaps her chopsticks at me.

"I could tell."

She drops her gaze. "But eventually I turned that anger inward."

"Why?"

"Because how could I not notice that my sister was in love? How could I be so focused on myself and my own love life that I didn't think to ask more questions about yours?"

Guilt hits me harder than ever before because I hate that Dahlia is taking this out on herself.

"Dahlia…" I try to work up the courage to tell her the truth, but what she says next makes me pause.

"I'm the one who's sorry, Lily." She glances up at me

with a trembling bottom lip. "I'm sorry for not being a good sister."

"Who needs a good one when you're the best one?"

She laughs to herself. "I don't feel like that lately."

Neither do I.

I decide to put the past behind us and hope she wants to do the same. "Can we stop avoiding each other now?"

She nods.

"Great, because I was wondering if you wanted to go shopping this weekend for the fundraiser gala?"

Her eyes light up. "It's been so long since we've gone shopping together."

"Yeah. I'm thinking we could make a day out of it."

Her gaze dips to my clothes—a simple black cotton dress and a jean jacket—before her entire face lights up. "You know what? I *love* that idea."

A shopping trip might not cure my guilty conscience, but some retail therapy always does wonders for the soul, and mine is in desperate need of a little pick-me-up.

The next morning, I pause working on a floral wreath for a funeral to answer an incoming call from my sister.

"Hey. What's up?" I ask.

"So…I have some bad news. It turns out Julian and I have an issue with our Chicago project that we need to address this weekend."

"Oh."

"I know." She groans. "We'll need to stop by the house sometime on Saturday, so I was thinking, what if we went on a weekend trip to the city instead? We'd have way more options than Grand Rapids too."

I scrunch my nose. Usually I don't mind hanging out with Julian and Dahlia, but I was looking forward to spending some time with my sister one-on-one.

We might not be twins, but she can sure read my mind like one. "I want us to have time alone together though, so I was thinking Julian and Lorenzo could hang out while we go shopping and have a girls' day."

I end up coughing from how sharp of a breath I take. "Lorenzo?"

"Yeah? Do you not want him to come?"

"No. I'm...surprised."

She chuckles under her breath. "I think it would be good for them to bond. Or, at the very least, grab a drink at a bar and glare at each other in silence."

The visual makes me laugh before I sober up. "I don't know... Is that a good idea?"

"Lily, you've avoided bringing Lorenzo to Sunday lunch for an entire month. Eventually you'll have to let Julian and Lorenzo be in the same room together, especially if it's serious."

Ugh. I hate that she has a point. "I guess."

"It'll be fun!"

Will it? Because the idea of going on a couples trip with my sister sounds like the final boss level of fake dating.

She expects you to be excited about this, not hesitant.

With a shaky breath, I say, "I'll have to ask Lorenzo—"

"He's totally going to say yes."

"How do you know?"

"Because why wouldn't he want to spend a whole weekend with you without Mom's rule about no sleepovers?"

Shit. That's totally something I'd look forward to if this was a real relationship because my mom is strict with boys. I'm talking *no moving in before marriage* strict—and definitely no sleepovers because apparently Dahlia and I are still virgins in my mom's mind.

My sister continues, "So, I'll have Julian book us two rooms. If Mom asks—which you know she will—tell her we're sharing one while the boys take the other."

Oh no.

No. No. *No.*

It hits me that I'll have to share a bed with Lorenzo because it will look too weird to ask my sister for a room with two queens.

Well, you did want him to admit that he wants you.

Perfect. This is fate smiling down on me. Really. I couldn't have planned this any better myself.

Then why are you so nervous about sharing a room?

Dahlia, completely unaware of my struggle, promises to send me the hotel info before she hangs up. I decide to get my call with Lorenzo over with so that way I can concentrate on the rest of my work.

"Are you okay?" Lorenzo asks first thing.

"Hi. Yes, I'm fine. Why wouldn't I be?"

"Just checking."

My heart, which was already beating faster after the

conversation with my sister, picks up speed. "About that... I'm sorry to bother you in the middle of the workday—"

Rustling on his end of the line makes my phone's speaker crackle. "No worries. Give me a second."

I hear him excuse himself from whomever he was talking to before I interrupted him.

"I can call back later if you're busy."

"It's fine." A door shuts in the background. "What's up?"

"So...I planned a shopping trip with my sister this weekend."

"And?"

"*And* it turned into a lot more than I originally bargained for."

"Lily, as cute as your conversational cliffhangers are, I'm in the middle of a meeting."

I stop listening once he drops the word *cute*. I mean, who could pay attention after something like that—

"So if you don't mind getting to the point..." His sentence hangs there.

"Right!" I'm in such a race to get the words out, I don't process my thoughts before saying them. "Uh, basically she wants us to join her and Julian on a couples trip to Chicago this weekend, and you and I will have to share a room—and a bed since I can't ask her for two queens without it looking weird—and she also wants you and Julian to hang out together while we go shopping, so I hope you don't mind."

It's so quiet, I have to check to make sure he didn't hang up.

"Are you still there?" I ask.

"Appears so."

"It'll be fun!" I repeat Dahlia's words.

"Should we review the meaning of the word?"

I laugh him off. "Maybe *fun* was a bit of a stretch, but it won't be the worst weekend ever."

"With Julian attending, I can guarantee it."

"Who knows? By the end of it, you two could become the best of friends."

"In that case, I'll start making our matching friendship bracelets."

With a laugh, I hang up the phone, and the smile on my face remains, along with a hint of nerves about spending an entire weekend with Lorenzo, showing him exactly what he's missing out on by denying himself what he clearly wants.

Me.

reflecting today's traditions

Choose your Legacy

CHAPTER TWENTY-FOUR

Lorenzo

Julian, Dahlia, and Lily are outside the Muñoz house when I pull into the driveway that Friday evening. Julian is in the middle of sifting through a toolbox in the back of his truck while Lily is looking at him, panicked.

I hop out of my G-Wagon and walk over to them. "What's going on?"

Dahlia glances up from her phone. "Julian tried to fix the fountain while we were waiting for you."

"Did you get it to work?" I ask him.

Julian shakes his head. "I told Lily she's better off replacing it."

She makes a face. "I want to keep it."

"Maybe I can call one of my guys to come take a look, but the parts alone are going to cost more than a new one."

Typical Julian, wanting to tear anything of value down.

"I'll cover the cost of fixing it," I say without thinking twice.

Lily glances over at me with wide eyes. "You don't have to."

I pull her into my arms as if it's the most natural thing in the world. With the number of fake dates we've been on, it has become second nature to touch her, to keep her close.

I've even come to enjoy the little flutter in my chest that occurs whenever we're in proximity to one another, which I never thought was possible.

"But you totally should fix it," Dahlia tells me while linking her arm with her sister's. "Lesson number one of dating a billionaire: When they offer their black card, you only ask, what's the limit?"

"There isn't one," Julian and I say at the same time before shooting each other a look.

"Well, thanks for the tip," Lily says with a sassy eye roll.

I grin before turning to face Julian. "Send me the bill?"

"Yeah, sure," he grumbles under his breath.

I was so distracted by the fountain that I didn't notice everyone's luggage packed inside Julian's truck until now.

"I thought I was driving," I say, keeping my tone light despite the tightness in my jaw.

Dahlia smiles. "Julian thought it would be better for him to drive since we'll need to stop by the client's house on Saturday morning."

"You can borrow mine." I tuck my hands into the pockets of my jeans—a move Lily follows with obvious interest.

I ignore the concerned crease between her brows. "I don't mind."

I'm an image of nonchalance while internally panicking at the idea of giving someone else full control behind the wheel. My hands start to sweat over the thought of sitting in the back seat while Julian drives, and if I'm not careful, everyone will notice.

"You know what?" Lily jumps in and ropes her arm around mine. "What if we take two cars?" she asks.

Julian shoots her a look. "And pay double the parking?"

Lily hits him with a glare. "Are you complaining about spending money when you dropped a thousand dollars on a prank last month?"

Dahlia laughs under her breath while Julian grumbles, "That was different."

Lily ignores him. "We'll see you at the hotel?"

"Sure," her sister replies, still looking confused but thankfully not pressing for answers.

Lily reaches for her bag in the trunk, but before she wraps her hand around the handle, I carefully move her out of the way and grab it instead. She follows me to my G-Wagon, giving her sister one last wave while I open her door. She has to use the step to climb into the passenger seat, and I get a glorious view of her ass in the process.

"Eyes up here, Vittori."

I slowly drag them toward her face. "Don't act like you don't do the same thing when I'm not looking."

Her mouth falls open.

I tap it shut with the tip of my finger. "It's okay. I like when you can't help yourself around me."

I shut her door with a grin and head to the trunk, where

I place her suitcase beside mine before checking all the tires once again.

I already did my usual routine back at my house because I didn't want to draw attention to myself, but my anxiety climbs when I see Lily in the passenger seat, depending on my driving to keep her safe.

Julian rolls down his window. "You all good?"

"Yup. Checking if I ran over a nail," I lie.

He reverses out of the driveway and leaves while I confirm that all the tires are in mint condition. Once I'm done with that, I pop open the hood and look over the engine.

The compulsion to assess every nook and cranny is proof enough that I'm slipping, but instead of being concerned over my safety, I'm preoccupied with Lily's. That much I can confirm as I assess the dipstick—despite having my oil changed last week—and the serpentine belt—looks brand new, because it is.

At some point, Lily climbs out of the SUV and leans against the side of it. "Want to talk about what's bothering you?"

I slam the hood shut and walk over to her side of the car. "In you go."

She steps onto the platform and climbs into the SUV. I reach behind her chair for the seat belt and clip it in place before tugging on the strap.

Before I move away, she reaches for my hand. "Lorenzo."

"Don't."

"We're not going anywhere until you talk to me."

"Fine by me. It's not like I wanted to spend the weekend with you and your overbearing family anyway."

Her eyes widen. "Excuse me?"

I want to rip my own hair out by the roots because why does she always push me to talk at the worst times.

Don't blame her for your lack of control.

Cazzo.

I can't look at her when I apologize. "I'm sorry. Driving long distances… It's a…" *Fuck.* I pause before losing the battle against my pride. "It's a *trigger*." I spit it out like poison.

"For what exactly?"

I stay quiet, hoping she gives up while knowing her well enough to predict she won't.

"I'm asking because I want to better understand you. That's all," she says in that calming cadence of hers.

With the deepest breath that makes my diaphragm burn, I answer.

"My OCD." There. I said it. It's not like I have done the best job hiding it from her. Not like I do with others.

"I don't know what it's like to have that diagnosis, and I won't act like I do, but regardless, being triggered doesn't give you the right to lash out at me like that."

"No, it doesn't." I hang my head in shame. It's been twenty years since I was diagnosed, so I should've learned to manage it by now, but lately I feel completely out of control.

"You don't want to end up upsetting the wrong person one day."

"I agree." I shut her door before getting behind the wheel. "Can we restart the weekend?"

She doesn't answer right away, so I follow up with "Please."

With a sigh, she nods. "Fine."

"Thank you," I say in earnest.

Out of all my cars, Lily seems to be the most interested in this one, to the point of her checking out the center console, dashboard display, and glove compartment. She even asks me a few questions about the way it drives after she notices the chair cushioning her when I turn.

"Do you like it?" I ask after hitting the button that turns on her chair massager.

She delicately traces the edge of the leather seat, and for one deranged second, I'm jealous of a chair.

You're…

No. Don't you even think about saying it.

She looks over at me with those doe eyes of hers and nods. "It's…fancy."

I make a show of connecting my phone to the display—a feature her dinosaur of a car is lacking, along with blind spot sensors and a dash cam.

"Imagine not having to use a portable speaker every time you want to listen to something," I say when music softly begins streaming through the car.

Her eyebrows shoot up. "Manny told you about that?"

"He was impressed by the system you jerry-rigged."

Her eyes fall to her lap. "I could've replaced the speakers, but then I would've had to cut back on buying clothes."

"Who needs functioning speakers anyway?"

"Exactly. I knew you'd get it." Her small smirk turns into a full-blown smile.

"Your dad gave you that car, right?" For some reason, I'm not ready to put the conversation to rest. When I think of Lily driving around town in that shitty car, I get this uncomfortable tightness in my chest that is impossible to ignore.

"Yeah. He bought it for Dahlia and me to share."

"That's a nice gift."

Her throat visibly tightens from her swallow. "Yeah. Money was tight, so we were surprised when he decided to get us a new car versus a used one."

"Only the best for the people's princess."

She groans. "You know about that nickname?"

I smile. "Impossible not to hear it whispered whenever you walk into a room."

She shoves my shoulder with a laugh. "Shut up. That's so not true."

I shrug. "If you say so...*principessa*."[I]

Her eyes roll.

"Not a fan? Okay. What about *cucciola*?"[II]

"Immediately no."

I choke on a laugh. "We'll have to workshop some options."

"I like the classics. Like *baby*. *Babe*. *Love*, but only if you're British."

"What about *amore mio*?"[III]

Her cheeks flush, and I officially have her new nickname.

As much as I want to keep the conversation light, I can't shake the idea of her driving an old car. "If your dad were

---

I **Principessa:** Princess.

II **Cucciola:** Puppy.

III **Amore mio:** My love.

here now, would he want you to be driving around in that car?"

Her hands, which were lying flat against her lap, curl into tight fists. "You're not letting this go, are you?"

"Do people typically give up by now?"

Her silence is confirmation enough. I tell myself not to push, to let it go and move on to another topic, but maybe that's Lily's issue. Maybe everyone is willing to give up at the first sign of upsetting her, and while that has its place, it shouldn't come at the price of her safety.

So you're her protector now?

My own hands tighten around the steering wheel. "What if there was another way to hold on to his memory without anchoring yourself to a two-ton relic?"

She glances over at me from the corner of her eye, likely assessing my angle. "I don't know."

I pull the dice from my pocket and hold them out for her to grab. Her fingers brush against the soft flesh of my palm, sending a few sparks scattering across my skin as she takes the dice.

"There are other ways to honor someone that don't compromise your own needs. With the Moirai, I was stubborn. I didn't want to accept that it wasn't the same buzzing casino my father built and managed, so I held on."

She rolls the dice between her fingers, back and forth like I do, clearly lost in thought. I don't want to interrupt whatever silent conversation she has going on inside her head, so I focus on the road until she is ready to talk.

"Letting go was hard, but I found a way to always keep a piece of it with me."

She is silent for a while after that, and I give her time to process what I said.

She turns in her seat to face me. "Let's say—hypothetically speaking, of course—I was ready to get a new car... Would you mind going with me to the dealerships?"

My breathing stutters because that was not what I was expecting her to ask.

"Sure," I say, knowing this is only the start of blurred boundaries and broken rules.

They say the road to hell is paved with good intentions, and me offering to help Lily find a car is the first step down a dark, obsessive path.

I can't say I'm sorry about it though.

At least not *yet*.

A few hours later, we finally make it to the hotel. Dahlia and Julian are already waiting in the lobby with our room keys, so we head to our rooms to drop off our bags, which are located on different floors.

Dahlia mentions our dinner reservation before we part ways, and I spend the time it takes Lily to get ready checking out reviews online. There are a few that make me pause, and my stomach is in knots by the time Lily steps out of the bathroom.

"What's wrong?" she asks as she brushes a hand down the material of her dress.

"Nothing." I head to the bathroom so I can wash my hands.

She follows me. "Are you upset about sharing a room?"

Not as much as I should be. "No."

"Then what's the matter?"

"I was thinking about dinner tonight."

Her lips turn downward. "Shit. I forgot."

I freeze. "About?"

"You don't like eating at restaurants."

My shoulders, which were already tense, bunch up. "Contrary to what you think, I'm not completely incapable of—"

"Whoa. I *never* said that."

"You might as well have."

"I'm sorry if it came across that way. I was only trying to support you."

"I'm not sure why you assumed I wanted that from you." My voice is snappier than usual, and she winces. "I'm sorry," I say immediately. "That was stupid of me to say."

She takes a deep breath, holds it for a few seconds, and slowly exhales through her mouth—a technique I'm familiar with. "Apologize by telling me why you reacted that way."

She could've walked out on me, but she is choosing to stay and give me a chance to explain myself, so I take it.

I stare out the window. "I don't want you treating me differently because you know about my OCD."

A wrinkle of worry cuts between her brows. "It's called *caring*, Lorenzo. I know it's an unfamiliar concept to you with the way your family has acted, but it's normal. Hell, it should be the standard, and I'm sorry people in your life made you think it wasn't."

"I'm—"

"I don't want an apology. I want you to do better, or else one day I'm not going to forgive you again."

She leaves the room without letting me get the last word in, and instead of being happy that she's gone, I'm worried about where she ran off to. We're a far cry away from Lake Wisteria, where she's accustomed to talking to random strangers without questioning whether they're safe or not.

I drop my head into my hands and groan.

One day you'll care about someone so much, you'll miss them as soon as they leave, my dad had told me when I asked why he called my mom as soon as she drove off for work.

Back then, I thought it was ridiculous. I mean, he saw her not even two minutes prior, and he was already calling her to talk?

I tug on the roots of my hair hard enough to make it hurt.

"I don't miss Lily," I say aloud, my voice full of false bravado.

I can't.

Or at least that's the lie I tell myself only five minutes later when I grab our hotel key off the dresser and head out to find her.

Becoming reliant on Lily feels like a fork in the road, where one wrong step could lead me down a path of no return.

A path riddled with complications, an expiration date, and, worst of all, *love*.

CHAPTER TWENTY-FIVE

Lily

Since we're all supposed to meet in an hour for dinner, I can't go very far, so I decide to explore some shops nearby. I need some time to cool off because I'm afraid of what might happen if I can't get out of this mood.

Caring about Lorenzo is frustrating, and it feels like a losing battle. He is hot and cold, making me think he cares one moment and leaving me confused and upset in the next.

There is no use denying that I like him. That's why his reaction back in the hotel room hurt me, because I took a chance and offered my support, only for him to reject me yet again.

No more though. I want to be chased, not be the one doing the chasing.

As if Lorenzo can read my thoughts from a mile away, he surprises me with a text.

LORENZO

Where are you?

ME

Went for a walk.

I'm impressed by my own maturity because I'd rather ignore him altogether.

LORENZO

Send me your location.

ME

I want to be alone.

LORENZO

Now I'm concerned.

I tuck my phone into my purse and head inside a store without answering him. More texts come through, but I ignore the notifications, instead flipping through the clothes on the racks.

I don't allow myself to check my new messages until five minutes have passed and I'm moving on to another store.

LORENZO

Tell me where you are.

LORENZO

I'm about to call your sister and ask her to find you.

LORENZO

Please send me your location. I promise to only check it when absolutely necessary.

I snort at the last one.

ME

Define absolutely
necessary.

LORENZO

At least three times.

ME

A day?

LORENZO

An hour.

I don't notice I'm smiling until I catch my reflection in one of the store's mirrors. With a frustrated groan, I'm about to toss my phone back into my purse, but I pause when a new text comes in.

LORENZO

Lily?

ME

Why are you acting like
you care about me?

His answer takes too damn long. I nearly give up on a reply, but then my phone vibrates.

LORENZO

You're important to me.

ME

Because of our
arrangement?

Three dots appear, disappear, and reappear again before a new message pops up.

LORENZO

No.

Who knew one word could say so much?

Lorenzo isn't done putting my heart through the ringer though, and his incoming text does an impeccable job of confirming that he does care, even if he doesn't *want* to.

LORENZO

If you refuse to send me your location, then at least give me proof of life.

I send him a photo of me blowing a kiss to the camera before dropping my phone back into my purse. I'm not sure what possessed me to send such a picture, but it's too late to turn back now.

While I'm scanning a rack of clothes, I grow increasingly frustrated with Lorenzo and the way he shut me out earlier, to the point where I shoot Rafa a text. If anyone can give me some much-needed insight, it's him.

ME

Quick question.

He answers immediately, which is promising.

RAFA

What's up?

ME

How did Ellie get you to open up?

My phone buzzes from an incoming call, and I answer.

"Hey," I say to Rafa.

"So much for a quick question."

I laugh. "I was curious."

"Because you're interested in doing the same?"

I pause in front of the window display. "Maybe. No." I pause. "Ugh. I don't know. I'm on the fence about it."

"Part of me wants to warn you against trying, but then I think of someone giving Ellie that kind of advice and how my life would've turned out if she had taken it."

My chest clenches. "Are you trying to make me cry?"

"No, definitely not, and don't you dare start, or else I'll hang up."

"Bruto."

"Brat."

I chuckle under my breath. "I hate to speed you along here, but can you please hurry up? I have to get back to the hotel soon."

"Is Lorenzo there?"

"Yes."

"Are you avoiding him?"

"Oh yeah. He deserves it."

"Good. Let him sweat it out a bit."

"Is that part of the strategy?"

"That and making him realize what life would be like without you in it."

"I can't exactly break up with him."

"No, obviously not, but you can talk about what the future will look like after the engagement is over with. Talk about your dreams. Talk about wanting to get married for real. Paint a picture that's so vivid, he knows if he's not the one making it happen, then you'll find someone else who will."

A bitter laugh crawls up my throat, but I swallow it. "And where am I supposed to find this future husband of mine?"

"He's standing right here."

I turn around with a gasp. "Lorenzo."

Rafa chuckles against my ear. "Best of luck. And don't forget what I said." He hangs up.

"How did you find me?" I ask, nearly missing the way Lorenzo's eyes dart over me while I slip my phone back into my purse.

"There was a sign in the photo."

"Oh."

"Yeah. *Oh*." He tucks his hand into his jeans. "Who were you talking to on the phone?"

"Rafa." I leave the store and start walking toward a store a few blocks down. Lorenzo follows beside me, blocking me from the busy street. It's such a small gesture, but it's the littlest ones that always send my heart into a tailspin.

"What did he want?" he asks while we're walking.

"Just checking in."

"Why is he so interested in your dating life?"

I shrug.

He pulls his hand out of his pocket and grabs mine.

I roll my eyes. "You don't need to hold my hand without an audience."

"Maybe I like the way your hand fits in mine."

The only reason I let his comment slide is because, damn, that was a great answer.

Neither of us says a word as I drag him into the next store. I expect him to let go of my hand once we get inside, but he keeps our fingers laced together until I escape into a dressing room with a few outfits in hand.

"So, about this future husband..." he says aloud, acting like there isn't a curtain blocking us.

"Yes?" I ask, my breath catching.

Was Rafa right? Is it really *that* simple?

"You're not thinking of jumping into a relationship right after we call off the engagement, right?"

I pause in the middle of taking my shirt off. "Why are you asking?"

"I didn't think much about it before."

There's no way it's this easy to make Lorenzo see reason, right? There has to be some kind of catch, or maybe Rafa is an outlier in this situation.

"Why wouldn't I move on? It's not like this is *real*."

He doesn't speak for a few beats. "Shouldn't you wait at least a year for optics purposes?"

Make him realize what life would be like without you in it.

"And waste more time? No. People will understand after you broke my heart and called off the engagement." Thank goodness he can't see my face right now or else he'd know something was up when he saw my smile.

"I think you should reconsider."

"Why?"

He pauses, the brief moment feeling like a minute. "It doesn't seem like a good idea."

I'm sure it doesn't.

I *almost* feel bad for Lorenzo, because he won't know what hit him until it's too late.

Like Eros, I've set sight on my target, and I won't stop taking shots at Lorenzo's heart until he has no choice but to face the truth about his feelings.

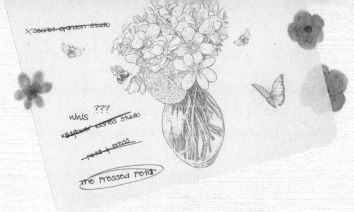

X secret garden studio

wws ???
wildflower washes studio

petal + press

The Pressed Petal

CHAPTER TWENTY-SIX

Lily

ahlia, Julian, Lorenzo, and I head to a restaurant near our hotel and spend most of our meal chatting about Lopez Luxury clients, Dahlia's TV show, and Lorenzo's campaign. Thankfully everyone steers clear of talking about Rose & Thorn, but my luck runs out when Dahlia faces Lorenzo with a suspicious smile on her face.

"So, Lorenzo...when did you realize you loved my sister?"

I groan. "Dahlia."

"What? I have a year of your love life to catch up on!"

"You couldn't ask an easier question?"

"Okay. Fine." My sister rolls her eyes. "What's stopping you from buying Lily a property so she can finally get started on the Pressed Petal?"

"The same reason I gave you," I reply, my throat working

hard to dislodge the ball of emotion stuck in it because *oh, shit*. I've avoided talking to Lorenzo about my dream, instead diverting every conversation back to Lavender Lane, and this is my penance.

Lorenzo wraps his arm around my chair, as if to say *I've got this*. "I've offered to help Lily in whatever way she needs," he replies, coolly. "But if she would rather do things her way, then I respect that. If she ever wants my help, I'm there to offer it."

That is…wildly accurate, and I'm genuinely surprised.

Dahlia sips her wine. "Good answer. Okay, now can you tell me when you realized you loved my sister? *Please*."

I don't even bother hiding my annoyance this time. "Come on."

"What? That should be the easiest question in the world." She takes a sip of her wine and waits.

I glance over at Lorenzo, and his face is a blank mask.

"You don't need to answer her," I say before shooting her a scathing look. "She should know better than to ask that."

He clasps my chin and turns my head until I'm looking into his eyes instead. "No need to be embarrassed, *amore mio*."

My heart repeats the same short pause from earlier, missing a beat at the nickname.

Dahlia perks up. "He has a nickname for you? *Cute*."

"Nothing is better than *sweetheart*," Julian grumbles.

"It's not a competition." She shoves his shoulder, and the corners of my lips curl, my annoyance from her overbearingness gone within a blink of an eye.

Lorenzo's warm gaze flickers over my face for a few drawn-out beats before he releases my chin and faces my sister. "I don't think there was an exact moment in time where I realized I loved Lily, but it was more a collection of small, impactful ones. Moments where I fell in love with her genuine heart or her quick wit or the adorable tell she has where her nose wrinkles whenever she wants to be honest but worries it might hurt someone's feelings. Not to mention she's confident, incredibly loyal, and so out of my league, I'm still surprised she gave me a chance."

I don't care what Lorenzo says.

I don't care what lies he tells himself.

He might not love me, but his words give me hope that there is a chance he could one day. Hope I haven't felt since I took the last gold coin my dad gave me and used my wish on *him*.

I hope Lorenzo is the one I've been searching for, I said before tossing the coin into my dad's fountain and watching it join the other ones at the bottom.

Maybe the wish wasn't a waste after all.

Or maybe Lorenzo's words right now were nothing but a *lie*.

My nerves are on high alert when Lorenzo and I return to our hotel room. Earlier the space seemed bright and open, but now the walls feel as if they are closing in around me.

Lorenzo asks me if I want to take a shower first, but the thought only makes my heart rate spike, so I let him go ahead of me. The soft click of the door shutting sends goose bumps across my skin, only to remain there when the shower turns on.

Don't be ridiculous, I tell myself before trying to distract myself with my phone. I scroll through social media until the bathroom door opens and a cloud of steam is let into our room.

Lorenzo walks through it, wearing nothing but a towel around his waist. He looks like one of Michelangelo's statues, meant to be ogled at from behind a red velvet rope.

Fitting, since I can look but not touch.

He ignores my existence as he heads to his suitcase and bends over, giving me a glorious view of his back muscles. He's leaner than other men I've dated but more defined in a way that makes me want to trace the dips and curves of his muscles with—

"Like what you see?" he asks without checking to confirm if I'm staring.

My eyes stretch to their limits. "How did you know..."

He turns around, hitting me with a smirk that makes heat pool in my belly. "I can feel you watching me."

"Is that a new thing?" With the amount of times I check him out, I'm praying so.

He shakes his head, sending my mind into a tailspin.

"Couldn't you have brought your clothes into the bathroom *before* you showered?"

"And miss out on your reaction to seeing me shirtless? Pass."

"So you admit to prancing around on purpose." I motion toward his glistening body.

He chokes on a laugh. "I did not *prance*."

"You strutted across the room like a damn peacock."

"Only because you stared at me like you were waiting for me to drop the towel."

"Did not!"

He walks over to me, my heartbeats matching the rhythm of his steps. "You've got something right..." He brushes the corner of my mouth, and a gasp gets trapped in my tightening throat.

I go to push him away, but when my hands land on his chest, I forget all about it.

He chuckles. "Do I feel as good as I look?"

"You're so self-absorbed."

"It's called being confident."

"You pronounced *conceited* wrong."

He chuckles, his chest shifting underneath my palms from the sound.

I *should* take my hands off him, but then I notice the way his heart is beating faster than expected—so fast, in fact, I think it outpaces mine.

An interesting development.

He's also affected, if not more, yet I couldn't tell based on his smug little smirk.

I'll show him. I drag my hand lower, tracing his abs one by one, his chest stalling as he holds his breath.

"You okay?" I ask innocently, batting my lashes.

"Just waiting until you're satisfied."

I look up at him with a smile. "With you, I'd be waiting forever."

With a little shove, he stumbles backward, and I jump off

the bed, grab my PJs, and slip inside the bathroom, all while laughing at the stunned expression on his face as I slam the door.

CHAPTER TWENTY-SEVEN

Lorenzo

After I get up on three separate occasions to check the lock on the door, I climb into bed for the final time. I keep to the right side of the mattress although I prefer the left, all because I don't trust the flimsy security latch meant to protect us from an intruder.

I've seen one too many videos on people breaking into hotel rooms, so the chances of me getting more than a few hours of sleep tonight are slim, especially when I think of who I'll be sharing a bed with.

If I didn't care about Lily, I'd choose my own comfort over her safety, but there is this undeniable need to…protect, right up there with my desire to *possess*. The urge has strengthened with every passing hour of our ruse, and I'm still not entirely sure how to navigate these complex feelings.

There are a few emotions hitting me all at once, and it's overwhelming after spending so many years on autopilot— existing but never truly *living*.

Lily, who suffers from the opposite issue, is unaware of my existential crisis. She sings along to a song while she showers, making it impossible to ignore her presence.

Water splashing against the tiles can be heard from the bed, and before I can rein it in, my imagination has a mind of its own and paints a pretty picture for me.

In this fantasy, Lily is standing under the hot spray, completely naked with soap sliding down her body. Her eyes are closed, so she doesn't see me stepping into the stall behind her. She lets out a gasp when my arms circle around her, but it's quickly cut off by a moan as I slide my hand over her stomach before I finally reach her—

The mental image is shattered when Lily drops something in the shower.

Fuck.

I grab the comforter and yank it up to my chin, silently commanding that my growing problem goes away before Lily steps out of the bathroom.

Despite my best efforts to distract myself, my thoughts drift back to Lily, and I blame her singing. I wish I could say it's bad, but on the contrary, she has a nice, sultry voice that doesn't match her bubbly, *pink is my favorite neutral* personality.

I'm tempted to sneak into the bathroom and shut her phone off, all because I don't like the idea of her listening to another man's voice while she's naked.

With a frustrated groan, I knock my head back against the linen headboard.

A minute later, Lily cracks the door open a few inches and pops her head out. "You good?"

"Yeah. Why?" I turn to look at her and wish I didn't.

Water sluices down her skin, dripping down her neck before disappearing underneath the white towel wrapped around her.

"I thought I heard a strange noise."

Just me dying.

Or at least it sure feels that way now. Even though I can hardly see her, thanks to the door blocking my view, I can imagine what is hiding underneath that towel. The thick white material does a good job concealing her curves, but her makeshift dress slips a little, giving me a glimpse of the tops of her breasts.

It takes every ounce of willpower to rip my eyes away from her. Once the door clicks shut again, I can finally exhale through my nose.

Ten minutes pass, and Lily exits the bathroom wearing a matching PJ set. There's nothing inherently sexy about the button-down set with navy-colored ribbons scattered across the white fabric, but my cock doesn't care. All Lily needs to do is bite her lip like she is right now, and my heart automatically starts pumping blood to the place it shouldn't.

Get a hold of yourself. I clench my hand around the comforter as she slides underneath the covers. She smells so damn good from whatever lotion she put on, and it only grows stronger as she tosses and turns in bed.

To distract myself from more thoughts of her, I unlock my phone and fiddle with the settings. The distraction only lasts for a minute until she rolls over and faces me with a huff.

"Can we swap sides?"

"No." I look over at the door, confirming it hasn't magically unlocked itself in the five minutes since I last checked.

She frowns. "Why?"

"I like sleeping on the right side of the bed." Or at least I do *tonight*.

"Same."

"Then what's the problem?"

She gestures between us. "I can't fall asleep like this."

"Then it's going to be a long night for you."

She groans. "Lorenzo."

"That's not exactly how I imagined hearing you say my name in bed."

"Think about it often?"

"Regrettably."

That comment earns me a smack in the head with a flying pillow.

I brush my still-damp hair out of my eyes before glancing down at her. She has her hand innocently tucked under her face, looking like an angel despite her wicked throwing arm.

"Do you feel better now?" I ask dryly.

"Nope," she says, exaggerating the *p* sound.

I reach over and shut off the lamp, giving her the universal sign for *please shut up*.

She lasts one whole minute before she speaks again. "What's the other reason you don't want to switch spots?"

I don't turn to face her. "Who says there's another reason?"

"I know you."

Those three little words have a massive impact on my psyche, like a wrecking ball tearing through the fortress I've built to protect myself.

"So what is it?" she asks, and I wish she'd stop.

"Aren't you tired?" I follow up with instead.

"It's hard for me to fall asleep in unfamiliar places."

"Likewise." I flop over and stare at the dark ceiling.

"Did you check for hidden cameras?"

"Do you take me for an amateur?"

She giggles, and I find myself grinning at the sound.

"How about trap doors?" she whispers. "I heard a story about a human trafficking ring—"

I screw my eyes shut. "Don't start."

"Sorry." She flips onto her back too.

"What do you usually do when you can't sleep?" I ask a minute later when I'm no longer tempted to get out of bed and check the lock on the door again.

"Listen to true crime podcasts."

"Next you're going to tell me you meditate to murder stories."

"Only on Mondays."

I make a noise in the back of my throat.

"Kidding!" She laughs. "I usually fall asleep with the TV on."

"I knew you were too good to be true."

She pinches my side, and I'm tempted to snatch her hand— strictly to teach her a lesson about touching me, of course. It has nothing to do with her being the first and only person I like holding hands with. Nothing at all.

"A lot of people do that," she says.

"I read somewhere that most of them end up single for life too."

"But not *all*, which means I only have to find one man who doesn't mind." Her grin is so wide, I can make out her white teeth in the dark.

Her comment kills my smile. The thought of Lily falling asleep in bed with another man has the power to squash my good mood.

"Put the damn TV on and go to bed." I force the sentence out through gritted teeth.

Her smile doesn't waver as she follows my command. The glow from the TV turning on makes me squint, but my eyes adjust as Lily flips through channels.

She eventually lands on an old rerun of *The Silver Vixens*, and I don't protest despite finding the outdated laugh track annoying. Eventually I stop noticing it because I'm paying more attention to Lily's laughs instead.

I could get used to this, I admit to myself.

After ten minutes, my eyelids start to drag, and next thing I know, I'm falling asleep without a single worry on my mind—a welcomed rarity.

And Lily is clearly the reason why.

CHAPTER TWENTY-EIGHT

Lorenzo

I wake up the next morning groggy and aroused, all thanks to Lily, who at some point during the night threw herself on top of me like a weighted blanket. Her thigh is draped over my erection, while her head is tucked underneath my chin, rising and falling with my shallow breaths.

I'm afraid to wake her up by moving, but I'm equally fearful of staying in bed because what happens once she finds herself wrapped around me like this?

You need to go. I will myself to get up, but there is something comforting about Lily's embrace. Multiple somethings, like the weight of her body. The familiar smell of her lotion sticking to my skin. The sweet little murmurs she makes in her sleep, the phrases incoherent.

I should categorize my curious reaction as just that.

Curiosity. But I know that it's much deeper than that, and I allow myself to explore it for a few blissful moments.

She makes me feel trusted, although she has every reason not to. Protective, because she looks so damn innocent cradled in my arms. And the most toxic feeling of all, so damn *possessive* that I want to be the only one she ever wakes up beside again.

Whoa. No.

Feeling possessive of Lily might feel *right*, but that doesn't change how it is all *wrong* for our situation.

We have a deal, and it's up to me to uphold it for the sake of my campaign and my sanity because once the obsessive thoughts start, the compulsions follow soon after, and an unhealthy cycle is born.

It physically pains me to leave our hotel room in search of the gym, but I need some distance. Except in the middle of my run, an image of Lily wandering around Chicago by herself flashes in front of my eyes.

In a rush, I'm hopping off the treadmill and heading to our room.

I need to confirm she didn't run off or something, I say while tapping the elevator button.

You wouldn't want her to get lost or hurt or worse, the voice replies, and my stomach sinks.

What's worse than getting hurt?

And now I'm thinking of apocalyptic-level scenarios, and I blame all Lily's true crime podcasts for the vivid imagination.

Maybe I need to buy a tracking bracelet or something so I can check on her from afar.

Yes, that's what I'll do. I'll order one as soon as I get back to the room.

The voice in my head is suddenly silent, and instead of being relieved, I only feel dread, knowing it got exactly what it wanted—a new compulsion to add to its growing collection, and one that will evolve the longer I'm in Lily's company.

That much I can guarantee.

Good news: Lily is still in our hotel room. The bad? She is sitting on the couch, weeping into her hands, her body shaking from the intensity of her sobs.

"What's wrong?" I ask, horrified by the tears running down her face.

She bristles before shaking her head. "Nothing."

I grab a tissue and pass it to her, hoping it helps me feel less useless.

It doesn't.

She doesn't look up from her hands to see it, so I pull them down and wipe at the corners of her eyes, where her mascara started running. "Tell me what's going on."

"Why do you care?" She looks up at me with those watery eyes of hers that threaten my self-control.

"I already told you yesterday—you're important to me." Whether I like it or not.

"How am I supposed to trust you after everything that's happened?"

"You don't have to, but if you choose to anyway, I'll work

on doing the same." I take a deep breath and hold it before adding, "I don't like seeing you cry or upset. It makes me feel helpless, and as someone who craves control, that is...difficult."

Admitting the truth aloud must've done the trick because Lily finally opens up about Daisy. I know most of the details already, but I pretend I don't. I soak up her emotions, from the brightness in her eyes when she talks about visiting Daisy to the way they glisten when she mentions someone wanting to adopt her on Monday.

I've spent most of my life being an emotional escape artist because feelings feed my anxiety. But with Lily, I'm more affected by her unhappiness than my own worries, and I'm driven by the desire to solve her problems.

"Do you want to adopt her?" I ask.

"I can't." Her voice cracks. "My mom's allergic."

"What about Rafa? He has a farm full of animals."

She shakes her head. "He's got enough going on with the ones he adopted."

"What's one more?"

She lets out a soft laugh, and it eases some of the pressure in my lungs like someone thrust a chest tube inside me.

"It's too much. He already told me so. *Twice*." A single tear rolls down her face, and I wipe it away, only for another to replace it.

More continue to fall, ruining my efforts to stop them. "I knew she'd find a home because she's the sweetest, cutest girl." *Impossible*. "But..." Her voice cracks, along with my resolve.

Fuck.

I take a step back and brush my hands through my wet hair.

I never imagined adopting a dog after the traumatic experience that happened with my last one, but I'm not opposed to the idea if it makes Lily happy.

If that is considered selfish, so be it. My actions will be balanced out by all Lily's selfless ones, like two weighing scales striving for karmic equilibrium.

"I'll contact the vet," I say, a bit too gruff.

She turns to look at me with wide eyes. "What?"

"I want to meet Daisy and see what's so special about her." Technically that is true.

"Why?"

I ignore her question and head to my suitcase. It's organized with the dirty clothes tucked into a separate bag, but I make a show of refolding my clean clothes.

She places a hand on my shoulder and wills me to turn around.

I don't.

"Lorenzo," she says in that too-sweet voice of hers.

You will not yield, no matter how sweet she sounds.

I start counting my underwear because why did I pack ten pairs for a two-night stay? Did I plan to shit myself multiple times?

Unfortunately Lily doesn't give up. "Since when do you want to adopt a pet?"

"It's a recent interest." *Now stop asking me any more questions,* I silently beg.

I should've known it was a wasted effort because she probes some more.

"Don't do this for me."

"I'm not." I'm doing this for me, the person whose mental health will benefit from her no longer crying.

And who knows? Maybe I'll grow to enjoy Daisy's company in my big, empty house.

Lily and I meet up with Julian and Dahlia for brunch before we split up again, this time the girls going off on their own. I'd rather hang out by myself than spend the afternoon with Julian Lopez of all people, but he won't leave my side.

"You good?" I ask when he pauses at the entrance of the first jewelry store on my list.

He looks around the sales floor, his face turning progressively paler. "Please tell me you're looking at buying Lily some diamond earrings."

"Has she mentioned wanting some to you?"

"Yes. It's a running joke by now."

"Then I'll add them to my list."

"You have a *list*?" He looks yearningly at a nearby trash can.

I bite my tongue to stop myself from laughing. An enthusiastic employee introduces herself, and after I tell her what I'm looking for, she is all too happy to show me their engagement ring options.

Julian looks ready to pass out, so I ask if someone can bring him a chair.

"This better be a fucking prank." He must not trust his legs either because he happily takes a seat.

I ignore him and focus on the dazzling rings.

"Lorenzo."

"Julian."

"This is all moving way, way too fast. Maybe you need to slow down—"

"The only opinion I'm interested in is which ring you think Lily would like most."

He checks out all the rings before shaking his head. "None of them."

I frown. "There has to be something here she'd like. This is the best store in all of Chicago."

He stares at the display full of the whitest, clearest diamonds money can buy. "It's not the store. It's the *color*."

The employee pauses. "Would she prefer something like an emerald or sapphire?"

Julian glances up at me. "If he can't answer that question, then he shouldn't be proposing."

Did I get outsmarted at my own game by Julian motherfucking Lopez?

No. I refuse.

Think, Lorenzo, I tell myself, refusing to fail Julian's test. He gave me a clue at least, so if a traditional diamond isn't what Lily wants, then there must be another color.

I can't see her wanting a sapphire—that much I know—while an emerald is trickier. She likes green, given the color of flower stems, so I mention it to the jeweler.

"We could do a peekaboo emerald in the band," she mentions, and I shake my head and think about the main diamond.

Pink is my favorite neutral, she wrote on her dating profile, and I want to smack my own forehead at ever questioning my abilities to guess what Lily would like.

"What kind of gemstones come in pink?"

There's a little glint in Julian's eyes that tells me I'm on the right path, and I've never felt better about proving him wrong.

So much for him hoping I wouldn't be able to answer the question.

Asshole.

"Pink?" The jeweler balks. "We've got sapphires and diamonds here, although the diamonds are significantly more expensive."

"Perfect. I want to see everything you have."

I must pass Julian's test with flying colors because he remains tight-lipped, stewing in silence as he processes me becoming an integral part of his life.

Till the election do Lily and I part.

CHAPTER TWENTY-NINE

Lily

My sister and I have spent the last two hours searching for dresses, and while Dahlia has found seven different outfits already, including two dresses for the fundraiser dinner, I've struggled to find anything that feels like me.

When I slowly began switching my favorite outfits with new, less bold pieces, I said it wouldn't be permanent. That I was only doing it temporarily while I sorted through my complicated feelings.

I justified it by saying I didn't want to be vulnerable. That I didn't want to express myself, whether it be with my words or through my clothes, and I most definitely didn't want to draw anyone's attention.

But was I really worried about other people, or was I more concerned about my skewed sense of self?

Because after my failed rebound after Lorenzo, I'll be honest: I didn't like myself very much. I felt desperate to improve my self-esteem when I hopped into bed with someone else, and I was ashamed for hurting that same person when I realized my mistake—although Richard can fuck off now.

But maybe it's time I forgave myself for the choices I've made.

Maybe it's time to *move on*.

Because how can I expect other people to accept me, let alone *appreciate me*, if I can't do the same?

The realization pushes me forward, and I'm reinvigorated as we head to another boutique on Dahlia's list. The gown in the window steals my breath, and I come to a full stop in front of it.

I feel like it was made for me, with colorful pink flowers and green leaves embroidered into the gauzy baby-blue fabric. The corset features smaller flowers while the tulle skirt is covered with larger floral brocade, the shape flattering yet still offering enough coverage to make my mom happy.

"Okay, now that's the look I was waiting for!" Dahlia drags me inside the boutique, where we are greeted with champagne glasses and a charming duo who are more than happy to remove the dress off the mannequin so I can try it on.

I'm ushered into a small dressing room and handed the dress while my sister sits right outside the door, sipping her champagne. The room has no mirror, so I can't see how I look unless I leave the fitting room.

"There's no price tag," I announce while stepping into the designer dress.

"I'm sure Lorenzo won't mind."

I look down at the dress with a huff. I can't help brushing my hand down the tulle skirt, hoping to find a single flaw to scare me away from buying it. The intricate details are even better up close, and the colors appear much more vibrant, the baby-blue color looking different depending on which light I stand under.

I step out of the room, and my sister sucks in a breath. One of the salespeople rushes over to help me adjust the corset, and she turns me around so I face the mirror.

My reflection stares back at me, and it's hard to hold my own gaze without getting emotional.

After spending so many months hiding—of disliking myself for mistakes I made and insecurities I couldn't ignore—I'm hit with a strong sense of longing.

"Does it come in black?" Dahlia asks the associate, clearly poking fun at me.

"Uh. No," she replies.

Dahlia fakes a pout. "Pity. My sister probably won't buy it, then."

I roll my eyes and head back inside the fitting room. Instead of taking the dress off right away, I snap a photo and send it to my mom before changing back into my clothes and walking over to the register.

When I open my wallet to grab my credit card, I find all of them missing except for a black one with Lorenzo's name on it.

I'm too impressed by his slick move to be annoyed when I swipe his card through the machine. My cheeks hurt from how hard I'm smiling, and it isn't only from the major hit to Lorenzo's bank account.

It's also because I leave the store feeling not like my old self but a better, more confident version.

And I truly couldn't be happier.

Dahlia and I are being driven to the next shopping location on her list when a new text comes in.

LORENZO

Why is there only one charge on my card?

ME

Because I only bought one dress.

LORENZO

How? You've been shopping for hours.

ME

Counting down the hours until we're reunited?

LORENZO

Impossible not to with Julian for company.

I laugh, making Dahlia glance up from her phone. "Is Lorenzo texting you?"

"Yes."

"Has he said anything about spending time with Julian?"

"Not really."

"I'm surprised they've lasted this long together without splitting up."

I chuckle, only to be interrupted by a new text.

LORENZO

Julian says Dahlia has spent an impressive amount on his card.

ME

She has.

LORENZO

Did mine get lost at that one store?

ME

I can buy my own clothes.

LORENZO

Never said you couldn't.

ME

Then why do you care?

LORENZO

It's a bad look.

ME

How?

LORENZO

They already think I'm poor now that I'm no longer in the billionaire club.

I can't help smiling to myself.

ME

What happened to not caring about billionaire pissing contests?

LORENZO

Turns out I'm not as evolved as I'd like to be.

ME

Did Julian bring out your inner caveman?

LORENZO

Yes. He's lucky I haven't challenged him to a death match.

ME

Don't. My sister will never forgive you.

LORENZO

sigh

LORENZO

Fine.

ME

Thank you.

LORENZO

Show your gratitude by spending more of my money.

ME

Doubt I can make much of a dent in your bank account, but I'll try my best.

LORENZO

Whatever car you pick tomorrow will make up for it.

The next morning, Lorenzo and I wake up early and go car

shopping. It takes us all day, but I finally walk out of the Mercedes dealership with a new SUV that is a newer, bluer version of Lorenzo's current one. I feel guilty for having a little pep in my step after years of fighting against getting a new car, but it disappears as I hop into the driver's seat.

Lorenzo lingers, not moving to close my door right away. Instead he props his arm against it and starts drilling me with questions I'd expect from a driver's ed class.

"You are aware I know how to drive a car, right?"

He rolls his eyes. "Yes."

"Then what's with the twenty questions?"

"You haven't had a new car in over a decade."

"Worried I'm going to crash it on the first day?"

His face pales, and I've never felt so insensitive in my entire life.

His parents died in a car crash! I yell at myself.

I scramble to come up with a better reply. "I'll drive below the speed limit. No, wait. I'll go even slower than that, so you'll have no choice but to leave me behind."

His hold on the door tightens, drawing attention to the veins in his arms. If I wasn't so distraught at the wild look in his eyes, I'd be going feral over his corded muscles.

Lorenzo takes a deep breath and reaches into his pocket. I expect him to keep his hand there, but he pulls out one Moirai die and holds it out for me to grab.

"Um, what am I supposed to do with that?" I stare at it, confused.

"Take it."

I gawk instead. "But it's yours."

"I want you to hold on to one of them for me." He curls my fingers into a fist before stepping away, taking a fragment of my heart with him.

"Are they lucky, by chance?" I joke, noticing the dark look in Lorenzo's eyes after he takes another step back.

"Maybe to you."

"In that case, I'm going to make a quick pit stop on the way home and buy a lottery ticket."

"Make it two?"

"Deal," I say with a smile.

His gaze lingers on my face for another moment before he heads back to his matching SUV.

I open my palm and stare at one half of his father's dice set. With how much Lorenzo panicked when one of them fell between his seats, I'm surprised he was willing to break up the pair so easily.

The romantic in me wants to hyper-fixate on the hidden meaning behind his gesture, while the down-to-earth realist plans to ignore the excited current spreading through my body because I don't need to get my hopes up.

He bought you a car, so consider those hopes no longer manageable.

It appears that my plan to have him realize he has feelings for me is going a bit too well, to the point where I'm waiting for the other shoe to drop. There is no way Lorenzo will easily accept he cares about more than my safety—not when he pushed me away the first time because of exactly that.

But unlike last time, I'm ready to put up a fight because I know what I want, and it's always been *him*.

We arrive in Lake Wisteria way after the sun sets, so I miss out on another Sunday lunch. Based on the Lopez-Muñoz group chat, I'm expected to bring Lorenzo to the next one. No *if*s, *and*s, or *but*s about it.

Like always, the Kids' Table group chat goes off with its own messages, but I don't read any of them until I safely pull into my driveway and park my new SUV.

RAFA

I wish I could be there.

DAHLIA

No, you don't.

I'm relieved that Rafa went to visit Ellie in Europe with her parents and Nico because that's one less person I have to worry about.

ME

It's the thought that counts.

JULIAN

If that's the case, then I'll *try* to be on my best behavior.

DAHLIA

I thought you two were best friends after Chicago.

JULIAN

Seeing as he's still making me give a speech this weekend, no.

I laugh, only to jump in my seat at Lorenzo knocking on my window.

"What are you doing here?" I ask, winded from the scare.

"I wanted to make sure you got home okay."

I open the door and step out of the car. "A text would've sufficed."

His brows draw together, and I wonder if he considered that option.

"Here." I retrieve the die from my pocket and hold it up for him to take.

He stares at it before shaking his head. "Hold on to it until we find out if we won the lottery or not."

I fight a smile and fail as I tuck the die back into my pocket. "I'll keep it safe."

He nods, his Adam's apple bobbing from his swallow. I'm tempted to stand on the tips of my toes and kiss it, but I hold back, instead brushing my hand down his chest. The way his breath catches feels like a reward and, even more so, a promise of what's to come.

Never in a million years did I expect Lorenzo to jump in and adopt Daisy. He might claim it wasn't because of me, and maybe he has his own reasons for wanting a dog, but there is no way I didn't influence his decision whatsoever.

We both know he would've been perfectly content spending the rest of his existence without canine companionship if it weren't for me.

I try not to make a big deal of it when he meets me at the animal clinic the next morning, ready to sign the adoption papers, but it's impossible once he meets Daisy, the world's cutest pit bull, while looking ready to bolt.

We've been in the private exam room for an entire minute already and he still hasn't let go of the door handle, his body tense.

"Lorenzo, meet Daisy." I take a seat on the floor, and Daisy takes it upon herself to turn my lap into a chair.

"This is Daisy?" The way his mouth opens and closes makes me laugh

"What did you expect?"

"Some kind of lapdog, or maybe a golden retriever. Not this…this…"

I scratch behind Daisy's ear, making her tongue loll out. "Beauty?"

"*Beast*," he hisses.

I press my hands over Daisy's ears. "Daddy didn't mean that, baby. He's just…overwhelmed."

There's a wicked gleam to Lorenzo's eyes, and I'd sacrifice my favorite pair of sneakers to know what's going on in his mind right now.

Daisy barks, and the deep bass sound has Lorenzo scrubbing a hand over his face. "At least it's not a yapper."

"Look at you searching for the positives."

"It's a short list, so don't get your hopes up."

I cradle Daisy against my chest. "Don't tell me you're backing out."

"I should." He releases the door handle and takes a step away from it.

Progress.

"But you won't," I say confidently. "Because that would make me very, very sad." I pop my bottom lip out and wobble it, making sure to soften my eyes simultaneously.

He stares at my mouth like he loves to loathe it. "This is a mistake."

My heart feels like Lorenzo is using it for dart practice. "What do you mean?"

His skin pales as he stares into Daisy's eyes. "I'm not qualified to take care of another living being."

Tension coils in my belly. "You take care of me, so how hard can a dog be?"

"For me, seems impossible."

"How so?"

"I had a dog once. Didn't end well." He speaks so low that I have a hard time hearing him.

My heart sinks. "I'm sorry."

"It was a long time ago." He carries on asking more questions about Daisy and what kind of care she requires, all while I wonder about Lorenzo's dog and why he gets that lost look in his eyes when he talks about them.

Lorenzo takes us shopping for pet supplies in Lake Aurora. He would've preferred to support local stores, but the vet recommended a specific food for Daisy to help her continue gaining weight.

I hardly recognize the town anymore with all its fancy new buildings and chain stores.

"What are you thinking about?" he asks as we drive down what used to be Oak Tree Road. It's hard to grasp that the winding street lined with stunning century-old oak trees became this generic strip of retail shops and strip malls.

"This place feels soulless."

"How so?"

"Everything I once loved about it is gone."

"Like what?" He keeps his eyes on the road, although they stray to take in everything I talk about next.

"The gigantic oak trees. The mom-and-pop shops. The *character*." I point to the brand-new pharmacy while wondering where the retro diner-slash-pharmacy went.

"This is exactly what I'm afraid will happen to Lake Wisteria," he replies.

"There has to be a better way to get your message out there."

"I'm working on it. I contacted the architects you mentioned, and they sent me the Lavender Lane plans."

"Morrison and Holmes?"

He nods.

"How did you pull that off?"

His eyes remain on the road, but they harden ever so slightly. "Does it matter? I got what we needed."

I wince. "Please tell me it was legal."

"Yes. All's fair in love and capitalism, and turns out they were willing to betray the Ludlows for a better contract."

"Hold on. You plan on hiring them?"

He leans back in his seat with an exaggerated casualness. "No. And even if I had the power to, I wouldn't, but that didn't stop me from copying them on an email and formally introducing them to my cousin and recommending their company."

"You still talk to your family?"

His smile borders on arrogant. "No, but the firm doesn't know that."

If there wasn't a tight ball of emotion in my chest, I'd laugh, but worry eats away at my amusement as I think over the news Lorenzo shared.

Yes, access to the architectural plans should help our cause, but everyone blindingly trusts the Ludlows, so what if the town assumes the mayor knows best? The Ludlow family has been running Lake Wisteria for years, and our local economy has only seen massive gains.

But what if…

"How many small businesses in town have you been working with?" I ask, the wheels in my head spinning so fast, I can hardly keep up.

"A lot."

"Rough number?"

"Fifty? I'd have to check my spreadsheet to make sure."

My eyes bulge. "Wow. Okay. That's more than I thought."

"Why are you asking?"

My mouth curls into a smile. "Because I have an idea."

CHAPTER THIRTY

Lily

The next week is pure chaos. Our relationship appears to be having a positive impact on Lorenzo's numbers, so his team is pushing harder than ever to keep the momentum going.

Since Lorenzo is busy preparing for the mayoral debate, I spend my free time with Willow, who is in much better spirits about the campaign now that the numbers are looking up. We meet multiple times at Lorenzo's place, wearing matching ruffled socks while workshopping ideas.

I try not to think too much of the basket of socks that appeared after my first visit to his house, but when Willow tells me she was amused by Lorenzo's selection, I'm pleasantly surprised to hear he was the one who purchased them. They may vary in color, style, and pattern, but they have one element in common.

They all represent things I love.

Some socks are more surface level with flowers, hearts, and bows embroidered or printed onto the material, while others remind me of conversations we had on the app—like Halloween-inspired socks for my true crime obsession or my very favorite, *The Silver Vixens*–themed socks.

That pair stands out from the rest, and I hope they bring me good luck as Willow and I talk through a few ideas for the campaign.

We want to encourage people to come forward and talk about how much Lorenzo has helped their business, but money is a sensitive topic, and the few people we've spoken to about it all have had the same answer.

We're grateful for Lorenzo's help, but we don't want people to know.

I don't plan on giving up at the first sign of adversity, but I'm running out of time before Lorenzo goes forward with Phase Two.

At least I can rest easy knowing I still have a couple of weeks left to figure out a better alternative. That's the only reason I'm able to relax on Saturday when Lorenzo surprises me with a spa day.

Him. Not Willow, which he specified in a text he sent me on Friday night.

My mom and sister are equally excited because he invited them as well, and we spend the day getting pampered. Our schedule is packed with massages, manicures, pedicures, and some type of body-wrap service that leaves our skin glowing. Lorenzo thought of everything, including scheduling me a blowout that leaves me looking like an Old Hollywood starlet.

Everything is so thought out, right down to the package that is waiting for me when I get home.

"What is it?" Dahlia waggles her brows at the black box.

I tug on the bow and pop open the lid to reveal eight jewelry boxes—one being a larger rectangle, and the others resembling ring boxes.

He wouldn't...

I'm relieved when I open the first small square one to reveal a pair of pink diamond studs that perfectly match my dress.

"He really does know you!" Dahlia shouts.

"Yeah," I say, drawing out the word. Julian must've told Lorenzo about the running joke because I've never spoken a word about it.

I open the next small box and find another stunning pair of earrings which are different from the first, with an emerald gemstone in the center that is surrounded by white marquise-cut diamonds.

"Oh my God." Dahlia checks them out while I reach for another closed box that holds a set of gorgeous rubies.

I continue until all seven small ring boxes are opened and organized to match the rainbow—a visual reminder of the conversation we had during our double date when I asked him about us coordinating outfits.

It looks like Lorenzo doesn't just want me to remember the colors of the rainbow.

He wants me to *wear* them.

I can't even wrap my head around the gift or the sentimental meaning behind it, let alone whatever my sister is saying before she bumps me in the shoulder.

"Open the last one!" She hands me the larger rectangular box.

I pop open the lid to find a dainty gold bracelet with three gold beads at the center. It's like one of those plastic friendship bracelets but with only two diamond-encrusted letters—an *A* and an *L*—separated by a diamond heart.

"What's the *A* for?" Dahlia asks.

I choke on a laugh. "It's a long story."

Thankfully she quickly moves on once she finds a card at the bottom of the box. "There's a note!" Dahlia shoves it into my hand. "Read it."

I put the bracelet down on the kitchen counter and open the card.

Put this on and never take it off.
—Laurence

"Who's Laurence?" She gasps. "Wait. What if they made a mistake and put the wrong letter?"

"It's a joke."

"And an expensive one at that." She brushes her finger over the letter *A*.

I ignore her question and pass the bracelet to my sister. "Will you help me put this on, please?"

"So long as you promise never to take it off," she teases.

Deal.

After all the effort I put into my appearance, I'm a little nervous about seeing Lorenzo. I had this whole plan set up, but now that I stare at my reflection in the mirror, I question if it looks like I'm trying too hard.

You did this for you, I remind myself.

With one last glance in the mirror, I head outside. My mom, who is also attending tonight's event, brings out her camera and snaps a photo of me like I'm going to my high school prom.

"*Mami*," I say with a groan, blinking away the black spots in my vision.

"*Eres tan preciosa*,"[1] my mom says, her eyes glistening like the stars sparkling outside.

The doorbell rings, and she rushes to go hide in the kitchen so Lorenzo and I can have some privacy.

I'm too nervous to open the door right away, so I stall in front of it, wondering what Lorenzo will think when he sees me.

The bell rings again, and with a grounding breath, I open the door. Our gazes connect like two sets of magnets. His eyes darken, the color turning from brown to obsidian as they travel down my body.

The dress isn't sexy, at least not outright, with the colors and floral patterns giving off a fairy-tale princess vibe rather than that of a confident seductress. But with the way Lorenzo stares at me, I feel like I'm the sexiest woman of all. And with

---

1   **Eres tan preciosa:** You're so beautiful.

how hot he looks in a tux, it's impossible not to feel that way, knowing *I'm* the one who will be on his arm tonight.

Eventually, and dare I say *reluctantly*, his eyes return to my face.

"You look…" He wipes his stubbled jaw. "*Bellissima*."[1]

Hopefully my layer of foundation conceals my flushed cheeks. "Thank you."

"Ready?" He holds out his elbow, and I take it once I grab my clutch off the coffee table inside.

"As ready as I'll ever be."

Turns out, I wasn't ready at all because Lorenzo is full of surprises tonight, starting with the one I wasn't aware of, hidden inside the inner pocket of his dinner jacket.

By the time we arrive at the fundraiser dinner, most of the guests have arrived and the cocktail hour is officially underway. The *casino night* theme I suggested is a hit, and all money spent at the different tables will go directly toward Lorenzo's Healing Hearts charity.

He hasn't talked about his personal connection to it, but I can tell it matters a lot to him, so I wanted to help in whatever way I could, including securing a few more silent-auction donations.

Julian and Dahlia arrived thirty minutes before us, so I

I **Bellissima:** Very beautiful.

hang out with them backstage while Lorenzo is busy checking in with Willow about some issue at the blackjack tables.

Julian paces behind the black curtain blocking us from the room full of people, looking like a caged beast as he mutters incoherent phrases under his breath.

"Is he okay?" I whisper to my sister.

"Not exactly." She smiles, but it looks strained.

"Why did I ever agree to help Rafa?" Julian groans.

"Because you're a good guy," I offer.

He scrubs his face. "Maybe I should be more like Lorenzo."

I stiffen. "What's that supposed to mean?"

"He's annoyingly confident," Julian replies.

"Right."

"Did you expect me to insult him?" He shoots me a look.

"Yes," I answer honestly.

Dahlia laughs. "Likewise."

"I'll have to learn to like him eventually, especially after tonight—" Julian cuts himself off rather abruptly.

"What's happening tonight?" Dahlia looks over at him.

Julian glances away, which only feeds my sister's curiosity.

"Julian," she says while grabbing his chin. "What is it?"

His gaze flickers over me before dipping down to her. "I'll talk to you about it later."

Dahlia gasps. "Why not tell me now?"

He tilts his head in my direction, and my sister's eyes go wide.

Dread settles in my gut now that the jewelry Lorenzo bought me makes sense. He must've picked it out while choosing my ring.

My heart takes up permanent residence in my throat, and my skin threatens to break out into hives at the idea of nearly two hundred people witnessing a proposal tonight.

I don't think I could've thought up a worse proposal if I tried.

Did you expect a romantic declaration of love for a fake relationship?

It seems silly to get upset about it, especially given our original agreement, but I can't help it.

Are you upset about the type of proposal or the fact that it's a fake one?

This kind of reality check would've been useful weeks ago, because how the hell am I supposed to tell Lorenzo we need to hold off on the entire fake proposal plan? Am I supposed to say that up until now I was fine with it, but now I'm having second thoughts because I *like* him?

Can I really tell Lorenzo that *Hey, maybe we should put everything on pause because there is a slight chance I might want him to propose for real one day?*

I'd laugh if I didn't feel like throwing up at the idea.

Take a deep breath.

There is no need to panic yet. When I see him, I'll pull him aside and tell him to prolong the original plan. Maybe even extend it by two more months—that way we can continue monitoring the polling numbers and see whether they continue to improve without going the extra step.

I abandon Dahlia and Julian so I can talk to Lorenzo about it. Willow points me in his direction, and I'm relieved to find him standing by himself out on the balcony, hiding from the two hundred people milling about the ballroom inside.

"Lorenzo," I call his name, and he turns with a smile.

The doors shut behind me, cutting us off from all the noise happening in the ballroom. It only makes the blood pounding in my ears sound louder.

"Lily," he says with a smile similar to the lawn signs around town, and I instantly know I'm too late.

CHAPTER THIRTY-ONE

Lorenzo

The more I thought about it, the more I liked the idea of proposing to Lily at the fundraising dinner. We're surrounded by her family and two hundred townspeople who will help spread the word about our love.

If this were a real proposal, I'd hesitate to pop the question because of the sour look on her face. For someone who orchestrated this entire sham, she doesn't appear the least bit enthusiastic to move on to Phase Two.

A tight ball forms underneath my sternum, growing larger as she stares at me with those pursed lips. Thankfully the knot loosens as she disguises her expression with an alluring smile.

If it weren't for the strain at the corners of her eyes, I would've believed it to be genuine.

I reach for her left hand and intertwine our fingers. Her diamond tracking bracelet catches my eye, and I smile to myself.

If I were less…well, like *myself*, I'd tell her about the hidden microchip disguised as one of the diamonds, but I don't want to run the risk of her taking it off. It's not like I plan on stalking her location constantly—I do have other important things to do with my day—but the ability to check on her at all times fills me with relief.

It's her fault. She forced me to care about her, to address my intolerable loneliness and possessive instincts, so she only has herself to blame.

Whatever makes you feel better about invading someone's privacy.

I lift her hand and kiss the inside of her wrist, right above the thin gold chain. She shivers despite the August heat, and for the briefest moment I imagine her having the same reaction somewhere a little more private.

Like in my bed, with me hovering over her, touching. Teasing. Kissing her wrist. Her shoulder. The corner of her mouth that always leads to me claiming her lips.

"Lorenzo," she says with a rasp, her voice a whisper hardly heard over the wind rustling through the trees.

I snap out of my fantasy. Out of the corner of my eye, I see some of tonight's attendees pressing their faces against the doors.

From their point of view, I'm about to profess my undying love for the woman standing in front of me, staring wide-eyed at me.

"I thought we agreed to wait two whole months." Lily's words come out strained, but no one would be the wiser given her inviting smile.

"I thought it would be best to surprise you instead. Make it look as real as possible and whatnot." I release her hand so I can reach inside my dinner jacket for the velvet box.

Before I have a chance to pull out the ring box, Lily slaps her hands against my chest, stopping my big reveal.

"But we still have two more weeks."

Is that panic I hear?

No. That can't be right.

I keep my smile in place because of the curious witnesses pressing their faces against the glass doors. "What difference would two weeks make? We've got a good momentum going now, so the sooner the better."

"I think we should hold off."

"Why?"

Her eyes go wide. Did she not expect me to ask her that question?

I lift her trembling hand to my mouth and drop a kiss above her knuckles. "Everything will be okay. It's normal to be nervous."

"No. I think this is a mistake," she whispers, but it feels as if the words were shouted in my face.

"What?"

"We should stick to being boyfriend and girlfriend. At least for a few more weeks while we wait to see the impact your debate performance has on the numbers. Plus with the article and the ads we're working on—"

"It'll be okay," I say. "I've got you." We can deal with whatever worries she has about the next phase together.

I slowly sink down to one knee. I'm not sure she is breathing as I pull out the velvet box and pop open the lid. The pink emerald-cut diamond ring is as close to perfect as one can find, and the two smaller diamonds on either side of the main gemstone highlight its beauty.

Julian was completely beside himself while I was designing it, so I know it's perfect, although the tear sliding down Lily's cheek makes me pause. Her face is flawless despite the endless waterworks, and I thank whoever did her makeup for the foresight.

"Liliana Guadalupe Muñoz," I say, suddenly nervous as I look up into her brown, misty eyes.

This isn't real, I remind myself.

But with her staring down at me, her hand shaking in mine—or is it mine shaking as I hold hers?—I allow myself a second to take her in.

I've snuck glances at her throughout the cocktail hour, because how could I not be caught staring at the most beautiful woman in the room, who is wearing a stunning blue ballgown that I bought her?

The color suits her. As does the confidence she exudes, different from how she was before but somehow even better.

From the jewelry I bought her to the dress she chose with me in mind, she looks like *mine*.

And her engagement ring will remind everyone of that.

Her breath stutters, and I chastise myself for leaving her hanging.

"I never expected us to be here tonight," I say, my voice

light and teasing. "When we began this…*relationship*, I was skeptical, but for the first time since I started this campaign, I can't help feeling a little hopeful."

I drop her hand so I can grab the ring from the box. "I know this isn't the proposal you dreamed of, but I hope the ring makes up for it."

Her watery eyes follow my hand as I slide the ring past her first knuckle. "You're supposed to ask if I'll marry you."

I shoot her a lopsided grin. "I don't like asking questions I already know the answer to."

Her polite smile hardly compares to the radiant ones I've grown used to, and I feel robbed as I finish pushing the ring up her finger.

A roar of applause breaks through the quiet, reminding me there is one last part to the show.

With unsteady legs, I stand to my full height and pull Lily into a kiss. Compared to our other ones, this time it's different. I can feel her hesitating, almost as if she is holding back, which isn't something I'm used to.

My suspicions are proven correct when she pulls away before I have a chance to deepen the kiss. She turns to face the crowd, who only saw her back throughout the proposal, and hits them with a stunning smile that never reaches her eyes.

Did you expect her to be happy about any of this?

No, of course not, but I didn't think her reaction would affect me to this level.

I want to pull her aside and ask her what's wrong, but Willow opens the doors. Another round of applause ensues, reminding us that the show must go on.

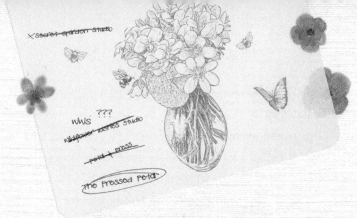

Secret Garden Studio

WWS ???

Wildflower Lashes Studio

Petal + Press

The Pressed Petal

CHAPTER THIRTY-TWO

Lily

I'm running on autopilot as Lorenzo and I walk through the crowd forming around us, my cheeks hurting from how hard I am smiling. I'm overwhelmed by how enthusiastic everyone is, and after the tenth iteration of "Congratulations," I'm ready to go home.

Lorenzo's arm remains a steel band around my waist, and while I enjoy his possessive hold, I'm also uncomfortably aware it wouldn't be there if not for the two hundred people surrounding us.

I've seen my mom have plenty of panic attacks over the course of my life, and I've had my fair share of anxious moments, but none of it compares to the way I feel right now.

I can't force enough air into my lungs. I try to breathe—try to calm the rapid beat of my heart by counting each inhale. When someone makes a joke, I laugh, but it comes out hollow.

The sound seems to gain Lorenzo's attention, and he excuses us before carting me away toward the private room where Julian and Dahlia were waiting earlier.

Oh God. The reminder of my family hits me like a gut punch, and I reach for my stomach.

"Are you going to be sick?" Lorenzo asks, panic bleeding into his question.

"Maybe." If not physically, then for sure mentally, because what did I agree to?

How did I end up being fake engaged to a guy I'm interested in, and how are we ever supposed to have a real chance at a relationship if half of it has been built on lies?

One second I'm bent over, and the next Lorenzo is lifting me into his arms and carrying me to the couch. I expect him to deposit me on it, but he takes a seat and cradles me in his arms. My thighs drape across his lap, and my dress poofs around us.

Being taken care of…being held in his arms like I matter…

I feel like I'm being torn in two directions, my heart splitting down the center as Lorenzo cradles me to his chest. Part of me cherishes this kind of connection after spending so long wishing for it while the other is terrified by it.

Terrified of *him* and how he is making me feel again.

"Are we going to talk about what happened out there?" he asks, tilting my body back so I have no choice but to look up at him.

"Is there a point? The damage is done." I hold up my left hand to show off the most beautiful diamond engagement ring ever to exist. It's difficult to look at it, knowing this ring is absolutely perfect and nothing will ever compare.

His brows furrow. "I thought this is what you wanted."

"It was."

"What changed?"

My heart is stuck in my throat, the beats growing with intensity as I consider whether to open up to him about my feelings.

If you don't, you'll keep going around in circles for the next three and a half months.

But if I do, there is a chance Lorenzo will shut down again, although this time it'll be worse because he can't run away. I'll be stuck with him, pretending to be a happy couple while dying inside.

I'm not sure what scenario I hate more, but I guess I'm about to find out.

"I wanted more for us," I say, choosing the path that could end with more heartache.

He tenses underneath me, the reaction tempting me to shut my mouth and never open it again, but no, I need to see this through until the very end.

"Lily," he drawls, a warning if I've ever heard one.

My shoulders feel heavy, the weight of my poor choices stacking on top of them like invisible bricks. "When we started this process, I thought there was no way in hell I'd give you another chance, and we both know you wouldn't want one either, so I didn't think there was much of a risk while faking it for the public. But the more time we spent together, the more I started looking forward to it."

I can't handle his blank stare, so I look away. "I wanted to hate you. I really did. But you're so damn…"

"Charming?" He cracks a smile.

"*Annoying* and persistent and so damn hard to dislike, especially when you open up to me because you don't trust *anyone*."

The timing between his breaths becomes smaller, and I press my hand against his heart to find it rapidly beating beneath my palm.

"Tell me I'm not alone in this," I demand, my voice strained. "Tell me you want me, that you feel this same, undeniable pull toward me, even if you're determined to not act on it."

He stares at me with that dark, brooding gaze of his. "I can't."

"Can't or won't?"

"Does it matter? Because either way, you're right. I won't act on it."

"Why not?" I want to shake him around. "Give me a good reason."

"Because I'll never be able to give you what you want. I *can't*. I'm incapable of loving someone else, and if anyone deserves the happy ending they want, it's you."

It feels like he's carving me open with every heartbreaking sentence that pours out of his mouth.

"How would you know if you haven't even tried?"

"Because people like me—people like my father—we don't love. We don't know *how* to. Instead we *obsess*, to the point of making ourselves sick over someone else." He teases the chain of my bracelet, and goose bumps spread up my arm from a simple brush of his thumb across my pulse point.

"Love *is* obsession. They go hand in hand."

"No." He shakes his head. "Love is good. It's *pure*. What goes on in my head…it's the complete opposite."

"Like?"

He laughs. "I'm not going to tell you."

"What do you have to lose? If your thoughts are so bad…if they're truly as awful as you say they are, shouldn't it scare me away for good?"

The corded muscles in his neck strain, and his fingers dig into the fabric of the couch.

"I think you don't want to tell me because what if I end up liking it?" I drag my hand up his lapel, noting how his breathing changes from my touch alone.

"What if I want to be obsessed over?" I lean forward and press my mouth to his ear. "What if I want to be *possessed*?"

I swear to God, Lorenzo *trembles*. The seams of the couch split from how hard his fingers are digging into the material.

I kiss the shell of his ear. "Because if you refuse to give me that, then I'll find someone who will."

His hand snaps up and wraps around the back of my neck, his firm hold sending a pulsing sensation through my lower half. "Stop."

"Why? I'm talking out scenarios with you since you're so invested in me getting my happily-ever-after and all."

Within a blink of an eye, Lorenzo flips us until my back is pressed against the couch and he's hovering over me. He keeps most of his weight off me, which is thoughtful, but I want more.

"You don't talk about other men while wearing my ring."

"Let me solve that problem, then." I reach to remove it, but he grabs both my hands and pins them above my head.

"Take that ring off and I'll superglue it to your finger."

"Sounds a bit drastic for a three-month engagement, don't you think?"

The strained sound that comes out of his mouth sends a wave of arousal through me that is so strong, I end up squirming underneath him. My eyes go round, and he hisses through gritted teeth when I accidentally rub up against his erection.

Because I can't resist, I repeat the move, this time making Lorenzo groan. "Who knew the topic of me getting with another man would make you so hot and bothered?"

Something visibly snaps behind his eyes, and the beast I was taunting?

He finally decides to reveal himself, and I instantly go from being the predator to becoming the prey.

CHAPTER THIRTY-THREE

Lorenzo

If I kiss Lily right now, in private without an audience, it will change everything.

I don't want to ruin the connection we've built over the last six weeks, but I also know I can't resist.

Not after she told me she wants to be *possessed*.

One kiss won't ruin an arrangement, right? We are two mature adults who have kissed plenty of times over the last six weeks, so what's one more?

My mind goes blank as I lean forward and brush my lips across her collarbone. She inhales sharply, and I smile against her skin as I leave a path of kisses across her chest. My mouth traces the delicate curve of her neck before it lingers at the corner of her mouth.

"Don't forget. You wanted this," I mutter against her skin.

She nods, her eyes glazed over like she's under my spell, only for them to slam shut when I seal my mouth over hers.

At first I'm reserved, teasing her with soft pecks that leave her squirming underneath me. Testing, teasing, *yearning*.

Only for the private moment to be shattered by Willow knocking on the door to let us know that Dahlia took Rosa home because she wasn't feeling well. Lily shoves me away, jumps off the couch, and calls her sister to figure out what happened.

Apparently Rosa's blood pressure was through the roof, most likely because of me not telling her about the proposal beforehand. A fact Julian is all too eager to gloat about once Lily and I find him backstage.

"How could you not ask for her permission?" Lily's eyes grow impossibly large.

"I didn't know I was expected to."

She bangs her head against my chest with a groan. "Lorenzo! No wonder she had high blood pressure."

"Looking back, I could've gone about the entire night differently."

"You think? I could kill you right now!" she whisper-shouts.

"Do you need a murder weapon? I've got a few tools in my truck that can do the job," Julian offers, speaking for the first time since we joined him backstage.

I flip him off without breaking eye contact with Lily. "I didn't realize her condition was so fragile."

No wonder she wants to protect her mom from the Ludlows and the NDA they talked her into signing. If my mom struggled with stress that bad, I'd do everything possible to stop an episode too.

Lily frowns. "She's not fragile, but I think anyone would have heart palpitations if their daughter got engaged out of the blue to a man they hardly know."

I rub the back of my neck, suddenly self-conscious. "Now I feel like an ass."

"You should," Julian replies, still looking a bit green.

"Don't you have a trash can to go heave into?"

"No, but do you want to lend me your favorite Ferragamos by chance?"

I'm about to reply when Willow gives us the signal.

I squeeze Lily's hip. "Ready?"

With a nod, she slips her hand into mine, and together we walk toward the parting curtains. Everyone is seated at their assigned tables, obscured in darkness as Lily and I take the center of the stage.

A spotlight follows us to the microphone stand, and I reach for it with my free hand. I'm not the type to get nervous while public speaking, but there is a slight flash of panic at the idea of divulging my past.

I've never been the face of the Healing Hearts charity before. Like most of my work outside of running for mayor, I prefer to keep my personal affairs private, and the small team at Healing Hearts knows that. They're committed to finding families who need support, so long as I keep supplying the funds.

Money can't bring loved ones back, but it helps with legal fees, medical needs, and mental health services that can add up over time, which is why I'm here tonight.

I hit the crowd with a dazzling smile. "Thank you, everyone, for coming out tonight to support Healing Hearts. Lily and I are happy to have you here."

She dips her head toward the crowd and places a hand over her heart.

I physically force myself to look back at the ballroom full of people when I'd rather stare at her.

"When I started this charity two years ago, I had recently found out that I lost two family members due to a drunk driver." My hand tightens around the microphone, and I banish the memory before it tanks my mood.

You're doing this for them.

Lily peers up at me, but I keep facing the crowd. If I acknowledge the sympathy in her gaze, I'll end up struggling to get through this speech, and it's hard enough talking about my parents' deaths as it is.

"Losing a loved one is one of the hardest experiences we can go through. Grief is a journey, and a never-ending one at that, and at Healing Hearts, we try to help families through the process by connecting them with services in their area and providing whatever funding they need. I'm aware that a lot of people don't have access to the same resources as I did, so I've made it my mission to give back to those who are looking to heal."

Lily places her hand right on top of my tux, right over my heart, which feels like it dropped to my stomach as soon as I started speaking.

"The silent auction will begin in an hour. So please enjoy the food, grab yourself a drink, and feel free to use the private car service we hired for the evening."

A waiter rushes over to us with a tray, and I pass Lily a champagne glass before grabbing my own. We both hold ours up in the air.

"And with that, I'm going to enjoy a dance with my fiancée."

Manny claps me on the shoulder, and I turn to find him scowling. I expected him to be in a better mood since Jane agreed to be his date, but something has clearly upset him, and I'm going to guess it has something to do with my surprise earlier.

The blank way he stares at me is unsettling because Manny wears his heart on his fruit-patterned sleeve.

He breaks eye contact first. "I'm starting to question if we're best friends."

"If me wearing your strawberry shirt wasn't proof enough, then I'm screwed."

He pushes me toward the bar. "That's the only reason I'm forgiving you."

"I don't think you could hold a grudge even if you wanted to."

"Oh, I'm pissed." He waves a bartender over, and we both order our drinks.

"I wanted to tell you," I say. "But I couldn't ruin the surprise, and no offense, but you can't keep a secret to save your life."

"Hm" is his only reply.

"How do I make it up to you?"

"Ask me to be your best man."

I laugh, thinking he's joking, only to stop when he doesn't join in.

"You're not joking?"

"My heart took a serious beating right now."

"Rest assured, if I have a best man, you'll be my guy."

"If?" He gawks. "What do you mean *if*?"

I walk back my answer to not raise suspicion. "We could decide to elope."

He laughs hard enough to gain some attention from those around us.

"What's so funny?"

"You're marrying into the Lake Wisteria royal family. You have no choice but to have a big wedding with all the bells and whistles."

"Sounds like my dream," I reply with a heavy dose of sarcasm.

"Don't worry—I'll be there every step of the way to help you out. It's my duty as your best man."

"I haven't even asked you yet."

"Yet? See, I knew I was your only option."

"Keep annoying me and I'll ask Julian to spite you."

He rears back. "You wouldn't dare."

"What if I told you his speech tonight is a test run?"

"So let's say—hypothetically speaking, of course—that Julian was to go missing. Would you mind if I step in to offer my endorsement?"

"Your friendship is the best endorsement of all."

He wipes at the corner of his dry eye. "That might be

the nicest thing you've ever said to me—at least up until you officially ask me to be your best man."

X secret garden studio

wws ???
wildflower washes studio

petal + press

the pressed petal

CHAPTER THIRTY-FOUR

Lily

Lorenzo and I spend the night working the room. We rub elbows with influential townspeople, play a few rounds of roulette with members of city council members, and sit through Julian's endorsement speech. For his own benefit, I'm glad he made it through the two-minute ordeal without throwing up, although he did break a sweat once he started talking about welcoming Lorenzo into his family.

I'm not sure if Julian's endorsement tonight will have much of an effect, but I hope if it does it's in a positive direction.

Once Julian says his goodbyes, Lorenzo and I split up so we can target different people like we had planned, which means I don't get him all to myself until two hours later once the final guests leave the ballroom.

"Have a drink with me?"

I should say no, but the way he stares at my mouth for a beat too long has me nodding along like I don't already have a steady buzz going.

He steps behind the empty bar. "What can I get you?"

"Another paloma sounds good."

He pops open a beer for himself before getting to work on my drink. His confidence shines through, and I could've mistaken him for a bartender if I didn't know he was the host of tonight's party.

"Do you have experience bartending?" I ask.

"Not officially," he vaguely answers.

"Could've fooled me." I watch him line the rim with salt before he walks around the bar and passes me the glass.

"Tips are encouraged." He taps his beer against my glass.

I stand on the tips of my toes and press my mouth to his. It's chaste compared to our earlier kisses, but it still makes my lips tingle, and my fingers itch to touch him.

"How's that?" Why do I sound breathy from an innocent kiss?

He wets his bottom lip, dragging my attention right toward it. "Better than anything money could buy."

"Says the millionaire who already has everything he needs."

"Not *everything*," he rasps.

I pop the straw into my mouth and sip, glancing up at him through my lashes like the tipsy little flirt I am.

"Want to go outside?" he asks, his voice gravelly.

I nod, and he leads me toward the same balcony where he proposed a few hours earlier. My heart beats faster at the reminder, only to grow stronger when I think about how we nearly hooked up afterward.

He stares out at the lake. The crescent moon reflects off the dark surface, and the small white caps look like little stars sparkling above.

"Thank you," he says quietly.

My head whips in his direction, finding him already staring at me. "What for?"

"Everything. I know you have your own reasons for helping me, but regardless, I appreciate it." He takes a long pull from his bottle without taking his eyes off me.

My body warms at his expression of gratitude, and while it isn't a long-winded one, it doesn't make it any less heartfelt.

"Putting my dislike toward the Ludlows aside, I do believe you're the better candidate. Hands down. No questions asked."

His brows jump. "Why?"

"You've been making a positive impact on this town for two years, in more ways than anyone knows. You care about Lake Wisteria—"

"Only because my mother loved it."

Lies, but not worth fighting him on right now. "That only supports my third point: You're incredibly loyal to those you find worthy of it." My voice catches at the end. I didn't expect that particular confession to make me emotional, but it seems to expose my own vulnerability.

I want someone to be loyal to me. Not because we're family or since we've spent our entire lives around each other, because I already have that. I want someone who supports me because we're a team by choice, not by circumstance.

I continue, hoping to keep my voice neutral this time. "It's only a matter of time before we get everyone to see the real you."

"I'd rather not."

"I know that, but you'll do it if it means winning the campaign."

He taps his drink to mine. "Cheers to that."

"And cheers to us." I lift my paloma higher, and the diamond on my ring catches a beam of light.

He reaches for my left hand and tilts it this way and that, as if he didn't design the piece. "Do you like it?"

"More than I want to."

"What's that supposed to mean?" He sounds more curious than annoyed.

"Whatever engagement ring I receive next will never match up to this one."

Instead of dropping my hand, he strengthens his grip. "Why do you keep talking about what comes next?"

"Because I'm not—"

"If you make a comment about your age, I swear to God—"

"You'll what?" I wrap my lips around the straw and suck.

He curses in Italian.

One point for me.

"And no." I drag out the last word. "I was about to say that I'm not going to sit around idly, looking like some jilted lover while living in the same town as my ex-fiancé."

A dark look passes over his face. "So what's your plan?"

I shrug, hoping to appear nonchalant despite the rising beat of my heart. "I hope to meet a man who makes me forget about everyone who came before him."

"And where will you find this…man?" he asks with a sneer, clearly struggling with the last word.

Has he not considered what comes next should we follow through with the original plan, or is he that blinded by his anxiety and desire to become mayor that he can't see what is so clearly right in front of him?

"Maybe I'll meet someone while traveling," I reply, and his gaze flickers with awareness. "Or maybe I can join a running club—"

"You already tried that," he spits out.

"Right. Then maybe another cooking class? That was romantic, and there were a few single people there," I suggest just to set him off. "Or I could expand my search to other towns. Lake Aurora has a ton of new residents, so maybe someone there ends up being a good match."

His eyes screw shut. "Can't you…stop talking about other people? We still have a few months, so let's…"

"Table it?" I offer when he struggles to come up with the rest of his sentence.

"Yes. For now." He forces a breath through his flared nostrils.

I exhale, allowing his request to sink in. He is clearly bothered by the idea of me with someone else, yet he still won't admit why that is.

And he never will unless you push him a little harder.

I have a clear vision of what I want, and I'm taking a gamble on if I've read Lorenzo correctly.

If not, my entire plan will blow up in my face and then the rest of our fake engagement will be riddled with a lot of awkward moments and sexual tension.

Only time will tell.

"No," I say, the word sounding far stronger than I feel.

His eyes snap open. "What do you mean *no*?"

I pull my left hand free from his. "I'm not going to stop talking about the future I want, so if you have a problem with it, then you need to do some soul-searching as to why that's the case."

I fist the material of my dress so I don't trip, and spin around, walking away. My heels clicking against the floor punctuate my dramatic departure, matching the erratic beat of my heart.

You're making the right call, I tell myself when Lorenzo doesn't rush to stop me.

I wasn't expecting him to run after me, but it still stings to know he didn't care enough to try. He let me have the last word, and for once, I wish that wasn't what happened.

After grabbing my clutch, I escape the ballroom and head toward the estate's valet area, where the car service is still set up, ready to take Lorenzo home.

A driver opens the door, and I climb into the back seat of the car, my chest twisting as I reach for my seat belt.

"Where to, miss?" the driver asks after taking his spot behind the wheel.

I give him my address, and with a nod, he takes off.

If this was one of my telenovelas, Lorenzo would've chased after our taillights in his thousand-dollar shoes, shouting my name until I noticed and asked the driver to park the car.

But unlike my fantasy, the rearview mirror remains empty as we drive away from the estate and the man who holds my future in his hands.

CHAPTER THIRTY-FIVE

Lorenzo

As I watch the car Lily jumped into driving past the front gates of the estate, I become increasingly more panicked. Her earlier words linger in the air, and I feel like I'm suffocating from how strained my lungs feel.

I hope to meet a man who makes me forget about everyone who came before him.

It's an insulting comment that disrupts my entire mindset. It seems like an unfair advantage for her to have, especially when I've spent the better part of my life mastering the art of control.

Maybe I'll meet someone while traveling, she mentioned, tempting me to pull some strings to get her on a no-fly list. That and having her blacklisted from Maria's cooking classes and the local running clubs. If possible, I'll also find a way to have her banned from crossing county lines, that way she never finds herself meeting anyone in Lake Aurora.

Becoming twisted up inside over her discussing a hypothetical situation is a whole new level of disturbed, and my thoughts are reeling as I consider her parting statement.

I'm not going to stop talking about the future I want, so if you have a problem with it, then you need to do some soul-searching as to why that's the case.

I slip my hand into my pocket and stroke my father's die. Lily still has the other matching one, which further emphasizes how much I care about her.

Which is why I *do* have a problem with her discussing a future where I cease to exist.

It becomes clear where my heart is at—or rather *who* has it.

But accepting the truth? That's a whole other issue.

I spend the short drive from the estate to my house on my phone, watching Lily's tracking dot as it travels across town before stopping at her house. My relief is temporary, gone as soon as I walk inside my house and am reminded of Lily all over again.

A basket of the most colorful embroidered socks sits by the door, ready for whenever she visits. The framed photo of us at the cooking class is featured front and center on the entryway table in front of the latest bouquet of flowers.

But there is no greater reminder of my growing affection toward Lily than Daisy, who comes running down the hall to greet me. A smile pulls at my lips, widening as she loses her footing on the marble floor and crashes into me, nearly taking me down with her.

If Lily was here, she'd be laughing at me taking a seat on the floor so Daisy can sit on my lap. I've made fun of Lily for doing so, and here I am, giving in to Daisy's wishes like I do with her mother.

I don't know what possesses me to snap a selfie of Daisy and myself, let alone send it to Lily, but I'm disappointed when she doesn't respond. Based on the time stamp, she saw it a minute ago, but my message remains unanswered.

Serves you right after doing the same.

Now Lily is the one with all the power, because piece by piece, I handed it over. There was no other option for me, and maybe I was a fool for thinking there was one.

So, instead of holding back and keeping my cards close to my chest, I send a second message—a first from me.

ME

> The only thing that would've made this picture better is having you in it.

Despite being exhausted from tonight's event, I can't seem to fall asleep. I've tossed and turned for an hour to the sound of Daisy softly snoring in her dog bed, and I'm nowhere near being closer to knocking out.

It probably doesn't help that I've checked my phone for any new messages from Lily more times than I care to admit. She most likely fell asleep already, so I scroll through our text thread because it's the only option I have.

Some texts bring a smile to my face, while others make me roll my eyes at prior messages I've sent. I tried so hard to create distance, whether it be not answering her right away or leaving her on read, only for me to be annoyed at receiving the same silent treatment.

Is it fair for me to feel snubbed at Lily leaving me on read after all the times I've done the same? No, but am I still justified about my feelings regardless? Hell yeah.

But mostly I feel bad that she went to bed upset with me.

I blame insomnia-induced boredom for my bad decision to redownload the Eros app and reread the messages Lily sent me.

There is one in particular that makes me pause my scrolling, and I end up rereading it twice.

ANA

> I didn't want to pretend anymore. Just like I don't want to pretend now. I don't care if you're Lorenzo or Laurence. I like you despite all the reasons I shouldn't, and it makes me hate myself.

I could've written the message right now, as it applies to our current situation so well.

Clearly pretending is catching up to me, if my inability to sleep while knowing Lily is upset with me is anything to go by. And yes, against all odds, I like her too, which is why I can't begin to fathom the idea of her moving on to someone else and building a life with them.

Not when I so clearly picture her in mine.

To further prove my point, I turn on the TV and drown out the sound of Daisy's heavy breathing. After flipping through the channels for a good five minutes, I settle on an old episode of *The Silver Vixens*.

I tell myself that it is the best show I could find, and I'm too tired to care if it reminds me of Lily.

I only have to find one man who doesn't mind, Lily said after I teased her about falling asleep with the TV on.

With a frustrated groan, I chuck the remote and find a comfortable position. I don't expect to be able to fall asleep, but eventually my eyes start to droop, and I end up drifting off to the sound of a nineties laugh track while wishing I was listening to Lily's instead.

The next morning, I struggle to get out of bed. If it weren't for Lily, I would've ignored my alarm, but I want to get to her house before she leaves for Mass with her mom.

Lily reads my text and opens the front door with a yawn, stunning me into silence as I take in her outfit. I was hoping last night's colorful gown wasn't a one-time exception, and thankfully it seems like my confident Lily is here to stay, and I couldn't be happier.

Despite not being a morning person, she took the time to pull off an intricate-looking braided hairstyle, making herself look like a princess with her cheerful sundress and high heels with butterflies on the straps. Her shoes are beyond impractical for the amount of walking we'll have to do, but they'll force her to rely on me for stability as we walk across the grassy parking lot, so I won't be complaining.

On the contrary, I'll buy a pair in every color to encourage such behavior.

She glares. "What are you doing here?"

"I thought I could start making amends with your mom by joining you both at Mass."

"She's not coming today."

"Why not?"

"She'd rather rest. If she feels better, she'll still go to lunch."

Shit. "But you're still going?"

She nods.

"Then let's go before we're late."

She looks like she wants to argue, but she clamps her lips shut and locks up the door instead.

When she teeters on the stairs, I'm quick to wrap my arms around her so she doesn't fall over. "Those heels will be the death of me."

"Good idea. I'll be dreaming of stabbing you with them all morning." She pulls back with a smile.

"Now I don't feel bad for thinking about them wrapped around my waist later."

Maybe I do like when Lily stops talking, but only when I'm the one making her speechless.

I open the door and help her into the passenger seat. Before she can reach for her seat belt, I grab it.

She huffs to herself. "I can do that."

"No one said you couldn't, but I like taking care of you."

She averts her gaze. "Don't."

"Don't what?"

"Make me think this is real." Her voice drops, and I feel guilty for being responsible for that doubt.

"What if I want it to be?" I ask, surprised by my own outburst. "Or what if it has been real between us for a while but I was too stubborn to accept it?"

"That's a lot of what-ifs."

"I only care about one." I snap her seat belt in place before kissing her temple.

"What if we gave this a try?"

CHAPTER THIRTY-SIX

Lorenzo

The universe is playing a cosmic joke on me because as soon as we make it to my car after Mass, Richard Ludlow is exiting his only a few spaces away.

I'm not sure why he is attending church when he's going to end up in hell, but I suppose the same can be said for me. Appearances are everything in this town, so we both play our parts, although I do wish his exterior matched his ugly personality.

He doesn't have to pass by my car on his way to the church, but he chooses to do so anyway so he can stop and say, "I hear congratulations are in order."

Lily and I stare at him.

He quickly dismisses me and focuses on Lily. "I'm surprised how quickly your relationship has progressed since you were sleeping with me not too long ago." He pauses, his gaze flickering over to my face.

Lily's eyes widen and her mouth opens, but I rope an arm around her and speak before she can.

"Were you expecting me to have some sort of reaction?" I ask, amused by the vein pulsing in Richard's cheek.

His brows pull together, forming a confused crease between them. "You know?"

"Did I ruin your surprise just now? Do you want a redo so you can have your big moment?"

He gapes like a dying fish. "You really don't care?"

"It's *my* ring on her finger, so why should I?"

"Fuck, man. I wouldn't be caught dead with a woman who fucked someone else to get back at me. I don't care how great she is in bed."

Lily sucks in a sharp breath, and I see red. She teeters on her heels from how quickly I release her and storm over to Richard.

He shrinks into himself as I get closer, only to flinch when I yank on his lapels and force him to stand as tall as his five-foot-nine frame allows.

My hand curls into a tight fist by my side, but I resist the call for bloodlust, choosing to fight with my words.

"Listen here, Dick," I whisper, so low Lily can't hear me. "Talk about Lily like that again— Scratch that. If you so much as look or speak to her—even to say *please* or *thank you*—I'll reach out to those *connections* your family loves to gossip about."

"W-what?" The word is broken up by his stammer.

I grin. "You know how the saying goes: Every lie has a little bit of truth to it."

"Are you…threatening to send the *mafia* after me?"

I pick a piece of invisible lint off his shoulder. "Don't be ridiculous."

He exhales slowly, right before I rip his false sense of security away.

"I'm *promising* to, should you so much as take a breath within a hundred feet of my future wife again."

All the color drains from his face.

I exert an admirable amount of self-control as I step away from him and head back to Lily, who is staring at us with brows that reach toward her hairline.

Richard storms off toward the church. Once he is no longer in our direct line of sight, Lily slumps against the passenger door.

"If he bothers you again, tell me."

She tilts her head back farther, her brown eyes looking more golden underneath the morning sun. "You can't protect me from him forever."

"Watch me."

CHAPTER THIRTY-SEVEN

Lorenzo

Good thing I have endless time to earn Mrs. Muñoz's forgiveness because she might be polite and accept the panna cotta I made early this morning as an apology for last night, but she has officially thrown her walls back up.

If I thought she was jumpy when I first met her, she's a whole new level of skittish, with her quickly escaping any room I walk into.

Not wanting to cause her any more stress, I ask her to have a word in private.

Mrs. Muñoz surprises me by going outside, and I follow her down an overgrown path that leads straight to Lily's favorite place. She hasn't told me why she adores the fountain so much, nor has she shared why her secret garden has been neglected, but I'll be sure to ask her about it now that the fountain is operational again.

Rosa takes a seat on the weathered bench. I keep a small but respectful amount of space between us, but we might as well be seated a mile apart from one another.

I decide to lead the conversation so she doesn't feel any pressure to. "So, about last night..."

She tenses beside me, her lips pressed together tightly.

With a deep breath, I continue, "I want to start off by saying I'm sorry. First for putting you in any position that would affect your health, and second for not taking you or your feelings into consideration like I should've."

She stares at the fountain instead of my face, not giving me much to go off besides my intuition.

"Asking Lily to marry me without talking to you about it first was a huge mistake, and I hope you can find it in your heart to forgive me. Honestly, I didn't think much about it, but I wish I had because you're one of the most important people in Lily's life..."

It's impossible to carry on with my apology once I notice the tears falling down Rosa's face.

"Rosa?" Panic bleeds into my voice because not once did I consider what to do should Rosa start *crying*.

I'm not sure if it's a good idea to hug her or if she'd prefer for me to leave, but then I think about her heart issue and if she should even be alone when she's distressed—

Rosa's hand reaches for mine, and she gives it a pat. "Thank you for fixing the fountain."

My eyes widen. "What?"

Did she hear a single word I said?

She wipes underneath her eyes. "When Julian told me it

was repaired, I thanked him, but he said I should reach out to you since you're the one who paid for it." Her gaze falls to her lap. "I wanted to thank you in person, and I planned on it yesterday…"

"But then I screwed up."

Her nose scrunches in the same way Lily's does. "I was definitely *surprised*, but what happened after wasn't your fault. My doctor warned me about what could happen if I got too excited—"

I cock a brow. "Excited?"

Her laugh is soft like her daughter's yet so completely different at the same time. "A little nervous too, but that's to be expected."

Her gaze returns to the fountain. "If my husband were there, he would've had something funny to say. He always had that way of making everything better and easing my worries." Her voice catches toward the end.

"I'm sorry for your loss," I say because I don't know what else sounds good in this situation, although I regret it as soon as the words leave my mouth.

"You know, people always say that, including myself, but I didn't truly understand what it meant until I had to go through it personally." I feel my throat getting scratchy as she continues, "Every time I'm reminded of my husband, it feels like I've lost him all over again."

She motions toward the garden. "This place…it was his. I should feel happy here, like Lily does, but it reminds me too much of him."

I felt the same way about Lake Wisteria at first. I couldn't look past my own grief because everywhere I turned, I was reminded of who and what I lost.

"But Lily..." She smiles to herself. "It's her special place."

"What happened to it?" It's a far cry from the mythical-sounding secret garden she described to me late one evening, and there is no way her mother hasn't noticed.

Rosa looks over at me with raised brows. "She didn't tell you?"

Shit. "Uh..." *Uh?!* I'm not the type to hesitate or flounder, and she is staring like I should definitely know the answer to that question.

Rosa's head tilts, and I know I've gone and screwed up.

But like an angel coming to save me, Lily magically appears from around the corner. I could kiss her for her impeccable timing, but I'm already pushing my luck around Rosa, so I hold off.

Lily's smile falls when she glances at the fountain, and both Rosa and I share a look. Neither of us says anything, but I can read Mrs. Muñoz's thoughts like they're my own.

What's going on in that pretty little head of yours, amore mio?

Lily clears her throat. "I was wondering where you two went off to."

Rosa's gaze swings between us. "Lorenzo and I were finishing up." She stands and walks over to her daughter to give her a hug. "I'll give you two some privacy."

We both watch her disappear around the corner, and from my angle, it looks like the overgrown hedge swallowed her whole.

I stand and head over to Lily, who went back to checking out the fountain. "What do you think?"

"It works." Her voice is strained.

"Now we have to fix up the rest of it."

A bone in her neck cracks from how quickly she turns to look at me. "What do you mean?"

"Your garden needs some love." I rub a speck of dirt off the side of the fountain, which could use a good pressure wash.

She stays quiet.

I speak up. "Your mom told me how much you love it here."

Her shoulders slump. "I did—I mean, I do." She shakes her head. "It's...complicated."

"For the record, the vaguer your responses, the more interested I become."

I pull her into an embrace so she has no chance of escaping this conversation.

"I don't know how to talk about it," she says, exasperated.

"There is a first for everything."

She swats my chest with a laugh, and the tightness in it lessens.

"Honestly?" She looks around the garden. "I couldn't deal with it...or myself, for that matter."

"What do you mean?"

She eyes the bench. "Can we sit down for this conversation?"

"Of course."

Once she takes a seat, I wrap my arm around her. "Comfortable?"

She seems to be with how she melts into me, but her quiet "Yeah" confirms it.

"So, you were saying?"

"My dad was big on two things."

"What were they?"

"A motto that was his catchphrase: *Un Muñoz nunca se rinde. A Muñoz never quits.*"

I nod. "And the other?"

"Wishes."

I shoot her a look. "How so?"

She flushes under my gaze. "You know. Like close your eyes, make a wish, and toss the coin into the fountain."

"That explains the coins. I was wondering about them when I dropped off your keys."

"It was something special I had with him. He and Dahlia had their own thing together, but this was mine. Anyway," she says, drawing in a gulp of air. "When I was little, he gave me this small bag of gold coins. There weren't a ton, but he told me to use them wisely."

She pauses, takes another breath, and says, "Nearly a year ago, I was down to one."

I'm not entirely sure where this story is going, but the way Lily hesitates to speak makes me even more curious.

"What happened with it?"

"I wasted it on the wrong guy." She doesn't break my stare, and I instantly know I fucked up in more ways than I imagined.

She used her wish on *me*, and I took that dream—that hope—and I destroyed it with my selfishness.

The thought... My stomach is in knots, winding tighter with every pained breath.

"Lily…"

She holds her hand up. "Wait. Let me get this out."

We sit there for a few minutes, the soothing sound of water cascading filling the quiet until she speaks again.

"After I ran out, I just…I didn't see a point. I didn't have any coins left, and visiting this place made me…so unbearably sad, to the point where I stopped making the effort. Running out of coins felt like I lost him all over again, and I couldn't deal. So, I let his special place rot, along with that final wish."

I'm the one struggling to keep eye contact now because how am I supposed to accept that I'm the reason for the pain in her eyes?

"I'm so sorry." My voice rasps. "I'm so fucking sorry. For everything."

She stabs another hole through my heart with her next sentence. "You say that, and I do believe you're sorry, but it doesn't take back the hurt you caused."

She stands up, and my arm falls to my side.

"We can't go back and change what happened. What's done is done, and I'd rather focus on my future."

My future. Not *ours.*

An important distinction meant to separate us, but I see it as a motivating one. Because that future she wants?

It doesn't seem so far-fetched anymore.

Her smile is sweet, and far warmer than I deserve, further adding to the acid burning in my chest.

She turns and walks away, leaving me alone. Instead of following her, I stand and walk up to the fountain, where I find twenty-plus gold coins sitting at the bottom of the basin, representing all of Lily's hopes and dreams.

I want her to tell me about every single wish, and I want to make sure she never has another reason to stop.

And I think I have an idea of where to start.

CHAPTER THIRTY-EIGHT

Lorenzo

I came into today's family gathering knowing that it would be tense, but I had hoped that after last weekend's Chicago trip it wouldn't be as bad as Lily's worst-case scenarios. She asked me to be on my best behavior, and I've been nothing but an upstanding gentleman this afternoon.

I remain levelheaded, even with Julian baiting me about my latest poll numbers and Rafa, who recently returned from Europe, glaring at me from across the table like I threatened to call animal control on him.

Meanwhile, Lily is a bundle of nerves and has spent most of lunch pushing food around her plate without eating any of it. It irritates me beyond measure to see her so uncomfortable among her family, and I want to fix it.

If I want Lily, then I have to accept that her family is part of the package. It's a foreign concept for someone like me, and perhaps if I share what my life was like before, they will give me more grace. Or at the very least, they might understand where I'm coming from.

You can't be thinking of opening up to strangers. What if they use your past against you? The insidious voice returns, louder than before.

If they do, I trust that Lily has my back, I reply, not giving the worried thoughts any more room to breathe.

"So..." I say, gaining everyone's attention.

Lily looks about ready to stab me with her fork, so I pry the silverware away from her and link our hands together before saying, "I'm aware yesterday's news came as a surprise..."

Dahlia interjects, "Seems to be a pattern for you two."

I shoot her a sharp smile. "And for that, I want to apologize."

Lily glances over at me and mouths, *What are you doing?*

I give her hand a squeeze, as if to say *Trust me*, before facing the rest of the table. "To be honest, I didn't grow up like you all." I motion toward the gallery wall of photos behind Rosa's seat. Photographs are only a snapshot of a moment in time, but given the decades' worth of memories, one can assume most of them were good ones.

Dahlia's head tilts, and Julian leans back in his chair, giving me the full weight of his attention. Rafa, who out of everyone here had a similar upbringing to mine, looks at me with compassion I wasn't expecting.

"What do you mean?" Rosa asks, her voice soft and timid.

"My uncle who took me in after my parents died wasn't exactly...loving, and he taught me not to trust anyone. So when you grow up in an environment like I did, you learn to keep your secrets or risk having them used against you."

The room is so silent after my confession that the ice machine across the house can be heard.

Lily, whose hand is still clasped with mine, rubs her thumb softly over my skin, reminding me why I'm talking about any of this.

I don't need to have a heart-to-heart about my upbringing. I've come to terms with my uncle being a piece of shit, and I've accepted that my cousins are too enmeshed in the family business to walk away from it now.

Josefina places a hand over her heart. "That sounds…"

"Like your family sucks," Julian offers, surprising me.

My lips curl. "That's putting it lightly."

"Do you talk to them anymore?" Rosa asks.

There are times I wish I could because I miss my cousins, but I can't reach out to them without getting pulled into Vittori Holdings drama. I'm building a life for myself that my uncle can't influence, but with new beginnings means letting go.

"No." I keep my answer short because I don't want any more questions about them.

"Well, from what I've read online, your uncle seems like a real piece of work, so it looks like you dodged a bullet," Rafa says.

"Literally or figuratively?" Julian asks with a smirk.

Rosa does a sign of the cross, and Dahlia jabs her boyfriend in the ribs while whispering something under her breath.

I lock eyes with Mrs. Muñoz. "While I'm clearing the record, I'm not in the mafia."

"I didn't—" she stammers nervously. "Lily said—"

"It's okay." Josefina pats Rosa's hand. "It's not like we weren't all thinking about it," she replies with a grin, and I return it with one of my own.

The conversation moves on to lighter subjects, and the tension slowly bleeds from Lily's body until she is laughing along with Rafa's story about getting pickpocketed while in Europe.

I'm pretty quiet, choosing to sit back and take it all in instead of inserting myself into every conversation. I've heard a lot about the Muñoz-Lopez families from Lily and people around town, but I've never had a chance to witness it up close.

And dare I say, I might be a bit...*jealous*?

No, that's not the right word for the emotions clawing through my chest. I'm happy for Lily and the life she grew up experiencing because it made her who she is, but at the same time, being surrounded by so much love reminds me of everything I lost.

I've missed my parents plenty of times, but right now, their absence feels unbearable. Like a hole in my chest that grows by the minute, threatening to consume me until there is nothing left.

I stand and excuse myself from the table. Everyone's eyes follow me out of the room, making the back of my neck itch despite me no longer being in their direct line of sight.

I escape into the kitchen, but the distance doesn't stop me from hearing everyone's low murmurs, so I head outside. Fresh air doesn't help as much as I'd like, and I end up fighting to get enough oxygen into my lungs.

When I'm this overwhelmed, I can't keep up appearances, so it's in my best interest to leave.

But before I can get into my car, Lily's voice stops me.

"Hey."

I resist the urge to lean my head against the window. "Hi."

I don't turn to look at her because then she'll know I'm not okay, and something about Lily watching me struggle with spending time with her family, which is something that clearly makes her happy and is important to her…

It makes me feel like I don't fit in her life the way I should.

"Where are you going?" she asks.

"Something came up."

"What?"

"*Lily*."

"Is everything okay?" She touches my shoulder softly, willing me to look at her. "You seemed fine, but then…"

With a deep breath, I face her. "No, it's not." The ugly truth spills from my mouth.

Her soft gaze flickers over my face before it falls to my hand clutching the car door handle like a lifeline. "All right. No worries."

I manage to keep my shoulders from slumping. "Thank you for understanding."

She cracks a smile, and it loosens the knot in my chest. "Do you care if I join you?"

I'm surprised after our conversation by the fountain, but I'll take her olive branch with open arms. "You want to come?"

"Yeah. You look like you could use a friend."

I let that one slide while promising to make my intentions very clear today.

"I'd like that, *amore mio.*"

She might be upset with me still, but the glimmer in her eyes is promising. "Let me run inside and grab my purse." She rushes up the driveway. "Don't leave without me," she throws out from over her shoulder.

I don't think I could, not unless someone physically removed me.

The grief I felt earlier is still heavy in my chest, but it feels slightly more bearable, and it has everything to do with the woman who always reminds me that I'm not alone, even in some of my darkest moments.

I never understood why my father gave up his entire life for my mother, but right now, I can see it clearly. Because when you find the one person in the world who *sees* you—who takes the time to collect every broken piece of your spirit and helps you put it back together—you don't let them go.

I made that mistake once, but I won't repeat it again.

That much I can promise.

Secret garden studio

WWS ???

wildflower wishes studio

petal + press

The Pressed Petal

CHAPTER THIRTY-NINE

Lily

"D o you mind if we pass by the cemetery?" Lorenzo asks as we drive away from the house.

"Um…no. Of course not." My palms start to sweat because the last time I went there was when we buried my dad. But for Lorenzo, I'm willing to put the memories aside and support him however he needs, even if it means doing something I usually avoid.

"Are you sure?" He takes his eyes off the road for a quick second.

"Yeah, but can we pass by the shop first?"

"Why?"

"I'm not going to show up to meet your parents empty-handed. That's rude."

Lorenzo parks in front of Rose & Thorn ten minutes later,

and I hop out to make a quick bouquet of my favorite pink flowers before rushing back to the car.

"It's the best I could do under a time crunch."

"She'll love it."

The ride to the cemetery is quiet, but in a soothing kind of way. Lorenzo keeps tapping his thigh in sets of threes, and I eventually reach over to hold his hand instead.

"You good?" I ask.

He nods. "I usually save visits for Fridays, but I felt... Today was..."

"Hard?"

"Yeah." He releases a lungful of air.

"I'm sorry...if my family triggered you, that is."

He shakes his head. "Don't apologize because I can't get over my grief."

His statement is so ridiculous, I can't help laughing, which causes him to hit a curb.

"Are you laughing at me?"

I suck in a few gulps of air. "Yes, because what do you mean you can't get over your grief? There's no such thing!"

His lips press together, and his furrowed brows are putting in extra work today from how hard I'm making him think.

"So long as you love your parents, you'll never stop grieving them, so the best way you can help yourself is to learn to coexist with the feeling." Now, if only I could take my own advice.

"You talk like it's that easy."

"It's not. I'm the first one to admit that I struggle with it."

"So what do you suggest?"

I give his hand a squeeze. "Sharing that pain with each other so we both feel less…alone."

He stays quiet for a minute while we drive through the main road of the cemetery.

"Thank you," he says as he parks in the lot.

"No need to thank me. This is what friends do." I reach for the bouquet.

"Lily?" He reaches for my hand before I can escape the car.

"Yeah?"

"I don't want to be your friend."

My heart takes a brief intermission. "Why not?"

He cups my cheek. "I'd much rather be your boyfriend, if that's an option."

I stop breathing altogether, but who cares. Oxygen is overrated.

"You…what?"

"I thought about what you said yesterday, and you're right—I am bothered by you talking about a future with another man because I so desperately want that man to be me."

My mouth falls opens, but no words come out.

"I don't want to lie to myself anymore about what we are. I don't want to *pretend*. I want you to be mine, not because of an arrangement but because you choose to be."

"You mean that?"

"With every fiber of my being."

"I'm supposed to believe you changed your mind less than twenty-four hours later?"

"I've been changing my mind for *weeks*, but last night forced me to accept what I've been denying for far too long."

"What?"

"If I had a thirty-year plan, you'd be the woman I would want to share it with."

Lorenzo once described falling in love as a collection of small, impactful moments, and this happens to be one of them for me.

I can feel it.

I slip my hand into Lorenzo's, and together we head down the cobblestoned pathway. He tells me about how he's visited the cemetery every Friday since he moved to Lake Wisteria, and I'm blown away by his commitment to visiting his parents' graves.

It's hard to not feel guilty when I don't do the same, but Lorenzo reassures me that I have the fountain, which is far less morbid.

When Lorenzo heads to his parents' tombstones, I hang back on the sidewalk, giving him space to talk to his parents. Their headstones look less weathered by time than the other ones nearby, and the bouquet Lorenzo picked up on Friday is placed in front of his mother's resting place.

I blink twice at it. "Oh God."

He looks up from his squatting position with a smile. "Not that you asked, but it was cute to watch you get jealous about them."

"I was not jealous." The words leave my mouth in a rush.

He stands to his full height. "You totally were."

"Okay. Whatever. Let's say I was a teeny, tiny bit jealous and pretend this conversation never happened."

"Are you kidding? I'm writing all about it in my diary tonight." I huff.

He smiles, only for it to go from smug to somber when he looks back down at the headstones.

"Ciao, Mamma e Papà." He starts speaking in Italian, so I have no idea what he is saying.

"Vi ho portato a Lily oggi, cosi potete finalmente conoscerla. Sono molto sicuro che la amereste piu di quanto amate me."[1] He looks back over his shoulder and smiles. It isn't blinding—not that I expect it to be—but it does reach his eyes, which look a little less haunted than earlier today.

He continues speaking for a bit before calling me over. I place the flowers I brought beside Lorenzo's bouquet before he wraps an arm around me and tugs me against him until there isn't an inch of space between us.

"Hi." I smile down at the headstones. "I'm Lily, your son's…"

"Girlfriend," he says without missing a beat.

Butterflies explode in my stomach because, wow. Okay. We're really doing this.

After all the time we've spent fighting against the inevitable, it feels like everything is finally clicking into place for us, and I couldn't be happier.

---

[1]   **Vi ho portato a Lily oggi, cosi potete finalmente conoscerla. Sono molto sicuro che la amereste piu di quanto amate me:** I brought Lily here today so you can finally meet her. I'm pretty sure you'd love her more than you love me.

"Yes. That's me. His girlfriend."

His eyes seem to sparkle.

We both turn toward the headstones. I stay quiet while he tells his parents about our weekend and about how much money he raised for Healing Hearts.

"Over a quarter of a million dollars. Can you believe it?" he says.

I smile at the wonder in his voice. It makes him sound younger and much less burdened from his chronic sadness.

He shakes his head in disbelief. "I still can't believe that Julian of all people dropped fifty thousand."

"Do they know about your history?" I tease.

"Yes, and they're very much Team Lorenzo. You, though? I'm not too sure."

I fake a gasp of outrage. "Are you *trying* to ruin my first impression?"

"Oh. They've heard plenty about you already, so no need to worry about that."

Something in my stomach flutters at Lorenzo talking about me to his *parents*.

If the man isn't in love with me yet, he is already halfway there, if that genuine smile on his face is anything to go by.

And I look forward to the day when he finally realizes it himself.

I'm not sure why I ask Lorenzo if he is okay with stopping by my dad's grave on our way out, but I do.

I mean, I know *why* I asked. The visit to the Vittoris' graves gave me courage, but it quickly wore off once we started walking toward my father's resting place.

My heart beats harder, blood pumping in my ears like my body can't tell the difference between visiting a grave and fighting for my life.

At this moment, it feels a bit like both.

Lorenzo must sense the change in me, and he wraps his hand around mine, keeping me grounded. "We could come back another day."

I appreciate his offer—I really do, but I shake my head. It feels wrong to visit the cemetery without paying my dad a visit, even if it is for only a minute.

If Lorenzo can manage this every Friday, I can make it through sixty seconds.

I *want* to.

I'm not sure what I was expecting when we arrive at my dad's grave, but a meticulously kept area and a floral arrangement of freshly cut yellow roses wasn't it.

My mom must visit more often than I thought, and guilt needles a hole through my chest.

Everyone grieves differently, I remind myself.

Lorenzo lets go of my hand and softly touches my cheek, cradling it with the palm of his hand. "Do you want me to give you a moment?"

"No." I dig my heels into the ground. "Don't go."

He dips his head and tucks me into his side instead, lending me some of his strength without saying a single word.

"Hola, Papi," I start, keeping my eyes drilled to the

tombstone because I don't trust myself not to cry if I look over at Lorenzo. "This is Lorenzo."

"Hi," he says, completely serious.

"I'm sorry I don't visit you here," I whisper. "But I think of you every day. I miss your laugh. I miss your jokes. I miss the sound of your voice, especially in the mornings because you were always my favorite alarm clock." I breathe through the pain in my torso. "I just...miss you."

I struggle to come up with much else. Maybe if I had known we'd be stopping by, I would've prepared a speech, but it was a spontaneous decision that makes me feel inadequate compared to Lorenzo's earlier visit.

"I don't know what else to say." My voice wobbles.

"Hey," he says, his smooth voice a much-needed comfort.

I turn my head to get a better look at him. "What?"

"There's no pressure to speak. We can stand here in silence for as long as you want, or we could go."

"You made it look so easy. I'm a bit jealous."

"I've been at this for a while." His smile is slow, and I appreciate every second of it.

Just like I appreciate *him*.

His strength. His resilience. The confidence he exudes, and the way he brings out the same in me. He makes me want to believe in myself again and my ability to handle anything that comes my way, because I know that if I struggle, he will be there to support me until I can hold my own.

I don't say the words aloud, but I feel them with every fiber of my being, and I hope one day I'll finally have the courage to share them.

CHAPTER FORTY

Lily

After our trip to the cemetery, Lorenzo asks if I want to have dinner together. Since I hardly ate much of my lunch, I agree, so we head back to his house, where he gets to cooking while I play with Daisy outside.

Once I tire her out, I rejoin Lorenzo in the kitchen, and we talk about random subjects, like what Healing Hearts plans on doing with all the money they raised. I tell him about how I tried and failed to win a silent auction item, which seems to surprise him.

"What were you bidding on?" he asks while checking an expiration date on the same bottle for a second time.

"Fifty thousand frequent flyer miles," I say wistfully.

"Where do you want to go?"

"Netherlands," I reply without hesitating.

"What for?"

I stare at him like he must be joking, except he doesn't laugh.

"Lorenzo. Do you know me at all?"

His eyes narrow. "I'm going to guess it has something to do with flowers."

"Yes!" I throw my hands into the air. "I was about to call off this entire engagement."

"I'll have to brush up on my international flower knowledge, then." His tone is teasing.

"Please do. I recommend familiarizing yourself with every important festival on the planet to be safe."

"My kind of trivia night."

I laugh. He smiles.

He goes back to cooking our chicken with his trusty food thermometer, which at one point reads 175 degrees.

"I think we're good," I say when I catch him stabbing the chicken in a fourth spot.

Lorenzo clearly takes food safety seriously, along with our personal safety, given the insane alarm system he has set up. Every time he lets Daisy outside, he disables it, and at one point I joke if he has a bunker.

The answer is *Not yet*.

After a minute, he still hasn't let go of the thermometer, so I pry it out of his hands.

"You good?"

He shuts his eyes. "I'm out of it today."

I want to broach a subject with him, but I don't know the best way to start.

Thankfully he sees the strained look on my face and asks, "What are you thinking about?"

"I was wondering...and please don't take offense, but I... Ugh." My nose crinkles.

"Lily. Just say it."

"Would it help if you talked to someone?"

He laughs so hard, he ends up needing to drink some water. "There's no way that's happening."

"Why not?"

"Because what good will that do?"

I place my hands on my hips. "Don't tell me you're one of those who don't believe in therapy."

"And if I was?"

"Then I'd ask what happened to make you think that."

He looks away. "I went before. Back in Vegas, but I didn't last long."

"Why not?"

"Turns out confidentiality has a price, and my uncle was easily able to pay his way into knowing everything about me."

My chest aches for all the shit his uncle put him through. "So this is a trust issue."

"Which is kind of a problem since therapy requires it, don't you agree?"

"Fair, but let me ask you a different question, then."

"What?"

"Do you trust *me*?"

He looks up at the ceiling before answering, "Surprisingly, yes."

His honest answer fills me with warmth, and I use it as

motivation to push the issue. "What if I know a therapist who couldn't be bought by anyone?"

"Everyone has a price."

"From what I hear, her hourly rate is expensive, but she's worth every single minute of it." My sister has said as much, but I can't personally confirm.

"What's her name?"

"Doctor Martin."

"Haven't heard of her."

"Exactly. It's by design, I can assure you."

He tilts his head. "How does she find new clients?"

"People find her, not the other way around."

He stays quiet as he serves us dinner, and we both sit at the island.

I don't expect him to give me an answer tonight, so I decide to give him an out. "Tell me you'll think about it?"

"If I were to say yes…" he says, and I hold my breath. "Don't expect much from it."

"Me? Never." I smile, feeling victorious against the demons holding him hostage.

We stick to lighter topics until both our plates are clean and we head to the living room. I should go home soon, but my will to leave dies when Lorenzo and Daisy climb onto the couch.

I join them because there is no way I can resist at least thirty more minutes of their company. Lorenzo wraps an arm around my waist, tucks me against his side, and passes me a remote.

"Put something on."

"What kind of mood are we in?"

"Whatever makes you laugh."

I dip my head so he can't see the goofy little smile on my face because there can only be one reason why he wants that, and damn if it doesn't make me fall in love with him a little bit more.

At some point, I must've fallen asleep on the couch during our movie night, so I'm surprised to wake up in Lorenzo's bed. He lies beside me, shirtless with the comforter draped over his lower half.

Compared to earlier, he looks at peace, with his hand holding mine like he couldn't help himself from touching me. I'm tempted to shut my eyes and fall back asleep, but then I notice the clock on his nightstand.

For once, I'm the one breaking my mom's curfew. Usually Dahlia is the one to do so with how often she falls asleep at Julian's house, and I always tease her about it because is falling asleep with her boyfriend worth sneaking back into our house at four a.m.?

One look at Lorenzo has me understanding that maybe my sister's reasons make sense.

I'm tempted to stay, but my mom has been through enough this week without me giving her another situation to hyperventilate over.

Rather reluctantly, I pull my hand back. Lorenzo doesn't wake up, but a furrow forms between his brows.

It dawns on me that Lorenzo is sleeping on the left side of the bed this time, and I have no idea why.

Not like you can wake him up and ask for an answer.

I slide off the bed, and I'm nearly halfway across the room when Daisy, who I didn't know had her own bed in Lorenzo's room, starts barking.

I try to shush her, but it's too late.

Lorenzo rubs the sleep from his eyes before slowly rising onto his elbows. "Sneaking out on me?"

"No," I say, although that's totally what I'm doing.

He smirks. "Were you planning on giving me a kiss goodbye?"

"Seeing as I'm not into somnophilia, can't say I was."

"I'm wide awake now, and even if I wasn't, you tripping the alarm system would've done the trick."

Damn. I can't believe I forgot about the system after him checking it multiple times last night.

I should ask him to type in the code so I can leave, but there's something about that smirk on his face that draws me in. Daisy quickly loses interest as I head over to Lorenzo's side of the bed.

Since I don't want him to gloat, I drop a kiss onto the top of his head like he always does to me and toss him his phone, which was on the nightstand. "Okay, now disarm the system. Thanks! Bye!"

He snatches my hand before I can escape. "Kiss me like you mean it."

"Then I'll never leave."

"If it were up to me, you never would."

Even if I could manage to get my legs to cooperate, there is no way I can go home after he spoke those words into existence.

"Fine," I say, feigning reluctance. "But first tell me why you're sleeping on the left side of the bed tonight."

His gaze darts to my mouth before returning to my eyes. "Turns out I don't like the idea of you sleeping closest to the door."

I might as well tattoo his name across my heart because the way it bleeds for him after that confession… *Yeah*.

There is not a single doubt in my mind that I am falling for this man, so I kiss him like I mean it.

Like I *love* him.

It feels like a first, and in some ways, it is. Without an audience or a story to tell, I can enjoy the feel of his lips pressed to mine without any rush.

No person to convince. No romance to fake. Nothing but me and Lorenzo, finally embracing what we've spent nearly a year avoiding.

Eventually I end up underneath him, staring up at his dark eyes.

"Stay," he commands.

"And risk my mom getting mad at me when she finds me missing tomorrow morning?"

"You can get home before she wakes up. Seems to work well for Dahlia." He kisses the corner of my mouth. "Are you done making excuses now?"

I pretend to think about it. "I suppose I can stay for a little while—"

He seals his mouth over mine, kissing me until I'm no longer able to form coherent thoughts. My head is full of white noise as Lorenzo kisses his way down my body before pausing at the top of my waistband.

When a man looks up at me like he is imagining all of the different ways he wants to make me come, the last thing I have on my mind is leaving.

So, I throw my inhibitions out the window and part my thighs. "Now it's your turn to kiss me like you mean it."

"You don't have to tell me twice."

My fingertips tingle with anticipation as Lorenzo slides my dress up my thighs until it pools around my hips, leaving me and my nude underwear on full display.

My brain has a difficult time keeping up with the fact that after so long denying our connection, we are finally together in his bed, the air heavy with anticipation.

"I've been thinking about this since last night," he confesses in a raspy whisper. "Before we were interrupted."

I tremble as Lorenzo drags his nose down my center, the deep inhale he takes adding to the growing heat in my belly, along with his soft kisses down the inside of my thighs.

"You told me you wanted to be obsessed over?" He rips my underwear off and tosses them beside me. "That you wanted to be *possessed*?"

"I want to be *fucked*, Lorenzo. Does that answer your question? Or do you want me to go into heavy detail about how I want you to fuck me so hard that my sore pussy will think of you all day tomorrow?"

He nudges my legs father apart with a smirk, and I shiver.

"If you're not thinking of me all week, then I didn't do my job right."

Oh.

I like the sound of that even better.

Finally, after what feels like forever, he leans forward and runs his tongue over my oversensitive center.

His enthusiasm is electric, and my body pulses with every stroke of his tongue. He proves to be an excellent listener who clearly pays attention to my moans, repeating the same moves with his mouth and fingers whenever I get louder.

His burning gaze locks onto mine as he rubs my clit with the pad of his thumb, only for my vision to go black when he curls his fingers inside me and strokes. I curse up at the ceiling, my entire body trembling as I fall apart.

I'm so out of it, I don't notice Daisy barking until Lorenzo is sliding off the bed to get her. He is walking funny thanks to his erection, and I take in the view of his backside as he carries Daisy outside and shuts the door in her cute little face.

She whines, but he must be taking the time to train her because she goes quiet when he orders her to.

"She wants to hang out with us." I pout as he climbs back onto the bed and crawls up my body.

"I'd rather her not interrupt what I have planned next."

I flash him a smile. "And what's that?"

"Whatever you want." He brushes his mouth over mine. "So long as it doesn't include us leaving this bed before I make you come again."

A man obsessed with giving me pleasure? I might've not won the actual lottery, but I sure hit the fiancé jackpot.

And with the way he smiles down at me, it makes me think he might feel the same way.

CHAPTER FORTY-ONE

Lorenzo

After an entire year denying myself what I want, I can't believe I have Lily sprawled out in my bed, looking up at me like I offered her the world. Little does she know, she's quickly becoming the center of mine, and I plan on spending the night showing her.

Given how she shimmies her hips beneath me while I remove her dress, her patience is running thin, so I placate her by pushing my thigh between her legs to ease the ache.

"Relax."

She grinds against me, smearing her arousal across my thigh. "Fuck me already and I will."

I dip my head and kiss a path down the column of her throat. "No need to rush."

She wraps her legs around my waist and pulls. "Lorenzo." She groans when I roll my hips.

"Again."

She repeats my name, although it's strained when my lips wrap around her nipple.

"Of course you have a thing for torture."

I smile as I trace a path of kisses across her before teasing her other breast. Despite her verbal protests, she slides her hands into my hair and holds me in place. I explore her body with my mouth, hands, and tongue before I dip a finger back inside her.

"I hate you," she says with a moan.

"Are you sure? Because your greedy little cunt seems to *love* me." I add another finger and hook it, making her pussy gush.

Maybe Lily is right and I do have a thing for torture because I could do this all night.

Too bad she doesn't seem to share my same enthusiasm for foreplay when she says, "I swear to God, if I don't come soon, I'm going to die."

With a chuckle, I kick my underwear off, grab a condom from the nightstand, and roll it on before returning to bed. Lily parts her thighs, and I situate myself between them so she can wrap her legs around my waist.

I lean forward and slide one hand underneath her head while I guide myself inside with the other. I don't dare look away from her face, so I take in the slight pinch between her brows before a look of pure bliss replaces it once I bottom out.

I touch my forehead to hers and give myself a second. I'm not the sentimental type, but something about this moment... about *Lily*...feels like I've been reunited with a piece of my heart I didn't even know I was missing.

Lily doesn't press me to hurry, instead cupping my cheek and crushing her mouth to mine, sealing the memory with a kiss that rivals them all.

My body is hot and feverish as I slowly slide out of her, a warmth spreading through me when I pitch my hips forward again. Slowly at first before the rhythm changes.

Lily claws at my back, her own arching as I find the perfect pace that unleashes a new side to her which I've yet to discover.

With every jerk of our hips, Lily's breathing grows more unsteady, only to falter when I suck on her nipple again.

My name has never sounded better than it does from her parted lips, and I cherish every groan, moan, and whimper that escapes her while she's in the throes of passion.

When I take her legs that are wrapped around my waist and toss them over my shoulders, we both sigh at the new angle. Her sounds of pleasure grow more intense, only to be cut off when I wrap one hand around her throat.

My hold is firm, and her eyes widen as I thrust deeper than ever before. I can feel her fighting off her orgasm. Can feel the way her breath hitches and her pussy spasms, yet she still won't let go.

I find the crook of her neck and suck hard enough to leave a mark. "What will it take to make you come?"

She flashes me a smile. "Wouldn't you like to know."

I slide out and slam forward again, making her gasp. When she still hasn't orgasmed, I alter my angle and hit the spot that has her moaning.

"Stop being stubborn," I say through gritted teeth, fighting my own orgasm. Sex isn't an activity I partake in often, and I've never been self-conscious about it until now, as I fight against the urge to come before she has a chance.

"But it's so much fun to see you fight your instincts." She laughs, and I snap.

I flip us over until she's on top, looking down at me with those doe eyes of hers.

"Let's see you fight yours." I wrap my hands around her waist and lift her all the way up to my crown, until I yank her back down with a hiss.

Her head falls back with a breathy exhale, and her hair tickles my thighs. She repeats the move with a curse, working herself on my cock while I sit and take her in.

That patience only lasts a minute until I'm hit with another urge to participate. I sit up higher against the headboard and pull her nipple into my mouth, sucking hard enough to make her squeak.

"Okay! Point taken." She places her hand against my chest and begins to rise, taking her heat with her.

Now I'm the one cursing to myself because *cazzo*. I'm addicted. Utterly, completely, unbelievably addicted to her.

When she slams back down, we both groan, and I reward her with my thumb pressing against her clit. We find a perfect rhythm, with her riding me while I jerk my hips until she finally shatters.

Wanting to join her, I hold her down and thrust until I finally follow her over the edge, diving headfirst into oblivion. Lily rides out my orgasm with me, not relenting until every ounce of pleasure is bled from my body.

She falls forward with a huff, and I wrap my arms around her, not quite ready to let her go.

I feel like a fool for wasting a year of our lives fighting what I should've been *embracing*. It was a grave mistake on my part, but I've learned from it and want to move forward. *Together*.

And for once the idea of becoming obsessed with someone else doesn't terrify me, so long as that person is Lily.

I wake up yet again to Daisy, although it is much closer this time because Lily thought it would be a great idea to let her jump onto the bed.

"Down," I command, but Daisy army crawls her way into my arms, giving me her best *please forgive me* face.

I cast Lily a sharp look when she giggles at Daisy licking my face from chin to hairline.

"You think this is funny?" I grunt under my breath before telling Daisy to get down.

Lily laughs louder when our dog refuses to listen.

I carefully slide out from underneath Daisy and roll on top of Lily. She squeals when I rub my slobbery cheek against hers.

"Stop!"

"Only if you promise to never let her onto the bed again." I have to draw the line somewhere, and this is a hard limit.

"It's only that she looked so lonely sleeping all by herself."

"She'll learn to manage."

"Should we get her a sibling?"

My eyes pop, and Lily laughs again. "I'm joking!"

Daisy flops onto her back and shows us her belly. When

Lily reaches over to scratch it, I snatch her hand back and hold it above her head.

"No encouraging her," I say.

"But look how cute she is." Lily pops her bottom lip out.

"For someone who claims they're not a morning person, you sure are wide awake."

"I blame your snoring."

I gape openly at her. "I do not snore."

She raises a brow. "Are you sure about that?"

Well, I'm not inviting people into my bed, so I can't confirm with absolute certainty—

"Relax." She kisses my jaw. "You sleep like a baby."

"How would you know?"

She winks.

"Creep," I say with a smile, because for some insane reason, I like the idea of her watching me. It makes me feel less guilty about doing the same earlier.

She checks the clock on the nightstand before jumping out of bed. "I need to get going before my mom wakes up!"

And just like that, our night together comes to an end.

I'm certain Lily cursed me, because as soon as I return to the house after dropping her off at hers, I instantly want her to come back. Clearly I'm not the only one who feels that way as Daisy drops to her belly in front of the door and lets out a whine.

I snap a photo and attach it to a message.

ME

Someone misses you.

She doesn't answer right away, so I head to the kitchen to clean up the mess I made this morning while I wait.

When my phone vibrates against the counter, I rush to check the new text.

LILY

Is she the only one?

With a smile, I reply.

ME

No, she isn't.

LILY

Did that hurt you to admit?

ME

Actually, it was easier than I expected.

LILY

I miss you too.

Reluctantly, I lock my phone and head to my home office so I can tackle the weekend's emails and review Willow's notes for tonight's mock debate. Lily is always on my mind, but I channel that fixation into my work because she needs me to win the election.

There is no other option for me because being defeated means her losing everything she cares about, and I won't let that happen.

When I'm not busy preparing for the debate and meeting with constituents, I am working on the Muñoz garden without Lily knowing. She thinks I'm too busy to spend time with her this week, and I am, but not for the reason she thinks.

Rosa is so excited about us clearing up the garden, she nearly ruined the surprise by telling Lily, but I caught her right before she sent a photo in the Muñoz-Lopez-Vittori group chat of me working in the backyard.

Julian pretends to still be bitter about the name change, but since he is the one who added me to the Kids' Table group chat, I think it's more performative than anything.

"*Gracias por el agua fresca, Señora Muñoz,*" Manny says before chugging half his drink.

"*Avísame si quieres más,*"[I] she says before disappearing inside.

"This is so good. I don't get how you could say no."

Because I'm all messed up in the head, I say to myself while taking a sip from my water bottle.

After a few more minutes, Manny and I get back to work. He hasn't complained once, not that I expect him to after he was the one who volunteered to help me with the garden when I texted him this morning asking for the address of his cousin's nursery.

Anything in the name of love, he declared before grabbing a trash bag.

And for the first time, I don't deny it.

Not even to myself.

I   **Avísame si quieres más:** Let me know if you want more.

X secret garden studio

WMS ???
Wildflower washes studio

~~pearl + pross~~

The Pressed Petal

CHAPTER FORTY-TWO

Lily

Outside of helping Willow and Lorenzo prepare for the debate, I've hardly seen my fake fiancé—or should I start calling him my boyfriend? He still pops into the shop to drop off some sweets or a cup of coffee, but he has been busy, and his visits never last longer than ten minutes.

The sporadic texts he sends me aren't cutting it now that I know what I'm missing, and while I'm hopeful that his schedule will ease up once he wins the election, I'm worried that his new job will only make our lives more difficult.

Before we admitted our feelings for one another, I didn't think much of what would happen to us once Lorenzo became mayor, but now I hope we can strike a balance eventually.

Get through the election first, I remind myself as I walk into the Angry Rooster Café. Maria waves me down from the two seats she saved for us in the back, and I head over there after ordering a coffee.

If there's anyone I can get to willingly come out to talk to the *Wisteria Weekly* reporter about Lorenzo and how much he's helped, it's Maria.

"Maria," I say, and she pulls me into a hug before ushering me to sit beside her.

We both take a seat and make casual conversation for a bit. She shares a few stories about this week's cooking school attendees, and I share a romanticized—or more so, *fantasized*—version of Lorenzo's proposal before we finally get to the real reason for today's coffee date.

I explain how I'd love for her to share her story with a reporter at the *Wisteria Weekly*. Our newspaper might seem small-time, but it's one area Lorenzo hasn't targeted enough, at least in my opinion as someone who still fills out the crossword puzzle every Sunday.

"I don't know..." She looks down at her lap, where her hands are bunched up.

"I know it's a big ask—"

"It's not that I don't want to help Lorenzo..." She exhales. "It's hard to talk about how our business was going under before he stepped in."

"I can only imagine." Given how successful her cooking school is, it's hard to believe that they were struggling to make ends meet, but then again, the restaurant industry has a high failure rate.

Maria holds her head high. "My husband is a proud man."

"Of you? I sure hope so because you're amazing," I tease, hoping to lighten the mood.

Her lips curl ever so slightly, so I count it as a win. "Ah. I see why Lorenzo loves you."

My blush is one hundred percent genuine.

"How could us being interviewed help him?" she asks.

"There's no guarantee, but I'm hoping if people see that Lorenzo's been helping this town succeed without any of them knowing for two years already, then perhaps it would help him stand out. As of right now, everyone credits the Ludlows for Lake Wisteria's success, and while they have helped, they're not the only ones responsible for the growth."

"No." She shakes her head. "I have a few friends who Lorenzo's helped too, and they all talk about how he gives so much while asking for so little in return."

I get choked up over her comment, and it isn't because of hormones or a piece of dust aggravating my contacts.

It's because someone sees Lorenzo as the incredible man he *is* rather than the villain he's not, and hopefully, once the *Wisteria Weekly* article is published, the rest of the town will too.

I won't stop until they do.

Between my job, meeting with the small-business owners Lorenzo works with for the *Wisteria Weekly* article, and all the election activities Willow has been planning, I'm run-down and struggling to keep up with the pace.

I don't know how Lorenzo manages everything, but his ability to juggle his personal, social, and political life should be studied.

When Lorenzo's campaign isn't monopolizing my time, then Josefina and my mom are with planning an engagement party—something they wouldn't take no for an answer on. I tried my hardest, but once they landed on a Saturday in early October, it was game over.

I'm too tired to offer much help, so I'm not sure what I'm agreeing to exactly. All I know is by the time Josefina leaves, we nearly have the entire event planned out.

I should feel relieved to be done with the majority of the planning, but then I receive a new message from Willow, asking if I want to swing by Lorenzo's house sometime today.

She follows up with another new text before I can ask what's up.

WILLOW

> Latest focus group was a shit show. He's already assuming the polls will reflect that.

Shit.

ME

> I thought he was closing the gap between him and the mayor.

WILLOW

> He is, but I think the engagement is backfiring.

ME

> How so?

My finger trembles as I hit the Send button.

WILLOW

People are worried about Lorenzo losing focus on the campaign.

I want to throw up. While Lorenzo had originally suggested against getting engaged, it was my great idea to up the ante because I thought people would take us more seriously.

You did try to stop him.

Yeah, but not soon enough, and now look. There is a chance his polls will come back better than ever after the debate, but there is also a risk that the engagement will set him back big time—to the point where he will never recover.

If we want Lorenzo to win, we need to think of something bigger than an engagement party, political debate, or *Wisteria Weekly* article about Lorenzo's entrepreneurial spirit.

But what?

I decide to pass by Lorenzo's house since he isn't answering my calls or texts. After Willow's earlier message, he seems like he could use the support.

He opens the door wearing only a pair of running shorts. His hair is damp from whatever grueling workout I interrupted, and his chest glistens, beads of sweat dripping down his toned stomach.

"Like what you see?"

I finally remember that I was born with the ability to speak. "Hard not to."

"Let me know when you're done checking me out."

"Thankfully, I can multitask," I joke before tearing my eyes away from his body. "Where's Daisy?"

"Groomer," he answers, straight to the point. "What are you doing here?" His tone might be gruff, but his actions are warm as he opens the door wider to give me room to enter.

"Willow told me about the latest focus group."

He shuts the door. "I warned her not to worry you about it."

"I'm more worried about *you*." With the debate happening this week, he needs to be at the top of his game, and the deep circles under his eyes don't give me that impression.

He runs his hands through his slick hair until it no longer gets in his face. "My business isn't the one at stake here."

"It was one focus group, Lorenzo. I'd hardly hedge the whole election on it."

He wipes his forehead with the towel he had draped around his neck. "The polls almost always reflect their comments."

"Well, this time could be different. I met with the reporter, and she's working on a front-page article about you and some of the businesses you've invested in. Those people want to help you and share their stories."

He shakes his head. "I don't know if that will be enough."

"It can help. Heck, learning about everything you've done to help give back made me see you in a completely new light, and I already knew a lot about you."

"And what happens if none of it is enough? What if we spend the next two months trying, and it still doesn't work out?" He shuts his eyes. "What if I *lose*?"

"I…I don't know." A cold feeling sweeps through my body as I take in his vacant eyes.

I understand Lorenzo losing the election is a possibility. Up until now, we've done a good job ignoring it, and honestly I'd like to hold on to that naivete a little while longer.

Lorenzo doesn't seem to feel the same way. "It's a reality we have to consider at some point."

"Why?"

He averts his gaze. "Because what if I can't do it?"

Goose bumps break out across my skin. "Do what…?"

His lips part, but he doesn't speak. Looks like I'm not the only one who wants to avoid an uncomfortable conversation.

"What can't you do?" I press.

His eyes shut, cutting me off from reading his emotions.

He has enough to stress about, I remind myself.

I grab both ends of the towel draped around his neck and pull him in. "We'll figure it out together if the time comes, right?"

He kisses the top of my head. "Sounds good."

It should, but the waver in his voice doesn't match the vote of confidence.

Desperately wanting to banish the last bit of heaviness from the air, I change topics. "Are you tired from your workout, or could I interest you in a little bedroom cardio—"

Lorenzo throws me over his shoulder, taking the steps two at a time.

"Gross! You're so…wet!"

The sound of his laugh echoes off the tall ceilings, and I feel ten times better already at the sound of it.

All my other worries melt away as Lorenzo and I spend

the rest of the night together, reassuring me of our ability to weather whatever storm comes our way together.

Little did I know, not everyone wants to get on the same life raft.

Some would much rather *drown*.

CHAPTER FORTY-THREE

Lorenzo

The expected crowd size for tonight's mayoral debate has doubled since the event was first announced, so it was switched to Wisteria High's basketball court—the biggest indoor venue available in all of Lake Wisteria. All free tickets were reserved within the first day, so it will also be live streamed in classrooms throughout the high school for those who want to watch.

Willow says she hasn't seen anyone this enthusiastic about an election before, and the voter-registration data reflects that. More people have signed up to vote in this election cycle year than any other year, so I should be happy, but this week's focus group spooked me, and my anxiety spiked to an all-time high.

I'll make up for the minor setback tonight and put to rest any lingering doubts about my ability to lead.

A door parallel to the teacher's desk I'm sitting at creaks open, and Lily walks inside the classroom, looking like the future mayor's wife in a periwinkle dress she bought with my credit card.

I never thought I'd enjoy buying something more than cars, but seeing Lily decked out in the clothes and jewelry I have bought her has me changing my mind. There is something incredibly satisfying about being able to provide for her, and screw Julian for insinuating that I couldn't.

I'm so distracted by her outfit, I don't notice her walking over to me with pinched brows.

"What's that look for?" I ask.

She takes a seat on my lap and drapes her legs across my thighs before she starts to undo the knot of my tie. "It's crooked."

"I must've messed with it."

"Nervous habit?"

I stay quiet.

She pauses her task. "Are you okay?"

Not really, but I can't admit that to her, can I? She's counting on me to pull out a win for the sake of Rose & Thorn, so I need to stay strong.

Or at least *appear* that way.

"Lorenzo?" she follows up when I don't respond.

"I'm fine," I say, my hand flexing as I resist the urge to touch my father's die.

"Then why can't you look at me?"

Because then you'll remind me of everything I stand to lose.

I didn't want to think of what it would look like to lose the election, but this week I could no longer ignore the hypothetical what-if scenarios.

What if my parents' murderer became the mayor?

What if I had to live in a town where I had to see his face all the time?

What if I had to sit back and watch Lily lose her shop because I couldn't beat the person who destroyed my family?

She nearly chokes me with how hard she pulls on the tie, and I wheeze.

"Are you trying to kill me?"

She hits me with a look of concern. "Didn't you hear me speaking to you?"

"No," I confess.

I'm quick to glance away, but she grips my chin and forces me to look at her again. "Want to talk about what's going on in that head of yours?"

"Not really."

"I assumed as much." She reaches inside her purse and pulls out the other Moirai die. "I didn't come here to talk anyway."

God, I love her for always knowing what I need.

Shit.

Love?

I mean, I've felt it during our time together, but I've never admitted it freely, not even to myself.

"What's that look for?" she asks, her gaze darting to my mouth.

"Thinking about you."

She readjusts her position on my lap so she can slip the die into my front pocket, reuniting it with its match. Her proximity to my cock sends a lick of heat across my skin, and blood begins to travel southward.

Her mouth curls at the corners as she walks her fingers up my chest. "I could help take the edge off a bit, if you want."

"We shouldn't." The plastic armrests beneath my hands bend from how hard I'm gripping them.

Her lips curl upward as she slides off my lap. If I was thinking straight, I'd reconsider the idea, but my mind goes blank as she sinks to her knees instead.

"Lily."

She ignores my protest and tugs on my leather belt, clearing the loops holding it in place before unbuckling it.

I should tell her never mind. I should shove the chair back, pull her up onto her feet, and fix her dress, which has ridden up to give me a better view of her thighs. Anyone could walk in on us, but the thought only sends more blood rushing toward my aching cock.

I hiss when she brushes her finger over it in the process of unbuttoning my pants, so I bite down on my lip and let her undo my zipper.

Fuck it. Five minutes is plenty of time.

My cock, which was already half-aroused with her sitting on my lap, thickens as she palms it over my boxers. I'm fighting a losing battle keeping my eyes glued to the door.

If anyone comes in unannounced, the desk will keep Lily and my dick hidden, so worst case is they'll see my face—

"Relax," she says, seeming to sense my panic.

She tugs my boxers down so she can free my erection, and my thighs tense as she leans forward. Her hair brushes across my thighs, adding another sensation to my already overloaded brain.

She laughs softly to herself. "You're way too wound up right now."

"Are you going to do something about it, or are you going to spend the next five minutes teasing me?" My gaze drifts back to the door.

"Don't you dare look away again." She gives my cock a single pump, and my eyes snap to hers.

The only way that's happening is if someone rips my eyeballs from their sockets because once Lily leans forward and wraps her pretty mouth around my cock, I'm a goner. Her wet heat envelops me, and warmth spreads from my groin to the rest of my body.

For a while, I thought there was something wrong with me because I'd heard men talk about sex and never related to their mind-blowing experiences. The few and far between encounters I'd had were unremarkable, and half the time I was more curious about finding out if my stance on intimacy changed than the actual act itself.

I eventually accepted that something was wrong with me...up until now.

Until *Lily*.

Because everything with her feels different. *Better.*

When I shut my eyes, she pierces my thighs with her nails, and I snap them open with a low rumble in my throat.

Our eyes connect as she drags her tongue up the shaft, and the knot in my stomach grows with every pass of her mouth over my length. I've completely forgiven her for the half-moon-shaped marks on my skin by the time she reaches the tip.

She swipes at a bead of arousal before she lets go of me with a *pop*. I'm about to protest when her tongue darts out, and she returns to tracing lazy paths across my length. Her teasing is torture as she fists my cock and slowly pumps until I'm leaning back in the chair with a groan.

"How much time do we have now?" she asks, and I curse.

"Four minutes."

She laughs. "Three more than I need."

Lily is my new favorite drug, and my brain is rewiring itself so I'm completely dependent on her.

Her strokes. Her licks. The way she takes me into her mouth and wraps her hand tightly around my length, her pumps matching the tempo of her tongue.

She dangles my orgasm in front of me, taking me closer to the edge, and I'm so. Fucking. Close.

"I'm going to come," I warn her, giving her an out.

My balls draw up, and my skin prickles, my release within reach. Lily must sense it, because her movements become hastier, and with one final, harsh tug on my cock, I come undone. Lily does her best to swallow everything, and I'm overcome with another wave of toe-curling pleasure as some of my cum slips out the side of her mouth.

I slump against the chair, and Lily releases me with a soft huff. If I was a gentleman, I'd offer her my pocket square, but I clean her chin with the pad of my thumb and smear it across her bottom lip.

Her tongue darts out, cleaning the mess I made before she leans forward and wipes my cock clean with the flat of her tongue.

I'm too blissed out right now to assist her, so she helps me by fixing my boxers and pants before redoing my belt. No one would suspect anything, and if they did, it's only because I'm unusually calm.

She looks up at me like she didn't make me come in three all-too-short minutes. If she didn't look impressed with herself, I'd be embarrassed because when have I ever come that fast in my entire life?

"Feeling better?" she asks.

"Yes. Impossible not to after that."

Her beaming smile is the only reply I get.

"Thank you," I say, my cheeks flushing because why the hell am I thanking her?

She giggles as I help her rise from the floor, which only makes my reaction worse. Not that she seems to care since she brushes the tip of her finger down the side of my face with a smile. "Aw. You're embarrassed."

"Shut up." I stand and button my blazer to give myself something to do.

"Is it because you came in less than three minutes?"

I'd walk away if I didn't enjoy her proximity so much.

She fixes my already perfect tie before leaning in, her mouth a few inches from mine. "Don't worry. I like knowing that you couldn't help yourself because it felt that good."

"Understatement of the century."

She kisses me softly, her lips ghosting mine. I don't want her to let go, so I deepen the kiss, tasting myself on her tongue.

I allow myself one minute to enjoy her company before I

pull away, not wanting to get riled up again before I head into the debate.

Lily offers me a reassuring smile. "You're going to do great out there."

"People *like* him." While I'll never relate to the feeling, I can admit that about Trevor.

She still thinks I'm doing all this for the greater good of the town, which wasn't my original reason for running, but it's quickly become a main one—right after helping save Rose & Thorn.

"So what if they like him? That doesn't make him the best choice for mayor." She smooths out an invisible wrinkle on my shirt. "*You* are, and it's time you show everyone out there why that is."

CHAPTER FORTY-FOUR

Lorenzo

After one last look at the clock, I remove my hands from my pockets and plaster on an approachable smile as I walk through the gymnasium doors. I step onto the makeshift stage located in the middle of the court, where Trevor Ludlow is already seated.

It takes an incredible amount of willpower to take a seat beside him knowing that he is here because he wants to take up his father's mantle, all while he put mine six feet underground.

Does he feel guilty when he sees me—the only child of two innocent people he accidentally killed—or does he pretend it was all a bad dream? His drunken memory of that night's events is probably hazy at best, although the same can't be said about his father, who was sober and all too willing to cover up the crime to protect his son.

Trevor reaches over and offers me his hand. I stare at it before putting on my well-worn mask and shaking hands with my parents' killer. As I give him a firm squeeze, I dream of crushing all twenty-seven bones while he smiles at me like a human version of a golden retriever.

His father sits proudly near one side of the gymnasium, smiling at his murderous son like he's the greatest gift on Earth. I suppose Trevor is a godsend when compared to Mayor Ludlow's other son, Richard, who sits beside him and looks like he's suffering from hemorrhoids.

Willow steps into my direct line of sight and tugs on her ear, giving me the signal to look more approachable.

I suppose staring at the Ludlow family with bloodlust doesn't give people the warm fuzzies, so I school my features and focus on the other bleachers full of townspeople. After a quick pass over the crowd, I turn my gaze to the woman who steals my attention every time we're in the same room.

Lily, who is sitting with her sister and mom, smiles and throws me two thumbs-up. The way she and the Lopez family are here to support *me* curbs any remaining negative feelings I have about sharing the same air as the man who killed my parents.

Tonight's moderator is a woman I recognize as the principal of the elementary school, Mrs. Singer. She steps up to the microphone that the townspeople will use to ask questions and addresses everyone. "Welcome to our first ever mayoral debate!"

That statement alone is questionable because how has this town been around for over a hundred years yet never had a competitive mayoral race?

"Since this is all very new, please be patient with us while we go over the rules." Mrs. Singer reviews the expectations, including silence from everyone unless they're chosen to ask a question at the microphone, before turning to face Trevor and me.

"Each candidate will have two minutes to answer a question and one minute for a follow-up rebuttal. A coin toss will determine who goes first, and we will switch off from there."

Without further ado, Mrs. Singer calls on the first person to come up to the microphone.

"In recent years, Lake Wisteria has drastically grown in population size, but some citizens, including myself, are concerned about the town losing its charm. So, what are some ideas you have to balance growth and opportunities with keeping true to our values as a town?"

A coin toss determines that Trevor will go first. He smiles warmly at the crowd, looking every bit like his father as he pulls the mic to his mouth.

It's the way his smile reaches his eyes that makes my stomach churn. Because how can someone appear so unbothered—so utterly *untouched* by the pain they caused—while I can't escape the haunted look in mine?

"Well, we've been fortunate to have so many people interested in moving to our town. It's been difficult to keep up with the boom in population, so we've experienced some growing pains while we adjust to the change, but what makes our town special isn't the size but rather the people who live in it."

He recites his response like he practiced it a hundred times, and after a second glance at the person who asked the question, I understand why. Of course Trevor and his father would infiltrate the crowd and plant a few of their most loyal citizens to ask questions.

He carries on talking about preserving the town square and Main Street, which are both ideas I agree with. I'm not surprised that he steers clear of talking about the Historic District, given his family bribing everyone on Lavender Lane into signing their NDA.

Trevor is finally cut off by the moderator. Everyone in the bleachers seems to like his answer based on their enthusiastic head nods, motivating me to do better.

Instead of remaining seated like Trevor, I stand up and face the crowd.

"Growth is a good thing. A great thing, honestly, but only in moderation." I pause and watch as some nod along to what I'm saying. "In fact, I'm going to play devil's advocate here and say what some of you will probably hate to hear."

People who were on their phones or whispering among each other during Ludlow's time look up or quiet down.

"We're becoming the Hamptons of the Midwest, and I don't mean that as a compliment."

A woman lets out a startled gasp near the top of the bleachers.

If there is one thing I've learned during my canvassing, it's that born-and-raised locals love the money the new residents pump into the town but they hate the idea of selling out.

Which is very much a possibility if Trevor is put in charge.

"Who here has visited Lake Aurora?" I ask.

Almost every arm in the crowd shoots up, including Jane's, who told me what it was like to witness how much Lake Aurora has changed.

"Keep your hands up and look around."

Bleachers squeak from all the movement.

"Now, who here knows someone who has lived in Lake Aurora?"

All the hands remain raised up high.

"And to those of you with your hands still raised, put them down if the person you know has moved away within the last five years due to circumstances related to the town, such as the cost of living becoming too expensive or the unstable job market."

Slowly, hands everywhere drop until there is only a small fraction left. Even Jane's hand is no longer raised because similarly, most of her friends and family moved out of their hometown once it began to change and the rent prices became unaffordable.

She told me as much during our double date, but I put all the pieces together once Lily and I witnessed it ourselves.

The silence in the room is deafening, but it says much more than I ever could on the subject, and I let the crowd sit with that discomfort before continuing.

"Lake Aurora faced the same predicament as us a decade ago, and their mayor decided to embrace change because they too were so very fortunate to have people interested in their town." It's poetic justice to use Trevor's words against him, and I enjoy watching the emotions flicker across his face.

Fear. Surprise. Uncertainty.

And soon enough, *defeat*.

"The town's council welcomed growth and expansion, and now Lake Aurora is struggling with an identity crisis. Mom-and-pop shops are having a tough time paying rent and keeping up with expenses with so much cheaper competition. Franchises are replacing family-run restaurants that were established fifty-plus years ago, turning their Main Street into a graveyard of boarded-up storefronts waiting for the next McDonald's to open up. Their rental market is at a record high, their infrastructure is struggling to support the influx of people, and community staples like their rec center have suffered from funding cuts despite the town's increased tax revenue."

I pause and allow what I'm saying to sink in. "Locals can't run away fast enough, and if we're not careful, our town will be next. So I'll throw the question back on you all and ask: How does one prevent Lake Wisteria from becoming another Lake Aurora?"

No one claps because of the event's rules, but the looks of fear on everyone's faces feel better than any round of applause I could receive. Not to mention the worried expression on Trevor's face as his wide eyes dart to find his father in the crowd.

"Mr. Ludlow, you have one minute to respond."

Trevor follows my lead and stands up, so I return to my stool and watch as he addresses everyone.

"My family has helped this town grow for a hundred years. I watched as my grandfather led us through the strawberry boom, and I saw my father navigate the inflation crisis that swept the nation a few decades later. I've studied their choices, not all of which I agreed with… Sorry, Dad, it was never a good idea to try to ban motor vehicles."

People laugh, and Mayor Ludlow waves his son off with a smile, his eyes full of pride. It makes me sick to see the two of them happy together when they should both be behind bars for their crimes.

Trevor grins. "I've learned from them because I always knew that one day I would want to follow in my father's footsteps."

My molars grind. I prepared myself for him using his family's legacy as a tactic, but stomaching it is a whole different issue, especially when the crowd is nodding along and eating up his words like they're gospel.

Trevor practically glows as he takes us down memory lane. "The town has entrusted us to lead them through the good and the bad times, and we've done our best to encourage economic prosperity while retaining what makes Lake Wisteria special. We can see Lake Aurora as what it is—a cautionary tale rather than a prophecy waiting to be fulfilled—and we can use that knowledge to better guide our decisions. They don't have the same history we do, and that's a good thing."

The energy in the room shifts, and the fear in everyone's eyes dims, replaced by hopeful expressions and soft chatter. Lily must hear something she doesn't like because she gnaws on her bottom lip, and Willow appears paler than usual as she looks back at a couple whispering behind her.

I can feel my victory slipping through my fingers. My gut instinct has gotten me this far, so I trust that if I don't win tonight's debate, I'll lose the entire election, and that is not an option.

Not because I want to avenge my parents, although that will always be a reason, but because Lily needs me to win.

Somewhere along the way, winning became less about getting payback and more about saving Lily, her mother, and their flower shop. I want to protect the life Lily built in this town by fulfilling the future she so desperately wants.

A future that I couldn't be a part of should Trevor become mayor. That much becomes painfully clear as I sit here, thinking of my past trauma that he caused.

I thought that maybe I could suffer through his time as mayor for Lily's sake, but I can't. I'd only end up driving myself crazy and push Lily away for good.

"Mr. Vittori, you have one minute to respond before we move on to the next question," Mrs. Singer calls.

I try to calm myself down, but Trevor's ability to charm the crowd and use their nostalgia as a weapon has rattled me.

Now is not the time to be nervous, I remind myself. Not when I have hundreds of people watching me, waiting to see how I can live up to the Ludlows' legacy.

I want to surpass it, not only for myself and my parents but for the woman I love.

"Mr. Vittori?" Mrs. Singer prompts, not letting me process my feelings.

I rise, noting the uncomfortable pang in my chest as I hold the mic up to my mouth. With a deep breath, I begin. "Mr. Ludlow speaks fondly of his father's legacy, and for good reason since the town has grown significantly. But I'm curious about one thing he said in particular." I shift to the side so I can look at him out of the corner of my eye.

"When you talk about wanting to follow in your father's footsteps, does that mean carrying on with his plan to destroy part of the Historic District? Because according to the architect at Morrison and Holmes, you paid them to draw up plans that require tearing down a lot more than five small businesses on Lavender Lane."

I swore to Lily that I would protect everyone who signed an NDA, including her mother, and the only way I could do that was by flipping the Ludlows' other source—the architecture firm. Maybe instead of manipulating the townspeople into signing NDAs, the Ludlows should've focused more on making sure the people they hired stayed quiet.

Trevor's eyes go wide, giving himself away, and the debate rules go out the window as the entire gymnasium breaks out into a roar of outrage.

Mrs. Singer does her best to get everyone under control. It takes a few minutes, but she calms everyone down by promising to give Trevor one minute to explain himself. I want to object but doing so would make me look like I'm intimidated, so I agree with the format change.

For someone who appeared nervous only two minutes ago, Trevor has a certain swagger to him that raises an alarm in my head.

And when he looks over at me and smiles like he won the debate, I freeze.

"What Lorenzo said is true—" He holds his hand up to quiet the whispers. "But what he failed to mention is that I would never make a decision like that without putting it to a vote."

I can see where he is going with this, and I don't like it.

"We did contact an architect to draw up some plans and a few construction companies to get quotes. I won't pretend that isn't the case, but we only did it so that we could give the town as much information as possible for you to make a well-informed decision."

I knew he'd go down swinging, but I didn't expect him to punch back this hard.

"I understand this might come as a shock to everyone, and I completely understand, but we Ludlows look out for our own, which can't be said about Lorenzo. He walked away from his family business when it got a little too hard for him." Trevor pauses, and I watch as his words and his victorious smile sink in.

Trevor faces the crowd. "Does that sound like a person who's loyal to you? Like someone who will fight when things get hard?"

For someone who was confident he could pull out a win tonight, I feel like the complete opposite right now, and the crushed look on Lily's face confirms it.

X secret garden studio

wws ???
wildflower washes studio

~~petal + press~~

the pressed petal

CHAPTER FORTY-FIVE

Lily

Willow suggested we both check on Lorenzo, but I decided it's best if I go in alone, so I say goodbye to my mom and sister before heading to the classroom I visited before.

I have no idea what to say to Lorenzo when I find him. His back is turned to the door and his head is hung forward, as if the weight of tonight's debate is crushing him.

It physically pains me to see him so dejected. I got a glimpse of it onstage, although he is always quick to shield his emotions, but now he has no audience to impress.

The full force of his disappointment hits me like a punch to the stomach.

My heels click against the floor, the fast beat matching the pace of my heart, as I walk up to the desk he is leaning against. I go to pull him into a hug, but he turns away from me.

Deep in my gut, I feel that the night is going to go from bad to worse.

"I want to be alone," he says gruffly.

"Doesn't mean you should be."

His reply is nothing but a drawn-out sigh.

"It'll be okay." I try to keep my tone upbeat despite the sense of dread growing inside me. I'm always the positive one. The *looks for a silver lining in everything* type of person, even when the sky is falling.

I can't be anxious about tonight. No. That won't do either of us any good, so I refuse to give my fears power over my actions.

"We will regroup and figure out the best strategy moving forward," I say.

"There is no other strategy," he lashes out, the corded muscle in his neck straining. "We're fucked."

"It was a bad night, yes. But we still have two months to—"

He laughs, but in a haunted kind of way. "Lavender Lane was the only card I had up my sleeve, and he called my bluff. He fucking called it, and I have no other hand to play."

I take a deep breath, in through my nose, out through my mouth, hoping the few seconds buy me patience. "I mean, the idea to let the town vote on the restoration was a surprise—"

"A surprise?" He slides his hands through his hair and tugs on the roots. "It was the best fucking idea that asshole has ever had, and trust me when I say it kills me to admit that."

Even if he said nothing, I would've seen the truth in his eyes, and it hurts to witness such a vulnerable moment from him.

"He had a few good comments, but so did you."

"Not nearly as many, and not nearly as good."

"You weren't listening to what the audience was saying. Not everyone is Team Trevor, despite what you think, and Willow can vouch for that as well."

He exhales loudly.

"Tomorrow we'll regroup and figure it out together." I reach for his hand.

He pulls it back. "Please go."

"No."

"I don't want you here." He refuses to look at me. "So leave. Now."

"I'm not going, so quit wasting your time." I stand tall. "I don't run away when things get tough."

That clearly was the wrong thing to say, and I instantly regret it when his entire face goes blank. It's unsettling, how quickly he can go from broadcasting his emotions to shutting down—a skill I'm sure he picked up during his childhood.

"I didn't mean it that way." The words leave me in a rush.

"It's okay if you did. It's not like it isn't true." His voice is clipped. Straight to the point, like we're acquaintances rather than lovers.

"Lorenzo," I groan.

He spins around, giving me his back. "Can't you take a hint? You're the last person I want to be around right now."

I stumble back. My chest feels like he punched a hole straight through it, but I hold steady, ignoring the ache.

He needs you, I say, fighting the urge to run as I roll my shoulders back.

"We'll get through this together."

"No, we won't," he says quietly.

This frustrating man. "I get that you're anxious—"

"Anxious?" He laughs again, this one more bitter than the last. "I'm fucking furious because he's going to win, which means we both lose everything." His voice shakes, and if I hadn't already realized I loved him for a while, him caring about what matters most to me would've done the trick.

"I don't want to think about what-if scenarios when there's still a chance you can win, but if the worst-case situation happens, then we'll figure it out. I can restart in another part of town—"

He shakes his head. "There's no *we*."

I jerk back. "What?"

He looks at me like I'm a stranger, and I can't help questioning if that's what he wants me to be.

"I'm not staying, Lily. If he wins…I can't." His voice cracks at the end.

I recoil like he struck me with his hand rather than his words. The ache is so overwhelming, I have to add some physical space between us, as if that would lessen the hurt.

It doesn't. Not even by a fraction.

"I thought…" That what? If he loved me, he would be able to put his pride aside?

He shakes his head. "I'll never live in a town where that mu—*man* is mayor."

His words hit me straight in the chest, like an emotional, battering ram threatening to shatter my heart into a thousand pieces.

"But..." *What about us?*

I don't realize I said the words aloud until Lorenzo looks up from his clenched fists.

"I like you." *But not love.* "I really do, but not enough to change my mind."

How does this even happen?

I believed that he was the one for me. That yes, while our story wasn't conventional, it was special in a way that no one could ever compare.

Maybe to you, but never to him.

Lake Wisteria is my home, but Lorenzo...he is my heart. I don't want to have to choose between one or the other.

"But I want to spend the rest of my life here."

"I know. But if I lose, I won't." He sounds completely drained.

I fail to notice the tears streaming down my face until Lorenzo wipes them away. Seeking comfort in his touch feels like I'm pouring salt in an open wound, so I pull back and wrap my arms around myself.

Pain flashes behind his eyes, but I refuse to think twice about it. He doesn't get to hurt me like this and feel bad about it afterward.

"Why am I not good enough for you to stay?" The question comes out as a sob, and I hate myself for being vulnerable.

"*No.* This has absolutely nothing to do with you."

I'd like to believe him, but I've seen this movie. Heard the same line from men I've dated. Quite a few times actually, and the ending is even shittier this time around.

I try to laugh it off, but with my heart breaking, it comes

out wrong. "I appreciate the attempt to make me feel better, but your decision does have to do with me. Because if you loved me, you'd stay. You wouldn't run away like Trevor suggested because you're supposed to be loyal to *me*, not an election."

His scowl deepens. "It's...complicated."

"Not when you love someone, it isn't."

He says nothing, and somehow that feels infinitely worse. Because I can't believe I read him wrong. So wrong in fact, I came up with an entire plan centered around helping him realize his true feelings toward me.

Feelings and actions I mistook for *love*.

If he truly loved me, then wouldn't he be trying harder to fight for us, to fight for the *town*?

He wouldn't give up because of one bad debate. He'd be figuring out how to show the town how wrong Trevor was about him.

Un Muñoz nunca se rinde...and neither should the person they choose to fall in love with.

It kills me to think of Lorenzo as anything but a strong, capable man willing to do anything to protect me, but it kills me *more* to see him quitting on me.

"I thought I could do it," he whispers.

"But you'd rather walk away. You'd rather *quit*."

"Yeah, I would. I'd much rather walk away with dignity than stay in this town for nothing," he snaps back, his voice sharper than a whip.

I flinch. "I'm not *nothing*."

He immediately jumps into apologizing. "*Scusami, amore mio*. I didn't mean it like that. You know that, right?"

Now I'm really crying, and there is nothing I can do to delay the tears once they start falling. He pulls me into a hug, and I don't fight him on it. Instead I melt into his embrace because it'll never be the same after tonight.

I won't allow it to be.

"I shouldn't have said that," he says, filling the silence when I don't speak. "I'm…distraught. Tomorrow we can regroup and come up with a new plan, and by next week we'll have the polls and post-debate data to review too. I…" He shakes his head. "It's no excuse, but my anxiety got the best of me, and I'm sorry. I'm so fucking sorry."

I don't ease his worries. I don't rush to make him feel better. I don't do anything but stand there in silence, processing how we got to this point.

He tilts my head back so he can get a better look at me. "Lily?" he asks, a crease forming between his brows.

"Yes?"

"Tell me you're still in this with me."

I look away and close my eyes. "Until the end of the election, yes."

"What?"

"You and me…we're done."

"Done how?" Each word is punctuated with a pause.

"I plan on following through with our original agreement." *Even if it's one of the hardest things I have to do.* "We can keep up with our public appearances, but if you don't plan on staying here if you lose, then everything else between us has to stop."

Tell me you've changed your mind, I beg one last time.

Fight for me as hard as you've fought for this election.

Whatever flame of hope I carried is snuffed out when he shakes his head. "I won't make you a promise I can't keep."

I want to curl into a ball and cry, because how can he look me in the eyes after everything that's happened between us and act like it doesn't matter?

"I see."

Maybe we were always doomed because neither of us is willing to sacrifice for the other. I won't leave, and he won't stay.

It's a tragedy that would make Shakespeare proud, and one I don't fully understand.

We were so close to that forever kind of happiness. I could feel it, could *see* it for the first time with Lorenzo after years spent searching for the right person.

Only to be blindsided in the end.

"I'll respect your wishes." He dips his head—a final death sentence to our relationship.

When I'm pulling away, I remember the bracelet he got me, and before he can protest, I unclasp it and hold it out in the palm of my hand.

"What are you doing?" His eyes go wild with...what? Worry? Anger?

Who cares.

"Clarifying where we stand."

When he doesn't grab it, I slip it inside his pocket, catching the way it clicks against his father's dice.

His throat visibly tightens. "It was a gift."

"One I only accepted because I thought..." Nope. Still can't say those three words aloud. "I thought wrong."

Better.

I don't know how I walk out of that classroom with my head held high. My rib cage feels as if it's cracking in half, each strenuous breath serving as a painful reminder of what happens when we fall in love with someone who won't love us back.

I should've stuck to our original plan, but no, I had to do something stupid and fall in love with the man who warned me against the very idea.

I thought love could conquer all...only to have it destroy me instead.

And I have no one to blame but myself.

Thankfully I don't run into anyone in the hallway or school parking lot, so I'm able to keep my cool until I get to my SUV that Lorenzo bought, all because he wanted me to be *safe*.

But really, who was going to keep me safe from *him*?

Once I get inside my car, I check out my reflection in the mirror and wince at the state of my makeup. When I go to clear the worst of it from underneath my eyes, I flinch at my engagement ring.

I want to yank it off and toss it out the window—or maybe ask Julian to bury it in concrete like Dahlia's old one from her previous relationship. The image of Julian bringing out the concrete mixer draws a smile from me, only for it to die when I realize that's a likely possibility.

Because should Lorenzo lose, I'll be expected to let go of everything associated with him, including our dates and—

Daisy.

Oh God. Another sob rips from my throat because we adopted a dog together, and I was too focused on myself to even think about her and what would happen should Lorenzo move away.

Are we supposed to split custody? How would that even work? Would he give her up entirely, or would he decide to take her with him and force me to travel to see her?

Assuming I even *want* to see him, because the thought of him moving on in another town without me feels like someone carved my heart out of my chest with a spoon.

I lean my head against the steering wheel and cry until I have no more tears left to shed. I'm not sure how long I sit there, losing my shit, but when I look up, the parking lot is empty except for one car.

And the owner leans against the trunk, looking straight at me like *I'm* the one causing *him* pain.

He has no right to look at me that way—to make me feel bad for him when I'm the one who put my heart on the line, only to have it rejected.

Mustering up the small amount of pride that I have left, I reverse out of my space and leave Lorenzo in my rearview mirror.

Tomorrow I'll pick myself back up and get ready to fake it, but tonight I'll allow myself to break for the very last time.

CHAPTER FORTY-SIX

Lorenzo

I deserve to suffer for the choices I've made, so I stand and watch over Lily as she breaks down in the middle of the empty school parking lot, fighting an intense urge to yank open her door, pull her into my arms, and promise her that I'll figure everything out.

I want to tell her that I love her and that I never want her to go another minute without knowing it. That I'm sorry, not only for hurting her but for letting her down in so many ways.

For making her cry.

For pushing her away multiple times when I could've been enjoying her company instead.

For not being strong enough to overcome my trauma, and for being too weak to share the burden with her.

I've never felt agony quite like this before, but I don't dare take my eyes off Lily. Don't so much as drop my gaze once, not even when my own eyes get misty when she curls over her steering wheel and sobs.

I want to rip out my heart straight from my chest and offer it to her as a payment for ruining us. For destroying the temporary happiness we shared and whatever hope Lily had of us making it out of this arrangement together.

You can still win the election. It's as if Lily is the one who spoke the words, not me.

She has always been the hopeful one. The wishful dreamer. The one who has brought out the best in me, and the one who's seen me at my very worst.

I failed her in more ways than the debate. I took her love for granted, and now I'll suffer through the consequences of my actions.

For the next two months, I'll accept whatever punishment she deems fit, all while fighting to save her business and the election.

I can't give her everything she wants, but that won't prevent me from giving her my all until the very end.

I follow Lily to her house. With her tracking bracelet stuffed inside my pocket, I can't resist the compulsion to make sure she makes it home safely.

I'm not slick about my intention either, so I anticipate her glaring in my direction when I park by the curb. What I don't expect is her stomping over to my car and pointing at the window until I roll it down.

"Quit following me around."

"I would if I could." Exhaustion bleeds into my voice.

Her eyes narrow. "What game are you playing?"

"I wasn't aware I was playing one."

She growls with frustration. "Go home."

"I will once you get inside." I lean back in the driver's seat.

"You don't get to do this."

"Do what?" I bite down on my tongue.

"Act like you care."

"Good thing I'm not acting, then, am I?"

"How can I tell? Our entire relationship has been a lie."

I breathe, hoping to expel some of my frustration through my mouth and failing after one attempt.

I'm too annoyed by her accusation to try again, so I pull out the bracelet from my pocket to show her who the real liar is here, and spoiler, it's not *me*.

Lily backs away. "I told you I don't want it."

I ignore her and open the app on my phone.

Her brows rise, right before they scrunch with confusion. "Is that…"

"A top-of-the-line model."

She covers her mouth with her palm.

"Tell me something, *amore mio*. Am I acting now?"

She shakes her head, anguish etched into the fine lines by her eyes and mouth. "Why are you showing me this?"

"Because let this be the last time you accuse me of lying." I hold the bracelet out for her to grab. "Now, do you want me to follow you around everywhere, or will you be a good fiancée and wear my gift?"

She stares at the bracelet like it might transform into a venomous snake.

"You need professional help, Lorenzo." She stares at me, her eyes a window to her crushed soul.

The only person I hate more than Trevor Ludlow right now is myself, because I'm the one who is making her miserable.

As much as I hate it, I won't make her a promise I can't keep either, so I'm put in an impossible situation.

"I'm only doing this because I don't want to see you more than I have to." Her fingers tremble as she reaches for the bracelet. She tries to put it on herself, but I intervene, allowing myself to seek comfort in her touch.

I pretend to struggle with the clasp to give myself more time. "Okay."

"You're a real asshole for tracking me without my consent, by the way."

"I'll never apologize for prioritizing your safety."

Her hands clench into fists by her side. "And who's going to keep me safe from *you*?"

Pain laces through me, starting in the back of my throat before weaving its way through my chest.

I never wanted to hurt her, yet that's all I manage to do.

With deft fingers, I secure the clasp and pull my hand back. "I'll see you on Saturday at the assisted-living facility."

"So that's it? Back to business?" Her body tensing, visibly bracing herself for my reply.

"Isn't that what you wanted?"

"Fuck you, Lorenzo." Her voice cracks, and my own heartbeat seems to slow as I replay the sentence in my head.

Lily has never spoken to me that way, and while deserved, it still *hurts*.

"Get some rest." For her benefit, I keep my voice cold and detached.

With another curse, she spins around and heads into her house while I watch from my spot on the curb.

Once the light in her bedroom turns on, I drive away, knowing that come tomorrow, everything between us will have changed.

I get home and am immediately assaulted with memories of Lily. Her basket of socks. The photo of us from the cooking class. The wilting bouquet that I'm supposed to replace tomorrow.

Everywhere I turn, I'm reminded of the woman who has infiltrated my life, turning it from shades of morally gray to a spectrum of colors that match her wardrobe.

I escape the entryway and head to the living room. Daisy gives up on sniffing my leg and disappears down the hall before returning with a pair of socks in her mouth.

"For fuck's sake." I wipe my face.

She drops the socks in front of me and whines.

"Your mom's not coming home."

She lies flat on her stomach and lets out another high-pitched noise.

"What?"

She nudges the socks with her nose, and I toss them onto the coffee table.

Since I can't stand looking at Daisy without thinking about Lily, I head to the liquor cabinet for a bottle of scotch. I slam one of the doors and accidentally scare her, so she takes off running.

I don't drink to get drunk ever. Doing so would take away my control, and I prefer to keep a tight grip on my reality. But tonight I make an exception.

I *need* to.

Because if I'm not thinking about Lily, then I'm ruminating over the debate and how I had to pretend I didn't want to kill Trevor Ludlow with my bare hands.

Outside of large town events like the Strawberry Festival, I've been able to avoid Trevor. He hangs around a very elite group of people, and since he hardly volunteers around town, we rarely cross paths.

But now that we have, I have a taste for a different kind of revenge. One that my uncle stole from me by not pursuing manslaughter charges before Michigan's ten-year statute of limitations.

I take a swig straight from the scotch bottle, the burn in my throat temporarily distracting me from the one in my chest. When that pain fades, I take another sip, and another, before the bottle starts to finally feel lighter.

Only that temporary relief is wiped away when Daisy returns with a new pair of socks, as if the first set wasn't torturous enough.

"Go to bed." I point at her dog bed in the corner.

She whimpers, but I keep my finger directed at her bed while taking another swig from the bottle. Reluctantly, Daisy heads to her spot with Lily's socks still in her mouth.

I turn away because the knot in my stomach becomes unbearably tight.

Fuck my uncle for allowing Trevor to get away with murder, and fuck the mayor for protecting his son. And fuck me, because now that I know what it feels like to love someone, can I blame the mayor for wanting to save his son?

The sympathetic thought sends me into a devastating spiral, and I end up taking a few more swigs of my drink.

I would do anything for Lily.

Anything but give her the one thing she desires.

I stumble over to the couch. My coordination is shoddy, so I trip on a stupid accent rug but still somehow manage to land on the cushions without cracking my head open on the coffee table.

I stare up at the ceiling and sigh. The sound is too loud, and the house is eerily quiet.

Better get used to the silence.

Before Lily changed my mind, I enjoyed the solitude. I craved coming home to an empty house, but now I can't think of anything more depressing.

Well, turns out there is one more thing, and it's being left on read after drunk texting my fake fiancée.

X secret garden studio

WWS ???
wildflower washes studio

petal + press

the pressed petal

CHAPTER FORTY-SEVEN

Lily

can't sleep, no matter how many episodes of *The Silver Vixens* I watch, so I decide to scroll through my phone instead. It's an idea that goes from bad to worse when a new message pops up from the last person I expect.

LORENZO

I'm sorry.

I'm so stunned by the random apology text that I ignore it until a new one pops up.

LORENZO

I don't want to go back to how things were before.

LORENZO

I want you.

LORENZO

Wait. No. Not like that.

LORENZO

Shit. I mean yes, also like that. But you
know what I mean.

LORENZO

Right?

I should put my phone away right now. Nothing good can
come from responding to his messages, and I'll only be making
this entire process more difficult for myself.

LORENZO

Please don't hate me.

I grab a pillow and shove it over my mouth to muffle my
frustrated scream.

LORENZO

And I'm s0rry about the track

LORENZO

Fracking bracelet.

LORENZO

Tracking bracelet.

LORENZO

I think I'm drunk.

I grab a throw blanket and tightly wrap it around myself
while I mentally count my breaths. The urge to lash out is
strong, but I hold off because I'd rather explore my emotions
than unleash them.

There are multiple reasons for me to be upset over Lorenzo's texts, but most of all, I'm mad at myself for caring about him despite the reasons I shouldn't.

I don't like to see anyone hurting, regardless of whether they brought it upon themselves or not, but somehow witnessing Lorenzo's pain is infinitely worse.

He put us in this position.

He is making us both suffer over his stubbornness.

Over his *pride*.

LORENZO

Will you come over and hold my hair back?

LORENZO

Please.

Another message comes through ten minutes later.

LORENZO

I don't feel so good.

LORENZO

Question: Does heartache get worse overnight?

Stubborn tears prick my eyes, but I blink them away because Lorenzo doesn't get to make me cry. Not anymore.

I lock my phone and stare at the artificial flowers hanging from my ceiling until my vision is no longer blurry.

Does heartache get worse overnight? he asked.

I'm bitter enough to wish mine does, that way I'll have a physical reminder of what happens when I fall in love with the wrong person.

I'm so miserable after last night, I end up asking Jane to cover my shift at the shop. I can't risk running into Lorenzo, who always picks up his two bouquets on Friday, so I spend my day working on a pressed-flower piece in the garage.

The bride has already messaged me once, asking how it was coming along, so I need to wrap it up before she gets annoyed at the wait time. Plus the work helps keep my mind occupied for a few hours, which is much needed after last night.

I don't expect Lorenzo to show up at my house later in the day, so I'm surprised to see him standing outside my garage, looking like he was run over by an eighteen-wheeler.

If I hadn't known he got drunk last night, the evidence would've been hard to miss today.

"Hey." He waves, and the easygoing greeting instantly pisses me off.

I walk out of the garage and yank the mask off my face. "What are you doing here?"

He tucks his hands into his pockets. "Jane said you weren't feeling well."

"So?"

"*So*, I wanted to make sure my fiancée was okay."

My eye twitches at my least favorite *F*-word. "Are you concerned I'll cancel on tomorrow's outing?"

"Should I be?"

"Nope," I reply.

His eyes close. "Lily, I—"

I interrupt. "Are you here to talk about the election?"

"What? No. I'm here to talk about us."

The sheer audacity of his statement makes me laugh. "Did you change your mind on leaving town if you lose?"

He looks away. "No."

One word has never felt more devastatingly final before.

Do not let him see you break again, I remind myself.

"Then there is no *us* to talk about." I readjust my mask and head back into the garage. "Goodbye, Lorenzo. See you tomorrow for our date."

I should be happy when he heeds my request and leaves, but I want to fall apart once he's gone. It's frustrating, and I feel like I'm being torn in two directions, neither of which are best for me.

And if I'm not careful, I'm afraid I'm going to break for good, and nothing can fix me once that happens.

Since I can't talk to my sister about my not-so-fake fake relationship, I turn to the only person who is both aware of my situation and also isn't directly tied to Lorenzo.

When I texted Rafa asking if we could meet up, he didn't try to figure out what was wrong. He told me to show up at his house whenever, so that's how I find him in his barn fifteen minutes later.

"Thought you'd like to see the kittens again." He opens the gate and lets me into the stall where the six of them are.

I take a seat on the floor across from him and grab the closest one, who happens to be the smallest of the bunch.

Neither one of us speaks right away, which is another thing I appreciate about Rafa.

Once I'm ready, I look up at him and say, "I'm sure you're wondering why I'm here."

"I think I can guess with one try."

I don't know whether to laugh or wince. "Is it that obvious?"

He lifts a shoulder. "I knew it was only a matter of time before Lorenzo screwed up. We all do."

"Great. Not that it even matters, but I wish it happened a little sooner."

"Like when? Before you fell in love with him?"

"I'm not *in love* with him," I huff.

Rafa shoots me a pointed look.

"Okay, fine. I *was* falling in love with him, but only because I thought he felt the same way." I cradle a kitten to my chest, needing the emotional support.

"What makes you think he doesn't?"

"Because he pretty much said so."

I go on to explain the conversation I had with Lorenzo, all while Rafa listens quietly, only asking a few follow-up questions when he needs further clarification.

"So he plans on moving away if he loses?"

"Yup."

"Damn. I didn't think his ego was that fragile."

"That's the thing. He has been fine living here with Mayor Ludlow in charge, but if Trevor wins, he has to move? It doesn't make sense."

"Has he been fine, though? Or has he made it seem that

way because he hasn't had any other choice right now while he's been campaigning?"

I sit with his words and process them. "I… Actually, I don't know."

"Maybe you should ask him."

"Why? It's not like it'll make a difference."

"Maybe, maybe not, but wouldn't you rather have all the facts?"

"So he can remind me all over again that he plans on leaving me? At this point, I'm asking to get hurt again." My voice cracks.

Rafa comes over and pulls me into a hug. "He could still win. There's still two months left."

"It already feels like he's given up," I admit, thinking back to the way he sounded after the debate.

Rafa releases me from his embrace, and the kittens return to our laps. "It sounds like he's jumping to the worst conclusion without any evidence."

"I mean, it was a bad night."

"From the little I heard this morning while grabbing coffee, it sounded like they both had some good points."

"Really?"

"I mean, I didn't hear much, but I wouldn't count Lorenzo out yet, and he shouldn't either."

"Truthfully, I don't know anymore. He and Trevor both looked terrible, so I'm not sure either of them won, but regardless Trevor definitely ended on a higher note than Lorenzo."

"How so?" he asks.

"Trevor brought up Vittori Holdings. Used the sale of

shares against him." I explain the situation with the *Nevada Sun* article and how it made Lorenzo look beyond petty.

"If people did some basic research, they'd understand the kind of man Lorenzo's uncle is and why Lorenzo walked away."

"But what if they don't?"

"Haven't you been talking to one of the *Wisteria Weekly* reporters?"

His random question makes me pause. "Yes, but it was more about Lorenzo and his connection to local businesses."

"What if the piece isn't only about that? What if Lorenzo opens up about his past and how he ended up here again?"

"I don't know. He's private about all that. Plus he strongly dislikes reporters." Not to mention I don't even know Lorenzo's true reason for returning to Lake Wisteria, so how can I ask him to share it with the town?

"Maybe that's part of his problem. People feel like they know the Ludlows, so they're more likely to trust them, while Lorenzo is still this enigma."

I bite down on my cheek. "I guess anything is worth a try at this point."

Everything except our relationship, that is.

At least according to Lorenzo.

I hit peak pettiness when I drive my old car over to the assisted-living center the next morning, and the downgrade from my luxury vehicle is worth the look of pure outrage on Lorenzo's face when I pull into the lot.

He seems to forget we aren't alone as he storms over to my car. I tilt my head toward the group of animal shelter volunteers parking close by, and he self-corrects his scowl into a smile.

"Good morning, baby," I say in a lighthearted tone that doesn't match the heaviness in my chest.

He gives me space to exit the car before pinning me against the door. "Did something happen to your other car, *amore mio*?"

I hit him with my most radiant smile. "It wasn't working."

"I'll text Manny and ask him to go check on it." He pulls out his phone and shoots off the text.

Shit.

Lorenzo looks up from the screen and zones in on my incriminating face. "What did you do?"

"Nothing," I say all too quickly.

He grabs the keys straight from my hand and pockets them.

"Hey! Give those back."

"Why? You won't be needing them anymore once Manny fixes your car."

"Still. You can't steal my keys." I reach inside his pocket, only to have him snatch my hand and lock our fingers together.

"Everyone come gather around!" Nura calls out.

"You can let go of my hand now." I keep my voice low.

"I *could*," he says, like that answers everything.

I can't let my true feelings show, so I put on a smile for the other volunteers forming a circle around Nura. It's difficult to ignore the little jolt in my chest when Lorenzo's hand tightens around mine, but I do my best to remember that it's all for show.

It has to be.

I remind myself of my purpose as Lorenzo and I are paired off with a dog and given our schedule for the day. We are assigned ten different people to visit, and our first two happen to be one of the town's oldest couples: Joanne and Lenny.

Joanne was Lake Wisteria's first-ever Strawberry Sweetheart—a title my sister also gained during the town's beauty pageant—so she is pretty well-known.

Lenny, on the other hand, is a grump who only softens for his one true love, which is why the frown on his face disappears as soon as Joanne smiles.

"Look at that dog, Lenny!" Joanne yanks on her husband's arm.

"I'm going deaf, not blind, woman." Lenny pretends to be miffed, but there is a sparkle in his eyes as he checks out the happy look on his wife's face.

Lorenzo and I shut the door to their one-bedroom apartment and take a few steps inside.

"It's so nice to have visitors," Joanne says.

Lenny's eyes drift toward the framed American flag hanging on the wall. Their only son passed before I was born, but his memory still lives on in their hearts.

"We thought you could use some company. This sweet girl's name is Angel." I point at the German Shepherd who has yet to be adopted after three months at the shelter.

"She doesn't look like an Angel to me." Lenny's nose scrunches.

"The same could be said for our pit bull, Daisy."

I laugh, only to regret it as soon as Lorenzo smiles at me.

Joanne beckons us forward. "Let me see her."

Lorenzo walks toward her, keeping the leash wrapped tightly around his wrist in case Angel thinks it's a good idea to knock Joanne and her walker over.

Joanne squints at Lorenzo. "Wait a minute. You're that guy on the TV."

Lenny squints. "Who?"

"He's running for mayor," she clarifies.

His gaze flickers over Lorenzo's dark hair. "You don't look like a Ludlow."

"Because I'm not." His jaw clenches.

"Thank God. The oldest one is a real twat. He used to run over my flower beds all the time, so I ended up slashing his tires once."

Lorenzo *laughs*, and the sound makes my chest twinge.

How am I going to survive another two months of this? I ask myself, fighting the urge to distance myself from Lorenzo and the uncontrollable responses he draws from me.

"And who are you?" Joanne asks me while Angel licks her hand.

"Lily. His fiancée."

"Oh!" Her entire face lights up. "You two will make the most beautiful babies."

Lorenzo wheezes, and my mouth falls open while Lenny looks like this is a typical Saturday.

"Don't mind her," he says. "She says that to every couple she sees, often without asking if they want children."

"Do not!"

He turns to us. "Watch. She's going to ask you fifty different questions about your relationship next."

"Lenny! Don't be dramatic."

"Twenty?"

"I'll start with one." Joanne huffs. "What did you think when you first met Lily?"

"Here we go," Lenny grumbles.

I expect Lorenzo to come up with a generic answer, but he surprises me when he says straight to my face, "At first I didn't want to like her, so I looked for reasons not to. She was bubbly and funny, and honestly, I never even told her this"—Joanne *squeals*—"but I found her to be intimidating. She knew what she wanted and she was completely and utterly unapologetic about it, and I feared that quality as much as I admired it."

Joanne's eyes go wide, and she's not the only one because consider me speechless.

Lorenzo doesn't take his eyes off me. "I had a set number of goals for my life, and most of them up until I met Lily were self-serving, but once I met her, she had this way of making me think about a future that was bigger than myself or this town. And slowly, little by little, the future she painted for herself… Well, I couldn't imagine anyone else standing beside her in that picture but *me*."

I wish his words were true, but each one of his actions lately tells me they're nothing but a *lie*.

CHAPTER FORTY-EIGHT

Lorenzo

Lily and I spend the rest of our Saturday taking Angel around the assisted-living facility. There is one nurse working who is particularly interested in her, so we stay a little longer so Angel can spend time with her after her shift.

By the time we leave, I'm exhausted, and Lily appears to be feeling the same given the way her eyes droop.

"I'll take you home." I shuffle her toward my car.

She scans the lot. "Wait. Where's my car?"

"Manny took it to my house."

"What? Why?"

"I thought I should keep your prized possession safe since there appears to be someone in your neighborhood who's tampering with spark plugs."

Her entire face turns red.

"How did you learn to remove those anyway?" I ask after sitting on the question all afternoon, ever since Manny passed by earlier to grab Lily's car keys so he could drop it off at my house.

She can have it back in two months—and not a single day before then.

If Manny thought my request was unusual, he didn't show it, most likely because I played it all off like some prank.

Lily kicks up some dirt with the toe of her shoe. "YouTube."

"I'm impressed."

She glances up at me. "The look on your face was worth it."

"Now I feel less bad about this…" I open my message app on my phone and show her my text thread with Manny.

MANNY

> Tell me again why you want me to remove Lily's engine?

ME

> It's part of the prank.

MANNY

> And the boot on the wheel?

ME

> Added safety precaution.

MANNY

> Would you like me to remove the steering wheel while I'm here?

ME

> Now you're thinking outside the box.

MANNY

> I was kidding.

ME

I'm not. Also, is it possible to take out the driver's seat? Just in case?

Lily shoves me hard. "What are you doing?"

"Keeping you safe."

"From what? The right to make my own choices?"

I laugh, which spurs her on.

"None of this is funny." Her voice shakes as her hands curl into fists by her side.

"I'm sorry." I sober up. "If you want the car, I'll give it back."

"In the same condition you stole it in?"

I stop grinding my teeth together long enough to answer her. "No."

"You're…"

"Yes?"

"The most infuriating man I've ever met."

"We both know that's not true." Not while Richard is alive, at least.

She walks over to my car with a groan and waits by the passenger side. I don't unlock it until I can grab the handle and open the door for her.

She doesn't climb in.

"You're not making this process any easier for me," she says softly.

"I can't stop caring about you, Lily."

Her brows furrow. "If the last forty-eight hours are a sample of what that looks like, I'm better off without it."

"These last two days have been hell for me too."

"Good."

Who knew it was possible to pack so much sass into one single word?

Wanting to prolong our longest conversation since the night of the debate, I play with one of her face-framing braids and say, "I scheduled a session with Doctor Martin."

The spark of anger in her eyes dies, along with whatever she was about to say when her lips part.

"I have no idea if it'll work out, but I'll try anything at this point," I add when she doesn't speak.

"That's...great. I'm happy for you."

I'm surprised by her comment. "Really?"

"Yeah. I still want the best for you." Her shoulders curl in on themselves.

"You say it like it's a bad thing."

"Because I'm the one who always gets hurt."

"Which is why I'm getting help." My arms become a cage, trapping her between my body and the car.

It won't be an easy process, but it could be a rewarding one, so long as I learn to work through my trauma and manage my anxiety, obsessions, and compulsions.

I *need* to.

I'm tired of running, both from my past and my future. It's a pattern that needs to end because, as much as it absolutely pains me to admit, Trevor called me out on my biggest issue during the debate.

I don't fight when things get too hard.

I *quit*.

And honestly I'm sick of running. Sick of hiding. Sick of pretending that life will get better without me putting in the hard work to make it possible.

Trevor already stole my parents and my childhood from me, so am I going to allow him to take Lily and our future away too?

No. Not anymore.

I'm going to fight for her and us, one therapy session at a time, because Lily is worth it, but more importantly, so am *I*.

I considered canceling a few hours before my therapy session, but Doctor Martin has a zero-tolerance policy for no-shows within twenty-four hours, so I have no choice but to attend.

Doctor Martin, a middle-aged woman with a Jamaican accent and braids adorned with golden cuffs, spends the next hour getting to know me and the constant grating voice in my head rather than making headway.

Discussing my OCD diagnosis isn't anything new. I've been to therapy before, but since I didn't trust the psychologist who reported to my uncle, I always held back. I was cautious with my responses, never quite letting anyone peek behind the curtain of my mind.

Today is different because I force myself to answer honestly and openly, not wanting my own stubbornness to prevent me from making headway. I respond to all of Doctor Martin's questions like a willing patient looking for answers to my life's biggest problems, and I'm rewarded with nonjudgmental commentary in return.

I didn't have high hopes when I began the session, but when the psychologist doesn't even blink twice at me describing the tracking bracelet I bought Lily, she earns some of my respect.

"Are you able to share more about other compulsive tendencies you have?"

I go through the basics, including my concerns with safety, food prep, and contamination, before I dive into my Lily-based worries.

"Sounds like a lot to manage." She scribbles something on her notepad.

"That's why I'm here."

"What made you want to take this step after…" She scans her notes. "Over twenty years feeling this way?"

"I need to figure out a way to manage my anxiety and process my past, both for myself and my girlfriend."

Her eyes soften behind her glasses. "Lily, right?"

"Yes, but right now our relationship is a bit…complicated."

"In what way?"

I explain my fake engagement because why not? Doctor Martin is paid to keep everything confidential, so the worst that can happen is her openly judging me for my choices.

"Surprisingly, you're not the first client to share a story like this."

I chuckle. "You seem to have quite the roster."

She nods. "But each one is different, so tell me a bit more about your relationship with Lily."

"She's…amazing. But I'm sure a lot of people tell you that about their…"

"Significant other?"

"Yes." Although I was about to say *fiancée*, because in my mind, I'm fully committed to Lily, regardless if she feels similarly.

I continue, "She is the one who encouraged me to go to therapy."

"Seems like you trust her opinion."

"I trust her with everything." I sigh. "Although I can't say she feels the same about me right now."

"How so?"

"I hurt her."

"What happened?" She jots more notes down on her tablet.

"How much time do you have?"

She checks her watch. "I'm all yours for another twenty minutes."

I give Doctor Martin a quick rundown of my life, from my parents being accidentally killed to me running for mayor against the man who took their lives. I explain how Lily still doesn't know because I have never figured out the best way to tell her, and now it might be too late.

"What do you mean by it being *too late*?" she asks.

"She doesn't want anything to do with me."

"Because you plan on moving away?"

I hesitate before saying, "Yes. Probably." I run a shaky hand through my hair. "I'm still deciding, but it's looking that way."

"And if you do leave, she won't move with you?"

I force a laugh. "No, and I wouldn't want her to. Lake Wisteria is everything to her."

"And what does Lake Wisteria mean to you?"

I pause, because shit. It feels like a far more nuanced question than I originally thought, so I hit her with a simple "I don't know."

I'm tired of that being my go-to response as of late. I used to be confident, but now I feel...

Lost.

Doctor Martin jots some more notes down. "Why don't you think about it over the week and we pick back up with it next time?"

"Actually...could we meet twice a week? I need to work through my shit and *fast*."

Her lips curl at the corners as she checks her calendar. "How does Friday at ten a.m. sound?"

I pull out my phone and add the session to mine. "I'll see you then."

I can't believe what I'm seeing. The paper a campaign volunteer handed me must be a joke because how can the latest polls look like *this*?

I don't want to believe it, but right there on the front page of today's edition of the *Wisteria Weekly* newspaper is a picture of Trevor and me from the debate, along with a short tagline announcing how there was no real winner.

I couldn't be happier about the polls included at the bottom of the front page because they're the best numbers I've seen yet.

Sure, I may not be in the lead, but I am *tied*, which is all the encouragement my team needs to keep pushing. We have to get out there and knock on more doors, visit town halls and attend PTA meetings.

I need to increase my overall appearances and talk to more people, giving myself as many opportunities as possible to refute Trevor's points from the debate.

"Holy shit." I drop the paper and shut my eyes.

This is really happening.

I want to share the news with Lily, so I call her without thinking twice about it.

"Is everything okay?" she asks with zero inflection.

I miss the way she used to answer my calls. She never shielded her emotions like this, and I took that generosity for granted.

"Lorenzo?" There's that same flat tone again, reminding me once more how I hurt her.

I swallow the lump in my throat. "I'm tied in the polls."

She is so quiet I can hear a set of pruning shears snapping stems in the background.

"This is better than any of us could've hoped," I add when she says nothing.

"Yeah."

"We're still in this."

She's too quiet, and it's all my fault.

"Lily?"

"Yeah."

"Talk to me."

"I have nothing to say except that I'm happy for you."

"I'm happy for *us*."

An awkward silence follows.

"Gotta go. A customer walked into the shop." Lily hangs up without waiting for me to reply.

It's for the best because I'm not sure what I would've said anyway. I could've called her out for lying about a customer since the signature Rose & Thorn bell didn't ring in the background, but I doubt that would've gone over well. Or maybe I would've begged for her to put aside all the hurt I caused and give me five minutes.

To what? Pretend like you weren't threatening to leave if you lost?

I wish I could take back all the doubt I placed in Lily's mind. All the *hurt*.

But there is no time machine that can fix my problems.

Only hard work and therapy, which is a process in itself.

My high from the news comes crashing down around me, and I'm left with an uneasy feeling in my gut for the rest of the day. I should be excited by my new numbers, but I can't shake the sense of dread taking root inside me.

You can fix this, I tell myself.

But what if you can't? the anxious voice replies, always threatening what little hope I have.

If I can't fix us, it won't be for a lack of trying on my part. I'll give her my all, and if that still isn't good enough, then I'll find a way to be *more* of whatever she needs.

Because Lily Muñoz is mine, and I'll stop at nothing until I become *hers*.

X secret garden studio

WWS ???
wildflower washes studio

Petal + press

the Pressed Petal

CHAPTER FORTY-NINE

Lily

Over the next three weeks after the debate, I keep to myself outside of planned outings with Lorenzo. At first I was nervous, but pretty much every time we go out, Lorenzo is quickly pulled into some kind of conversation with a townsperson, which is a relief.

If I could find a permanent third wheel to follow us everywhere, I would.

Lorenzo seems very accommodating lately. He even offered to return my Corolla—in fully operational condition—to which I told him no. Truth is I love my new SUV, and the thought of driving my old car is becoming progressively more difficult the longer it stays sitting in Lorenzo's garage.

After I asked him if he could find a new owner for the car, Lorenzo surprised me with a custom keychain using the

Toyota car badge—a memento I wasn't emotionally prepared for but am grateful to have dangling from my new key fob.

Whether Lorenzo's good mood is due to the recent polls or him attending therapy, I'm not entirely sure, but I make the most of it and ask if he wants to meet with the *Wisteria Weekly* reporter.

He says yes, so Nicole is going to meet us at Lorenzo's place in an hour for the interview.

I'm in the middle of getting ready for it when my sister walks into my room and shuts the door. She takes a seat on my bed, and I turn away from my vanity so I can get a good look at her.

"What's up?" I put down my eyeshadow palette.

"Why isn't Lorenzo coming to Sunday lunch tomorrow?"

"He's busy."

"Doing what?"

I shrug. "Campaign stuff."

Her head tilts curiously. "He wasn't able to make it last week either…or the week before that."

"He's had to focus on the campaign after everything with the debate. I'm sure his schedule will free up after the election in five weeks."

She tilts her head. "Is everything okay?"

I don't break eye contact, although it's difficult to maintain my sister's stare with how closely she is looking at me. "Sure. Why wouldn't it be?"

"Oh, I don't know, maybe because Rose & Thorn could be torn down and you'd have to restart somewhere else?"

"Right. Obviously I'm not okay about that," I answer,

suddenly feeling an onslaught of guilt for not thinking about my shop. With everything going on between Lorenzo and me, it didn't feel like much of a priority.

"See! That's the look right there."

My brows rise. "What look?"

"Like someone kicked Daisy."

The reminder of my dog sends another spike of heat through my chest.

"And that!"

I can no longer hold her gaze. "You're the one who brought up Rose & Thorn."

"Only because you *forgot*."

My gaze snaps back to her face. "I didn't forget." I've been...distracted.

"Maybe not entirely, but I know you." A line of worry forms between her brows. "I didn't pay close enough attention to the signs before, but I'm wide awake now, and I won't accept you telling me you're fine when clearly you're not."

I'm overwhelmed by emotion, and I don't do a good job hiding it.

She walks over to me and leans against my vanity. "What's going on?"

My eyes water because how do I explain to my sister the mess I've made of my life?

"I can't tell you." My voice cracks. I want to—I really do, ever since the very first night when Lorenzo and I committed to the plan.

"Why not?"

"Because you're going to get mad at me." I fidget with a

loose thread on my dress—a cute pink one that makes me feel confident even on the lowest of days.

"I won't."

"You say that *now*…"

"And I'll say it again after you share whatever has been bothering you for the past few weeks." She reaches for my hands and wills me to look at her. "I want to help you however I can because I don't want to watch you fade away." Her eyes flicker across my face. "Not again."

My eyes water, not only for Lorenzo and what our relationship has become but for myself. Dahlia is right. I did fade away.

But not anymore.

"I appreciate the thought, but I don't know if there is anything you can do to help me." I grab a tissue and dab at the corners of my eyes because no, I refuse to ruin my eyeliner after spending ten minutes on it.

"Don't count me or Julian out yet."

"Are you volunteering Julian without asking him?"

"I think it's better than Lorenzo extorting him, no?"

Her unwavering loyalty and support gives me the courage to share the truth about my situation, regardless of the outcome. If Lorenzo gets mad at me about it, so be it.

If he hadn't hurt me first, then I wouldn't even be in this position, so he's to blame.

Dahlia is quiet as I explain why Lavender Lane was singled out by the Ludlows and my situationship with Richard. I then open up about my fake relationship with Lorenzo, who I used to know as Laurence.

The more I share about my situation, the messier it sounds, but Dahlia doesn't judge me or vocalize her thoughts. She does hit me with an arched brow when I talk about how I naively thought I could get out of the engagement unscathed, though, and I guess I deserve that one.

I'm winded by the time I finish explaining everything up until now, minus Lorenzo's confession as to why he needs to move away if he loses.

When another minute passes without my sister saying anything, I start to panic.

"So you *are* mad."

She shakes her head. "This is…wow. I need a few minutes to process how you faked an entire relationship." Her gaze drops to my hand. "And are engaged!"

I shut my eyes with a groan. "Don't remind me."

"What were you thinking when you agreed to all that?"

"I was desperate."

"*Clearly.* But now you're saying that you genuinely have feelings for Lorenzo, so it's not really a fake relationship, then?"

"Technically yes—or it *was* real, but now it isn't again." My nose wrinkles. "Ugh. It's complicated, okay?"

"Was there ever a time it wasn't?" she deadpans.

I force a laugh.

She starts to rub her temple. "I'm starting to get a migraine."

"Same." I sift through my purse and pull out a bottle of Advil. We both knock a couple back before resuming our conversation.

"All right. I'm ready for your judgment." I bring it on with a flick of my fingers.

"I *want* to give you a hard time about this, but I'm pretty sure you're doing an incredible job of that, so I'll refrain from judging too harshly."

"Thanks for your generosity," I reply dryly.

"But…"

"I knew you were holding back."

She chuckles. "An anonymous dating app? Seriously? You were practically begging to be catfished!"

If my bed wasn't so far away, I'd grab a pillow and launch it at her head.

"Well, what happened was way worse!"

"Can I see the app? I'm curious how it looks."

My cheeks flush as I redownload the app and log back in. With how Lorenzo and I left things, I don't expect to see a new message notification in the corner from *Laurence*.

"Laurence! Like the note he left with the bracelet." Dahlia clicks on the inbox because she's a nosy brat.

"Hey!" I push her away before she can see the screen before me.

The last message has a time stamp from two days ago, but the ones before that… There are probably fifty unread messages in our chat, with the oldest one dating back to about a month ago.

Shocked doesn't scratch the surface of how I feel.

Lorenzo has been using our old chat like a diary, and I almost feel like I'm in the wrong for reading the messages, even when I know he wrote them here on purpose.

Because I can't help myself, I read the newest ones first, ignoring the way my sister does the same from over my shoulder.

LAURENCE

Doctor Martin had asked me to think about what Lake Wisteria means to me, and I finally figured out my answer three weeks later.

LAURENCE

At first Lake Wisteria was a place to escape to, but over time it became my home, and that is all because of you.

LAURENCE

If our situation was different, I'd want to spend forever in this town, and I want to spend forever with *you*.

Warmth spreads through my body, and I reread that sentence three times before Dahlia startles me.

"What does he mean by 'if our situation was different'? Does he not plan on staying here?" she asks.

"Not if he loses."

"What? Why?"

"I…I honestly don't know."

She stares at me, probably gauging how serious I am. "And you haven't pushed for an answer to literally the most important question of your entire relationship?"

"No." I stare down at my lap.

"Lily," she groans. "You have to ask him why. If not for you both to overcome it, then for closure."

"But what if it proves that I'm not good enough?"

"Did you read his messages? Because he might be a man with many issues, but none of them seem to be about *you*," she says right as the doorbell rings.

"Shit! What time is it?"

"Five."

I look at my half-finished face of makeup. "I can't go out there looking like this."

Dahlia stands with a smile. "Oh, don't worry. Lorenzo and I have a few things to catch up on."

"Dahlia…"

"I'll buy you ten minutes, so get to it." She escapes my room, careful not to trip over the random obstacles in her way.

"Be nice to him!"

"I will be, right after I give him hell first."

I almost feel bad for Lorenzo.

Emphasis on the *almost*.

I come out from my room ten minutes later, dressed and ready for our meeting with the reporter, fully expecting my sister and Lorenzo to be in the middle of a conversation.

Except I find Lorenzo sitting by himself in our living room, looking down at his phone.

"Where's Dahlia?" I ask.

He looks up and doesn't answer my question right away. Instead he takes his time checking me out. I've worn this dress twice in front of him already, but he stares at me like he's never seen it—or me—before.

Butterflies break out in my stomach, a betrayal of the worst kind given our situation. Because regardless of how good he makes me feel, we are over.

Even if he won the campaign, I wouldn't take him back. Not when he didn't feel like he had a good enough reason to stay before the results.

"My sister?" I ask again while he checks out my heels.

He clears his throat. "She had to go. But before she left, she said to remind you to ask me why I insist on moving away if I lose."

I wince. "Great." Typical Dahlia, always inserting herself into situations that I can handle myself.

"So, you told her about us?"

"Yup." I grab my purse off the hook by the front door.

"Why?"

"She knew something was wrong, so I couldn't exactly hide it from her anymore."

His frown reaches his eyes. Wanting to avoid looking into them, I open the door and wait for him to exit before I lock up behind him.

"And you told her I'd leave?"

I wait to answer him until we're in his car—some black retro sedan I don't recognize—and away from any pesky neighbors. "Not at first. She asked me to show her the Eros app, and then she saw the last couple of messages you sent—"

He snatches my phone straight from my hands. "You redownloaded the app?"

"Yes."

"Interested in meeting someone else?" He types in the password, but it fails. He scowls as he tries another code and unlocks my phone.

Mother—

"Daisy's gotcha day? Cute, but too obvious."

"Give it back!" I reach for it, but he easily keeps my hands away while deleting the app.

"Lorenzo!" I shout.

"While I'm here…" He goes ahead and deletes the entire dating app folder I had.

"When you leave, I'll redownload them, and you won't be around to prevent it from happening."

His gaze burns a path down my body. "What will the town think of you cheating on me?"

"It's not cheating if you leave me."

He ropes my ponytail around his hand and tugs. His mouth finds the hollow part of my throat, and he kisses it right before sucking at the skin.

I half groan, half moan.

"I'm not leaving you, and tonight I'll prove it once and for all."

CHAPTER FIFTY

Lorenzo

The meeting with the reporter was all Lily's idea. When she first mentioned it, I was against the suggestion given my past experiences with the media. But seeing as the *Wisteria Weekly* is a far cry from the easily influenced *Nevada Sun*, I go along with her plan.

If I want to win, I need to make the most of every opportunity, which is why I invited Nicole over to my house for an official interview. Lily is the ultimate hostess, apologizing on Daisy's behalf when she nearly sends Nicole into a wall, and I can picture her doing the same for years to come.

Thinking about Lily and our future seems to be happening more often than not lately. It's clear I love her, and therapy has only further cemented the idea in my head, although I haven't wanted to admit it aloud, but I'm done lying to myself.

Besides her smile and laugh, I love how compassionate and patient she is, and I admire how she doesn't back down from her promise, even though I can tell it is difficult for her to spend time with me each week.

I love the way she has turned my home into her own without knowing it, and I love how easily she fits into my life like she's always had a place in it.

And once Nicole leaves, I'll tell her that.

It takes me ten minutes to determine that Nicole is nothing like the *Nevada Sun* reporter, and I should've assumed as much because Lily would never put me in that kind of position to begin with.

Once we get past the pleasantries, Nicole pulls out a notepad and her phone. "I appreciate you both taking time out of your Saturday to meet with me. I'm still catching up on a few things after I got sick last week."

She hits the Record button on her phone.

"No worries." Lily smiles.

"We appreciate you wanting to speak with us." I reach for Lily's hand and lace our fingers together.

Nicole glances at our clasped hands before looking up with a smile. "Lily's told me so much about you."

"All good things," Lily adds. "Except for you not being a Detroit Lion's fan."

Nicole places her palm against her heart. "I'm still processing that one."

"How much will it cost me to have that fact excluded from the article?" I tease.

She grins. "Are you kidding? That's making it onto the front page."

"There goes the election…"

The reporter laughs. "While we're on the subject, let's talk more about that. What pushed you into running?"

I consider repeating the generic statement Willow and I have gone over what feels to be a hundred times, but I offer a new one instead.

"I believe the town is facing a hypothetical fork in the road, and it is up for them to decide which path to take. Both can lead toward prosperity—where one brings money and wealth to a select few while the other allows for a higher quality of life for everyone. I've been clear about where I stand, which is why I'd rather step up now and fight for a town I believe in than sit back and wish I did something about it later."

Nicole writes down notes while I speak.

"And with Lily's shop on the line, I wouldn't be able to live with myself if I didn't give this campaign my all."

Lily squeezes my hand, and I look over to find her staring at me with a wobbly smile.

"Thank you," she says.

Nicole glances back and forth at us before asking, "Your shop is on Lavender Lane, right?"

"Yes," Lily replies, her voice dejected.

"That's quite the coincidence that the Ludlows chose that street, then." Nicole jots more notes down with a frown.

I scoff. "I don't believe in those."

"Neither do I," she replies, and I like her even more.

"Will you tell me more about this architect firm they hired?"

I go into detail about the firm, and then Nicole asks me about Trevor's biggest sticking point: Vittori Holdings.

"Do you still keep in contact with your family?"

"No. It's not a subject I like to talk about," I add. "While I care for my cousins, it's no secret that my uncle and I parted ways on bad terms, so I've had to cut myself off from everyone to protect my peace, and anyone with complex family dynamics can probably relate to that."

The reporter writes down a few more notes before asking, "Is that why you sold your Vittori Holdings shares, or were there other factors at play?"

"Yes to both of your questions. No one wakes up one day and leaves a billion-dollar company without justifiable cause, so my decision was a long time coming, and my uncle's choice to tear down my father's legacy was the final straw. All those rumors about me selling my shares because the investors weren't happy with me were false. The company's value didn't tank solely because of business choices I played a part in making, although people were quick to make me the scapegoat.

"Long story short: My values didn't align with that of the company's CEO, who unfortunately is my uncle. Of course he took my departure personally. He expected me to fall in line with the other board members, but I refused to be part of a company that prioritizes greed over morals. I'd rather stay true to myself than become a sellout, so I left."

Lily's eyes soften at the corners. I wish I could read her thoughts, if only to know what brought out that look from her.

Nicole's pen flies across her notepad. "It's a different kind of loyalty."

"Exactly," I reply.

Trevor let the town assume I wasn't loyal, and I'm correcting the narrative. By the time Nicole is done, he will look like the ass while I keep coming out on top, hopefully with Lily by my side.

Nicole glances up. "If you don't mind me asking, what brought your parents to Lake Wisteria originally?"

I explain my mom's childhood briefly and my parents meeting in Vegas before saying, "After my parents got married, my mom wanted to leave Vegas, and since my dad's biggest priority was to make her happy, they ended up moving."

She nods. "And then you followed in their footsteps."

"It felt like the right path to take."

"Imagine if you hadn't." She glances back and forth between Lily and me.

"I don't like to think about it." I kiss the back of Lily's hand, not for show but for comfort.

Nicole raises her brow. "I'm curious—you could've moved anywhere in the world after selling your Vittori Holdings shares, but you chose to come back here. Why is that?"

"There was something about Lake Wisteria that felt… right. So, I took a chance and moved back, and soon enough, it started to feel like *home*. Not only because of the town and the people in it but because of one specific person."

I look at Lily while I say the last part so she knows I'm speaking to her as her boyfriend rather than a fake fiancé. "Lily showed me what my life could look like, and it's that vision that keeps me motivated. It holds me accountable and pushes me to want the best for this town, both for her and the future family we want to raise here."

"That's beautiful." Nicole clears her throat, but I don't take my eyes off Lily.

I watch the way her eyes water as what I said sinks in, and I know that I can't go another day without telling her how I feel because doing so in front of strangers feels wrong.

She deserves all my words, even the ones she doesn't want to hear, and tonight she's going to hear them. Whether she decides to reciprocate them is up to her.

"I'm proud of you for meeting with the reporter," Lily says once I return to the living room after seeing Nicole out.

"Really?"

She nods. "I know it was the last thing you wanted to do, but I think it'll be good for the campaign."

I take a seat beside her. Before she can protest, I pull her in before calling Daisy to take a seat on her other side.

She might let out a huff of disapproval, but the way she sinks into my side is promising.

I kiss the top of her head because I can't resist. "Thank you. For all you're doing to help me win. It means more to me than you'll ever know."

She pulls back all too soon, her face going blank. "We all benefit if you do."

"Yeah, that's true, but I like to think you also do it because you like me."

"So?"

"So, it means all that much more to me."

"Lorenzo…" she warns, but against what, I'm not entirely sure.

"Do you still like me?" I ask.

"I thought you didn't like asking questions you already know the answer to."

"I need to hear it," I answer honestly.

"Why?"

"Because I'm losing my mind without you."

"I'm right here."

"Yes, but it's not the same." The knot in my stomach tightens. "I miss you." I whisper it like a confession. "I miss you so damn much, Lily, and I didn't think I was capable of missing someone this badly."

"How is that even possible? I've seen you almost every day these last three weeks." There is a hint of disbelief to her tone.

"Yeah, but things between us are not the same."

She exhales slowly through her nose. "What did you expect would happen after the debate? Did you expect me to keep putting my heart on the line for someone who isn't willing to do the same?"

"No, of course not. But I didn't know how difficult it would be to watch you pull away."

Her lips purse with distaste. "Don't try to guilt-trip me."

"I'm saying this because I'm trying to be honest and open about my feelings instead of keeping them to myself. That's all."

Yet you haven't told her about your parents and Trevor yet.

I want to, but what if she thinks I'm only telling her now because I want her to forgive me?

Fuck. The thought of that happening makes my stomach turn.

"It doesn't matter anymore. We're done." Her voice breaks at the end.

I should respect her boundaries, but I can't. Not at the expense of losing her altogether.

I can see it happening slowly, right in front of my eyes, and if I don't do something about it fast, it won't matter whether I win or lose the election.

Because I would've already lost her, and the thought of that happening is unfathomable.

"If we're done, then kiss me. Show me how unaffected you are by our connection—show me how much it doesn't matter," I taunt because screw it. Let her show me since she's so big on actions.

She rears back. "What?"

"You heard me." I pause. "Prove to me that we're over, and I'll never ask you about our relationship again."

She shakes her head. "No."

"No, you don't want me to do that? Or no, you're too scared to accept that we will never be over. We weren't a year ago, and we sure as hell aren't now."

Her eyes spark with anger. "Why are you doing this?"

"Because I can't let you go."

"I never wanted you to." Her confession sits heavy between us.

"Good, because I won't." I slide my hands through her hair, keeping her head in place. "I'm sorry for ever making you believe I could."

Her eyes shut, and I lightly tug on her strands so she reopens them.

"I was a fool for thinking I could walk away. I'd rather spend the rest of my life in therapy, working through my personal issues if it means I get to come home to you every day."

She shakes her head.

"You might not believe me now, but I won't stop until you do," I say with absolute certainty. "I'm not running away or giving up if I lose the election, which is why I've started therapy now rather than later. Because win or lose, I want to stay in this town and build a life together. It won't be easy. I won't deny that, but I do know you're worth it.

"A few months ago, I stupidly said you were too much for me, but the truth is, *I'm* the one who wasn't enough. I'm still not, and I'm not sure I ever will be, but that won't stop me from giving you my all, and I'm sorry that my actions made you question that."

Her eyes water. "What if you change your mind?"

"I won't. So long as you want to stay here, then I do too."

"You need to stop saying all the right things."

I hold her chin. "Why does that upset you so much?"

She looks up, giving me a clear view of her eyes welling with tears. "Because I don't *want* to believe what you're saying."

I lean forward and tilt her head, leaving enough room for her to be in control of whether she wants to kiss me.

"What are my actions showing you, then?" I ask instead.

Her eyes drop to my mouth. "I don't know."

"Yes, you do." I brush her bottom lip with my thumb.

She shakes her head.

"Did you read all my messages on the app?"

She hesitates before nodding.

"Then you *know*, Lily."

Her chin wobbles. "It doesn't matter."

"Why?"

"Because I was tricked by your actions before, and I thought…" Her face turns progressively more red.

"You thought what?"

She tries to avoid my gaze, but I cradle her face and force her to look at me. "Tell me."

"I thought you were falling in love with me," she whispers.

"Ask me," I command, and she shakes her head. "Ask me how I feel," I repeat.

Her eyes screw shut. "I wouldn't believe you anyway."

Pain laces through my heart, sharp and all-consuming. It makes me want to lash out, but I hold back and refocus my energy into more productive emotions.

I cup the back of her head. "The only liar here is *you*, and I'll prove it."

I seal my mouth over hers before she can say anything else, and I won't let her go until she finally accepts the truth once and for all.

CHAPTER FIFTY-ONE

Lily

A person can only take so much before they break, and Lorenzo saying he misses me ruined my plan of staying away from him today.

I could *see* the truth in his sad eyes and in the dark shadows cast underneath them, as if he has been sleeping poorly like me since the debate. I see it in the text messages he sends me throughout the day, checking in on me despite having access to my location through the bracelet he gave me.

Every time I remind myself that I should be angry at him, the emotion is quickly replaced by another one any time we are in the same room.

Sadness, since being in his presence reminds me of his betrayal.

Love, because no matter how many times I lie to myself, I know it won't go away overnight, and maybe it never will.

But most of all, I am *fearful*, knowing that if I accept his actions as honest ones, then I'll run out of reasons to be mad at him. And if I'm no longer angry at him, then I have no reason to stay away.

Not a single one, other than the fear of him hurting me again.

I try to hold on to that thought, but once his lips meet mine, I forget all about my anger. My fears. Everything fades into the background, my worries becoming white noise as he kisses me.

Against all my instincts, I shut my eyes and allow myself to enjoy the moment. Sparks scatter down my spine as he slides his hands through my hair and holds me in place, his lips a soft cushion for mine.

He takes his time, and he intentionally drags out our kiss, forcing me to catalogue every single way my body responds to his.

My stomach flips. My breath stalls. My heart stops before finding its rhythm again. All from a stupid, simple *peck*.

To keep him from gloating, I deepen the kiss, my arms circling around his neck so I can pull him. He follows my lead, and I hate him for it.

I don't want to be in charge. I want my brain to shut off for a few minutes and allow him to take control so I don't blame myself when all this comes crashing down around me.

The next few minutes play out like snapshots in a movie, almost like an out-of-body experience.

Me climbing onto Lorenzo's lap so I can comfortably kiss him without hurting my neck.

Him standing with my legs wrapped around his waist, only breaking our kiss so he can safely walk up the stairs.

Us kissing against his bedroom door with Daisy whining on the other side, her high-pitched sound making Lorenzo pull away from the door and toss me onto the bed.

I don't recognize myself as I get rid of Lorenzo's shirt and pants before yanking his boxers down. His erection slaps against his toned stomach, and my mouth waters with anticipation.

When I reach for him, he seems to snap out of his lust-induced daze and takes a step back.

"What are you doing?" I hiss.

He stands at the foot of the bed and presses his clenched fists into the mattress. "I don't want you to regret this tomorrow."

"I won't." Or will I?

I can't think straight with the way he looks at me, his eyes a window to his beautifully broken soul. "This isn't only sex for me," he says softly, as if I didn't feel his words down to the marrow of my bones.

"What else could it be?"

"You know."

My chin lifts defiantly. "I'm getting tired of you saying that."

"I'd love to say something else, but I'm waiting on you."

"Why?"

"Because you have all the control here."

Do I? Because I feel like a prisoner in a cage of my own making, and Lorenzo is my warden. I'll spend forever tied to him, whether it be due to the strings of fate or by shackles of lust.

He climbs onto the bed and crawls slowly toward me, his hands brushing up the length of my calves, then my thighs, before they land on my hips.

His smile is arrogant as he lifts my dress high enough to reveal the wet spot on my underwear.

"Tell me what else this could be, baby."

First *amore mio*, then *baby*? I'm a goner in two different languages—that much becomes clear from the way my stomach clenches.

"I'm not your baby." My voice trembles, whether it be from adrenaline coursing through my veins or anger at him for dragging out this process after being the one to initiate it.

"Do you prefer *amore mio*?" He slips his hand under the band of my panties and pulls them slowly down my thighs.

"I prefer that you put your mouth to better use."

"How quickly that happens depends on *you*."

I spread my legs wider and tilt my hips in a universal sign to say *Put your mouth on my pussy, please*. He moves forward, close enough for the tip of his nose to trace my soaked slit, and goose bumps explode across my body.

He reaches over and nips me in the thigh. "You're so damn hard-headed."

"Why does it matter if this means anything to me?"

"*Everything* about you matters to me."

My scoff comes out forced.

Lorenzo takes a deep breath and groans against my center, and I swear, I nearly give in. I'm not the stronger Muñoz sister, and I don't want to be if it means denying myself what I want.

"Is it so hard to believe?"

Yes, I want to say.

"You're my fiancée, Lily," he replies, as if that's supposed to answer any lingering doubts.

"None of this is *real*."

He drags two fingers through my wetness before bringing them to his mouth and sucking on them. "Tastes pretty fucking real to me." His tongue darts out to lick them clean, and my lower half throbs as I picture him doing the same to me.

He then yanks my thighs wide open as far as they'll go, making me gasp when he shoves his face against my core. His possessive hold on my thighs tightens as he inhales.

"Smells that way too." The tip of his nose presses into me, and my eyes flutter closed before they snap open again when he sinks two fingers inside me. He unleashes a low laugh that rolls through me.

"If this isn't real, then why are you soaked for me?" He doesn't let me answer. "Why are you in *my* bed, wearing *my* ring, lying beneath me with your legs spread and your greedy pussy begging to be filled?" A third finger joins his other two, and my back bows from the pleasurable stretch.

I can't answer him, and even if I wanted to, my mouth and brain aren't cooperating long enough to formulate a coherent sentence.

"Do you need more proof, *amore mio*?" He hits the spot that sends my eyes rolling into the back of my head. "Or are you ready to admit that this is real?"

I somehow manage a single word. "No."

"Good." His lips curl into a knowing smile as he pulls his hand out, grips my thighs, and wrenches them open. "You know I love a challenge."

My eyes widen.

His are two glittering orbs, privy to something I'm not. "Fight me all night long on this if you feel the need to. I promise I'll enjoy every second of it. But make no mistake—you're not leaving this bed until you admit the truth about us."

I huff. "You can't keep me here forever."

"Why not? It's not like you'll hear me complaining."

His words…the look in his eyes…it's too much yet also not enough at the same time.

I go to slam my thighs shut, but his fingers dig into my flesh, holding me in place for his viewing pleasure.

"Lorenzo," I say, my lower half throbbing for some kind of relief. "Please."

"I know, baby. Don't worry—I'll take good care of you."

He says it like a promise. Like he is making a vow that has no expiration date, and I'm inclined to believe him.

He gets comfortable between my legs, his shoulders nudging my thighs as wide as they'll go as his mouth hovers over me.

His arrogant smile would make anyone wave a white flag of surrender because I already lost. I know it, he knows it, and my aching pussy knows it too, that traitorous bitch.

"Fuck." My back bows when he finally puts his mouth to good use.

He somehow mastered my body in a way that makes me

feel like he's been familiar with it for years. He knows exactly how much pressure it takes to make me moan and how to tease me until I'm grinding against his face, begging for some kind of relief.

He provides me with a continuous wave of pleasure. One that rolls through me with every stroke, lick, and flick of his tongue, my orgasm rising like the crest of a wave until it finally breaks.

I black out at some point, and during that time, Lorenzo crawls up my body and seals his mouth to mine. His fingers sink into my hair, and he cradles my head as our tongues intertwine, the taste of me flooding my mouth.

I could kiss him for the rest of my life, and it will always feel like the very first time. Butterflies exploding. Sparks flying. A heat spreading through my lower half, pulsing every time he rocks forward.

I'm gasping by the time he finally pulls away, and I open my mouth to protest, only for a moan to slip out when he kisses a path across my jaw, along my throat, straight down toward the swell of my breast. When my dress becomes an annoying barrier, he slides his hands underneath and pulls it over my head. My bra follows a similar fate until I'm completely naked and at his mercy.

Lorenzo traces the curves of my breasts with his fingertip, my nipple pebbling when he grazes it with his nail. I arch my back when he flicks his tongue across the sensitive peak, and a jolt of desire ricochets through me as he sucks.

I'm squirming and covered in a few love marks by the time he slides a finger inside me again. We both groan at the same time, his sounding far more tortured than mine.

He adds another finger, which adds the slightest bit of pressure. "You want more, baby?"

My core spasms when he curls his finger.

"Do you like it when I call you baby?"

I shiver from the way the pet name naturally rolls off his tongue.

He nips at my abused bottom lip when I don't answer him.

"No." I lie when he finds that sensitive spot inside me.

"It's okay to admit it." I can *hear* him smiling, but I refuse to open my eyes to check. "Because I like it too."

"Look at me," he demands, halting his movement.

When I realize he won't continue unless I listen, I follow his command. His eyes are a blazing fire, threatening to consume me until there's nothing left but ash.

"Do you want more?" he asks, his voice raspy, as if he is the one being pleasured right now.

"Yes," I confess with a weak voice.

He slips a third finger inside, stretching me until I can no longer keep my eyes open.

"Let me make you happy." The way he says it makes me think he is talking about more than sex. Again.

"I'll be the happiest after I come."

He chuckles while continuing his slow, blissful torture.

"Please." I reach for his cock and find pre-cum dripping from the tip.

"Depends on if you're ready to accept what's happening between us."

He sucks in a sharp breath when I tease the head with my thumb, collecting his arousal before bringing it to my mouth.

His sharp eyes follow my tongue as it darts out to taste his pleasure.

"How do I taste?" His husky voice hits me like a powerful aphrodisiac.

"Like *mine*."

"Look who's the possessive one now." More arousal coats his crown, a clear sign of how he feels about our mutual obsession.

I want to take him into my mouth, but Lorenzo seems to have other plans as he pulls his fingers back.

He lines his cock up, only to rear back with a curse. I never thought I'd enjoy a man forgetting to put on a condom, but Lorenzo being so out of his mind from lust makes me smile.

His body is visibly trembling by the time he puts a condom on and returns to his spot between my thighs.

"You okay?" I ask when he doesn't speak.

He wraps a hand around his shaft and drags it across my slit. "I will be."

I wrap my legs around his waist to draw him closer. His control is far better than mine, because with every swipe of his tip over my dripping center, I feel my hold on reality slip.

"Lorenzo," I whine, my voice unrecognizable to my own ears.

"Tell me what we both need to hear."

We. Not him. Not me. But *we*.

"I want you to fuck me," I say, hoping it does the trick.

He abandons his idea and reaches underneath my ass to lift me up instead. "Try again."

"I need your cock inside me. Right. Now."

His fingers dig into my flesh hard enough to bruise. Since his hands are occupied, I reach for his dick, but he has my hands secured above my head before I can touch him.

"Since you're having trouble, I'll give you a hint. Three words. Eight letters—five of which are vowels."

"I hate you."

His kiss is punishing. *Brutal*. So damn possessive, I'm convinced my lips will carry the evidence of his abuse for days to come.

"I'm feeling extra generous with you today, so I'll give you one more try."

"Why are you doing this?" Frustrated tears spring to my eyes.

"Because I want a chance to say it back."

I feel like he wrapped his hands around my throat rather than my wrists. "You love me?"

He stares at me, his face a blank slate of nothing.

The walls feel as if they're closing in around me, and my ears start ringing, drowning out whatever Lorenzo is trying to say.

We can both admit how far we've fallen, but what if it isn't enough? Lorenzo could change his mind tomorrow about staying, and—

He releases my hands so he can cradle my face. "Hey."

I don't respond.

"Take a deep breath."

I follow his command.

His mouth curls. "It'll be okay, all right?"

"How do you know?"

"Because so long as I love you and you love me, we can get through anything together. That much I can promise."

A single tear falls down my cheek, and he kisses it away like it never existed. He then kisses my cheeks. The tip of my nose. The corner of my lips, the top of my forehead, and the curve of my jaw.

I've never felt so loved in my life. So *cherished*. Maybe that's why I finally give Lorenzo the three words he has been waiting to hear.

"I love you," I say as I fight to keep the tears at bay.

His sharpness melts away, his eyes softening in a way that I've never seen happen around anyone else.

"I love you too," he repeats—first in English, then in Italian—as he sinks inside me.

He says he loves me as he drives into me, his pace going from soft and slow to deliriously unrelenting. He says it while he leaves kisses on every inch of my skin within his reach, and he works the same phrase out of me a few times.

But nothing compares to the way I *feel* loved when we both finally come. He cuddles me first, and then he kisses me until I'm breathless again, which was probably a strategy to keep me in bed while he grabbed a washcloth from the bathroom and cleaned me up.

When the post-orgasmic haze disappears and the warmth from earlier fades, I'm left feeling cold, pulsing dread because can I really trust what Lorenzo said?

Has our situation changed, or did we only complicate it more with deeper, more complex feelings?

"Don't," he says, as if commanding me will stop the mix of guilt and panic brewing in my stomach.

I can't look at him as he grabs a fresh pair of underwear for me from the dresser. They're not a pair I purchased, but they're the same brand he yanked off me earlier.

His attention to detail should make me happy, but it only makes the fear growing inside me worsen.

"Lily. No. You don't get to doubt us now." He climbs back onto the bed and cups my cheeks. "And you do not get to regret telling me you love me. Do you hear me?"

"But what if—"

He slams his mouth over mine, kissing me until I forget about whatever I was protesting about.

His breathing is ragged by the time he pulls away.

"Get angry at me. Yell at me. Ask me a hundred questions, and I'll answer each one honestly—"

"Tell me why you said you'd leave if you lost the election."

His lips press firmly together.

"You promised to be honest."

He nods. "I did." He slowly slides off the bed and heads to the closet.

"Where are you going?" I rise onto my elbows.

The closet's automatic light switches on, revealing a row of dresses in all shapes, materials, and vivid colors. Not a single black stitch to be accounted for.

If I didn't have a bigger task to focus on, I'd ask him when he bought all those clothes for me. My guess is sometime before the debate.

Lorenzo disappears around the corner and returns carrying one of his T-shirts. I throw it on while he pulls on a pair of new boxer briefs.

"So?" I say once we're both no longer naked.

"Do you want a drink for this conversation?"

"Do I need one?"

"Maybe."

I shake my head. "I'll take Daisy though."

He opens the door and calls her name. She runs down the hall and skids to a stop by his feet, and I expect him to order her to the dog bed in the corner. Instead he pats the mattress, and she jumps onto the bed and curls into a ball beside me.

That should've been my first clue that I wouldn't like whatever he is about to share, but it's the second one that makes me uneasy. Because Lorenzo is visibly *trembling*, and I'm no longer afraid of how he could hurt me but rather what could've hurt *him*.

X secret garden studio

WWS ???
wildflower rushes studio

petd + press

The Pressed Petal

CHAPTER FIFTY-TWO

Lily

When I saw the look in Lorenzo's eyes, I knew I wasn't mentally prepared for this conversation, but I didn't realize how unequipped I was until he begins talking.

"Trevor killed my parents."

"Trevor...Ludlow?" I ask, too shocked by the news to fully process it the first time.

He nods.

The faint ringing sound in my ears grows louder as I mentally spiral. In my head, ten different questions pop up, none of which make it past my parted lips.

Lorenzo begins pacing the space in front of the bed. "He was out late, drinking at some bonfire with all his friends."

Even though I know how this story ends, my throat still closes up like someone wrapped their hand around my neck.

Lorenzo continues walking back and forth, his body riddled with tension, and his hands visibly shaking. "Trevor could've walked home if he wanted to. He lived that close to the beach where he and his buddies were drinking. But no, he decided to *drive* like an entitled, reckless brat who thinks they're untouchable."

Thankfully I'm not standing because I'm hit with a dizzy spell. I concentrate on Lorenzo, as if I'm lost at sea and he is my horizon.

"If he were my friend, I would've stolen the keys straight from his hands, but clearly Trevor was surrounded by all the wrong ones. Or maybe they tried to block him from driving, but they clearly didn't try hard enough because who tells a Ludlow what to do?" The bitterness in his tone isn't directed at me, but it feels like it with how harshly Lorenzo speaks.

"No one," I murmur.

He nods, the movement short and stiff. "So, he drove, and still to this day, I'm not sure where he was going because he ended up on the opposite side of town—" His sentence ends with the break in his voice.

"No." Acid crawls up my throat at an alarming rate.

"If he drove straight home... If he paid attention to where he was going, my parents might still be here today. No, I'm sure they would be because Trevor wouldn't have hit them. He could've gone home and slept it off, and my parents would've never ended up dying in a ditch."

He whispers the next part, sounding more like the ten-year-old child who lost his parents than a bitter adult with a score to settle. "They would've come back home to *me*."

I don't notice I'm crying until Daisy starts licking my face.

"For a while, before I found out the truth, I blamed my parents." He looks down with shame. "Why did they insist on driving the sick dog to the vet in the middle of the night? Why couldn't they wait until morning?

"The dog didn't even make it. Not because of the accident, which he miraculously survived, but from kidney complications." His pain is a living, breathing entity, and I absorb it like my own.

With an experience like that, I'm surprised he wanted to adopt Daisy.

Because he wanted her for you.

Daisy butts her head against my chest, and I wrap my arms around her neck while wishing I could hug Lorenzo instead. Something tells me he needs to get this out without any interruption, so I hold off.

"Eventually I learned the truth about everything that happened, and it made me sick." The words tumble out of him without any pause, and he isn't the only one who feels sickened by the news. "Trevor called his dad first. Can you believe that? Not 911, but his *dad*."

My heart pumps furiously in my chest.

Lorenzo shakes his head with disgust. "And then the mayor called his brother, who was a deputy at the time."

I'm so disgusted by the entire cover-up, I can't begin to describe how I feel about it, but I think my expression must do the job because Lorenzo frowns when he turns to look at me.

"It was more than an abuse of power. It was…"

"One of the most awful things a person can do," I answer.

His voice drops. "I'll never know if they could've gotten help in time, and that's what haunts me most. It keeps me up at night sometimes, thinking about their last moments and whether they were bleeding out in front of each other, praying for help but never getting it."

I'm full-on sobbing by this point.

"How did you…" I can't even finish the sentence because it's too horrible. To think that not only did Trevor Ludlow kill Lorenzo's parents but then tried to cover up the crime?

Absolutely unforgivable.

"How did I what?" Lorenzo asks softly. "Find out about everything?"

I nod with tears streaming down my face.

"I hired one of the best private investigators in the nation to get to the bottom of the case. His methods were expensive but effective."

"And he connected it back to Trevor?"

"Yeah. There were too many coincidences to ignore."

"How did your PI figure out it was him of all people?"

A dark look passes over his face.

I don't like it, so I ask, "What?"

"Will you take my word for it when I say that I'm certain I have the right guy?"

"You don't want to tell me," I state, not sure how to feel about that.

"Only because it wasn't legal."

"What did you do? Break into the mayor's house?" I laugh it off, only for the sound to die halfway out of my mouth at the serious look on Lorenzo's face.

His lips press together. "Not exactly…"

"You know what? I'd rather not know."

"I thought so." Some of the tension in his shoulders loosens.

"But if you have evidence, why not come out with it?"

"Michigan has a ten-year statute of limitations for manslaughter, so even if I wanted to, I couldn't."

My heart sinks. "Fine, but you could tell everyone and prevent him from becoming mayor, right?" There has to be something Lorenzo can do.

He halts his pacing and sits on the edge of the bed, between me and Daisy, with one hand on my calf and the other on our dog.

"Not without admitting my own crimes, I can't. It isn't worth the risk, and it would be challenging for people to accept illegally obtained evidence anyway."

My idea of forcing Trevor to leave town dies. "Oh."

He offers me a reassuring smile, as if I'm the one who needs comfort, not him, the man running for mayor against the person who killed his parents.

The same man he would have to see for the rest of his life should he choose to stay here because of *me*.

An arc of pain shoots through me.

"What?" he asks, searching for whatever caused my pinched expression.

"If you lose…" It wouldn't affect him because of his ego like I had falsely assumed but because he would lose to the person who took already took everything away from him.

Of course he can't live here if that happens, in a town where people let him down yet again.

His gaze flickers across my face, and wrinkles of concern appear across his forehead. "Don't worry about that."

"How can I not?"

"Because we have five weeks left and I finally caught up to him in the polls."

"He killed your parents, Lorenzo. That's..." My eyes burn from unshed tears. "I completely understand why you don't want to stay, and I would never ask you to." I look down at my lap in shame. "I wish you'd told me sooner." The last sentence comes out as a whisper.

I would've never given him such a hard time about leaving if I had known, and the guilt is eating me alive. "I'm sorry for treating you the way I did—"

"You're not allowed to blame yourself." He scoots me over and pulls me into his arms. "You didn't know because I didn't want you to, so anything you said or any way you acted was completely justified."

I nestle deeper into his chest and mumble the words that have been lying on the tip of my tongue. "If you lose, you shouldn't stay."

His arms wrapped around me stiffen. "I am."

"No." I fight like hell not to cry. "You can't." I won't let him, which is why I say, "There are other towns nearby where we can have a fresh start."

"We?"

"Yeah, *we*. Do you have a problem with that?"

He looks at me like he isn't sure what to do with me.

Same.

He shakes his head.

"Good," I say. "Then let's focus on winning and take it from there." I hope to change the subject with a quick pat on his chest.

He kisses the top of my head before reaching for the remote. "What are you in the mood for?"

"Something happy, please."

He flips through the channels before landing on a nineties comedy about a girl with a computer-operated closet full of amazing outfits and an interest in playing matchmaker for two teachers.

"The things I would do for a closet like that," I say as I watch the blonde girl pick out her outfit for the day.

He smirks. "That could be arranged."

"Speaking of closets…" I tilt my head back so I can look up at him. "When are we going to talk about yours?"

He raises the volume like an ass.

"I saw all the clothes," I speak louder.

"Mm-hmm," he replies.

"Were you planning on showing me anytime soon?"

"Not until you told me you love me."

"Why?"

"I'm not interested in buying your love. Where's the fun in that?"

"I already love you, so that's not possible."

He rolls on top of me, keeping most of his weight off me. "Say it again."

"I love you."

He claims my mouth like he does my heart, an unapologetic takeover of my mind, body, and soul.

"Again," he says after breaking away.

"*Te amo.*" I brush the hair out of his eyes.

"*Anch'io ti amo, amore mio.*"

"I know, baby." Which is why I'll never let him go, not now that I know for sure he loves me back.

Wherever Lorenzo goes, I will follow, whether it be a few towns over or across the world.

Plus if Trevor wins, I don't want to stay here anyway for multiple reasons, but most of all because I could never put Lorenzo through that kind of pain.

He shouldn't have to choose between the woman he loves and his own mental health, and I won't allow him to.

It will be hard, but I can restart anywhere, so long as it's with him.

"Well, well," Dahlia says the next morning, scaring the shit out of me as we both sneak back into the house at the same time.

She gives me a quick pass. "From the state of your hair and makeup, I take it Lorenzo finally cleared up a few of your issues?"

I blush. "Shut up."

"Oh, no. I'm going to keep pestering until you spill some deets."

I'm tempted to ignore her as I head to the kitchen, but that'll only encourage her. "Not much to share."

"You spent all night together, and based on the bags under your eyes, I don't think you did much sleeping." She waggles her brows.

"I hate you." I grab a protein bar from the pantry.

"I'm only saying…" She smiles.

"Yes, we talked things out and we're finally in agreement on a few things. Does that satisfy your curiosity?"

"Come on. Give me a little more than that." She bats her lashes, and I reluctantly concede to her request.

"We talked about our future."

Her grin widens. "And?"

I glance away for this next part. "If he loses, we're going to move."

"What?" she whisper-shouts. "You can't leave! Not when I moved back here."

I make a face. "I love him, Dahlia, so if he wants to go, then I'll follow him."

"Why isn't he willing to stay if he loses?"

I can't tell her about his past without his permission, and honestly I doubt I'll ever ask for it. That's Lorenzo's story to tell, and if he doesn't want to, I'm not going to pressure him into doing so.

Instead I say, "I don't want to stay here if Trevor wins either."

Let her think it's because Trevor wants to tear down my business and Richard is an ass, which, while important, aren't the deciding factors.

Lorenzo is.

Dahlia raises her chin. "Then we need to make sure he wins."

"*We?*"

She nods. "I'm not going to let my baby sister and her man get run out of the town they love."

"And how are you going to do that?"

She cracks a smile I'm way too familiar with. In my experience, it can either end with the best results or temporary jail time.

I have no idea what Dahlia has planned, but I can only hope it leads to promising results because the campaign and my future in Lake Wisteria are counting on it.

CHAPTER FIFTY-THREE

Lorenzo

As much as I want to spend the next few days with Lily, I have an election to win, so I resist the desire to hole up in my house with her. She is always understanding of my busy schedule, and she doesn't make me feel bad when I have to cancel our weeknight dinner because a city council member wanted to meet with me.

She asks for nothing except two things: that I continue going to my therapy sessions no matter how busy I get—I reassure her that I have no intention of stopping, although there are some days where I'm tempted—and that I start sharing my location with her on my phone.

I went from being the stalker to becoming the stalked, and I'm not mad about it since I still do the same with Lily's bracelet app. Doctor Martin says we will have to work on my checking behavior eventually, but I'm still holding off.

I'd rather tackle my other compulsions first before I approach any Lily-related ones because I know those will be the hardest to manage. Her safety is on my mind often lately, along with her emotional well-being, which needs to be protected at all costs.

The only times Lily and I get together over the next week are always in public, surrounded by way too many people. People who like to politely interrupt us to ask us about our upcoming engagement party or chat with me about my stance on random topics related to the town.

I've always had people pull me aside to ask about small-town issues that relate to them, but now it is happening more than ever before, which is a positive for my campaign but a negative for my social life.

Lily is a good sport about it, and she never gets annoyed, even when I end up spending twenty minutes of our cake-tasting date talking to the couple seated next to us about the impact of Ludlow's budget cuts on the recreational center. Nor does she seem the least bit bothered when I get pulled aside during Trivia Night at Last Call because a constituent wanted to speak to me about affordable housing for seniors.

Next thing I know, we garner attention from a group of people sitting nearby, turning the double-date night with Julian and Dahlia into a mini town hall. Last Call's owner eventually brings out a mic for me to use, and I spend the night informally answering questions while Lily, Dahlia, and Julian watch from our booth.

Julian claps me on the shoulder as we're walking out of the bar a couple hours later. "I do not envy you whatsoever."

"Likewise." I give him a once-over.

He ignores the jab. "I don't know how you do it. If I had to stand up in front of that many people and speak…" A shudder rolls through him.

"I don't think about it while I'm up there."

"I'm honestly impressed."

"Are you…complimenting me?"

He takes a deep breath and holds it.

I grin. "I'm sure it kills you to admit such a thing."

"I think this whole conversation took five years off my life, yes."

We both laugh, which makes Dahlia and Lily turn to face us.

"Oh my God," Dahlia says.

Lily gasps. "Did they become besties?"

"No," Julian and I reply at the same time.

Dahlia and Lily laugh.

"We're…" Julian stammers.

"Poking fun at each other."

Dahlia bats her lashes. "And now they're finishing each other's sentences?"

Lily nods with a smug smile. "Definitely besties."

By the time Saturday comes around, I'm overstimulated and ready to take a break from socializing, but Willow scheduled a huge door-knocking campaign with all the volunteers, so I have to participate regardless of my desire to rot on the couch.

When I arrive at the campaign headquarters with boxes of doughnuts and coffee, I'm surprised to find seven new people waiting beside all the other volunteers. Lily, Dahlia, and Rosa stand next to Josefina, who looks like she dragged Julian here against his will. Ellie, who has always been supportive in my brainstorming meetings with Willow, smiles in my direction while Rafa watches her.

All of them are wearing *Vote Vittori* shirts, and I won't say it makes me sentimental, but it does mean more to me than they'll ever know.

I didn't notice Daisy until Lily walks over to where I am standing, watching everyone with a slack jaw and raised brows.

"Hey." She kisses me on the cheek.

"How did you get them all to agree to this?"

She shakes her head with a laugh. "It wasn't me."

Daisy rises onto her hind legs and places her paws on my stomach, giving me a better view of her bandana with a *Daisy for Vice Mayor* slogan on it.

"Cute touch." I rub underneath Daisy's jaw, which makes her tongue fall out of her mouth.

"Thanks. She's part of my strategy today." Lily winks.

I quirk a brow. "How so?"

"She's an attention magnet, so all I need to do is sit in the park and people will come up to me in no time."

I chuckle under my breath. "No one will be able to say no to talking to you—with or without Daisy."

"Good! Because we all made a bet to see how many people we can get to talk to us today, and I can't lose."

"A bet?" I ask, amused by the idea of them competing against each other.

"Yes. Winner gets to pick a car from your collection and drive it around for a day. Loser has to wash dishes for the next four Sunday lunches."

"Did you…"

"Also invite Manny and his mom to participate because he's always asking to drive your Ferrari? Why yes, I did."

"Lily…" I warn.

"You need all the help you can get!"

"I'm going to kill you." *With orgasms,* I say to myself. Many, many orgasms, some of which will be delayed because what was she thinking, offering up my car collection like a prize on one of those game shows?

I fake a lunge, and she darts away with a squeal.

"See you later!" She disappears out the front door of the office with her clipboard, leaving me with the biggest smile on my face.

She's lucky I love her, but not nearly as lucky as I am to be loved *by her.*

Halfway through today's canvassing, I take a break and head to the Muñoz house so I can meet up with a delivery man. I couldn't have planned today better if I tried since Lily is going to be occupied for most of the day.

"Sign here." He passes me the clipboard.

I sign the invoice while his team carries the last item into the backyard. I show them where to place it and take a photo of the garden, now that it is complete, and send it to Rosa, who has done a good job keeping Lily away from the backyard.

Thankfully Lily has been so busy with work and the campaign that she hasn't wandered outside yet, and Rosa has assured me that she'll make sure she doesn't until the engagement party, which Lily still thinks is taking place at my house.

This entire plan, which has been on my mind for a while, feels more special now that Lily and I are finally on the same page.

I hope my actions leave no room for misinterpretation this time, because there is no question in my mind that I love Lily Muñoz, and I'll spend forever making sure she never doubts that—or me—again.

CHAPTER FIFTY-FOUR

Lily

'm in the middle of reorganizing my closet—my pastels are back, along with all my accessories and expanding shoe collection—when my sister shouts my name.

"Lily!"

I come out running, only to skid to a stop when I find Dahlia sitting on the living room couch, with one hand in a bag of potato chips and the other holding the remote.

"What's wrong?" I ask.

"Hold on!" She presses a button, and I watch as she rewinds to the beginning of an ad playing on the TV.

It takes me a total of five seconds to realize it's a political one that was paid for by Trevor Ludlow.

"Who is Lorenzo Vittori?" An ominous voice plays in the background.

I take a seat and watch as Trevor's team goes on to include pictures and short clips of Lorenzo over the span of his adult life. Most of the photos are from his time before he moved back to our town, and if I weren't annoyed by the blatant attempt at a negative ad, I'd roll my eyes.

Because oh, how scandalous of Lorenzo to go out on a date with another woman.

And wow, Lorenzo was caught playing poker? Must be a gambling addict, then.

There are a few photos of him at the Moirai, two of which were taken after the hotel was destroyed. It breaks my heart to see Lorenzo standing in front of the resort with sunglasses on his face despite the gloomy day.

Doesn't take a genius to guess why that is.

In the middle of the ad, it takes a turn, and the focus switches to Trevor Ludlow and all his contributions to the town, including his time as city commissioner before he dropped the position to run for mayor. His list is short, and his photo montage is giving major out-of-touch nepo-baby vibes, down to the final clip of him driving his cigarette boat across the lake, waving at the camera like he won an Academy Award.

"Who told him driving around on a half-million-dollar boat was a good idea?" I ask.

"I don't know, but they deserve a handwritten thank-you note from Lorenzo because that was incredible." Dahlia dabs at the corner of her eyes. "The way he picked up a few pieces of trash on the shore? Someone hand that man a community service award."

"There's no way Ludlow's focus groups actually had positive feedback about that."

"What if they wanted to secretly sabotage him?"

My eyes light up. "You're a genius!"

"I thought we established this decades ago."

I grab a pillow and launch it at her head. "I've got to call Willow."

"About what?"

"We need to see what people think of the ad."

"Why?"

"Because if they hate it as much as we do, then we need to find a way to run it around the clock."

Dahlia looks impressed. "Oh my God. That's diabolical."

I flick my hair over my shoulder. "I know."

"Go! Get to it, my evil little protégé!" She practically pushes me off the couch, and I run back to my room and call Willow to explain my plan.

Turns out three different focus groups had a ton of feedback about the ad, most of it in line with our own opinions of Trevor. So, Willow pulls a few strings at the local station to have it played every hour across multiple channels.

Everyone is talking about it by the end of the week, and although the Ludlows were able to have the ad completely removed from the television, the damage is already done.

Trevor Ludlow is officially deemed out of touch, and today's Sunday special of the *Wisteria Weekly* highlights the divide between Trevor and his constituents by noting his achievements—or lack thereof—when compared to Lorenzo.

A Tale of Two Locals, the title reads.

One man was born and raised here, and the other was forced to leave.

Nicole briefly covers Lorenzo's backstory, including how he started Healing Hearts two years ago as a passion project, before she dives into what has happened since then.

She also met with a professor at our community college who analyzed the kind of economic impact Lorenzo's investing business has had on the town.

Even for someone like me who hates statistics, the answer is an obvious one.

To remain unbiased, Nicole dives into Trevor's past and discusses his accomplishments as city commissioner. I had no idea he took credit for the town's budget cuts, so I'm sure everyone will be surprised to hear that he was the one who suggested to reduce funding for schools and the rec center so the town could finally break ground on the country club project.

The Historic District is hardly mentioned in the article, which is a bummer, but I suppose Nicole can only fit so many bad ideas on one page before it begins to look biased, although it clearly isn't.

Trevor was interviewed as well, but his answers were lacking, so if he gets upset about the front-page piece, he can only blame himself. But in order to do that, it would require him being self-aware and holding himself accountable, and if the article proves anything, it's that he lacks those abilities.

I'm not the only one who thinks so. According to the polls, which come out the next week, the town agrees with me because for the first time, Lorenzo is in the *lead*.

X Secret garden studio

wws ???
Wildflower lashes studio
~~Petal + Press~~
The Pressed Petal

CHAPTER FIFTY-FIVE

Lily

My sister insisted on us getting ready for the engagement party at Lorenzo's house because she thought it would save us the trouble of having to drive over there. We're the type to run late to everything, so I agree.

Lorenzo paid for a team of people to help us with hair and makeup, so Dahlia, Josefina, my mom, and I get the full work-up. Josefina suggested I use the same people for my wedding day, and I nod along, knowing full well it will be a while before that.

I'm trying to take our relationship slow, although it doesn't help that to the public, we're engaged.

Lorenzo on the other hand has fully embraced his status as a fiancé, even going so far as handpicking my engagement-party dress. It is perfect, with the baby-pink dress nearly looking white in certain angles.

There is a note attached to the tag, and I escape into the bathroom to read it.

I couldn't picture you wearing anything but your favorite neutral.

There is no signature, but I could recognize Lorenzo's fancy scrawl anywhere.

My sister pounds on the door to remind me of the time, and I force myself to put the note away and get dressed. The midi dress fits like the seamstress had my exact measurements in mind.

When I step out of the bathroom, three gasps fill the air.

"Que belleza," my mom says at the same time as Josefina's, *"Mira ese vestido."*

My sister says nothing since her mouth is hanging wide open while she openly gawks at my new shoes—another hand-chosen gift from Lorenzo.

"How are you going to walk outside in those?" she asks.

"I'm sure that was Lorenzo's intention." He loves for me to cling to him almost as much as he likes carrying me when my heels start sinking into the ground.

My mom checks her phone and shrieks. "We've got to go!"

"Relax," Dahlia says.

"The party is right outside," I remind them.

All three of them look at each other like a perfectly-timed sitcom.

"What?" I ask.

"The party isn't here," Dahlia responds without saying anything else.

Everyone ignores my questions as we all climb into Dahlia's

sedan and head toward the south side of town. Dahlia pulls onto Lopez Lane, which is pretty empty.

"Where is everyone?" I ask.

"They'll be here in an hour."

I'm too shocked by the time change to ask any more questions, so I stay silent as my sister parks in front of our house.

"Wait here for Lorenzo," Dahlia says before disappearing into the house with my mom and Josefina.

It takes a few minutes, but my fiancé walks through the side gate with a breathtaking smile on his face, wearing a form-fitting, navy-blue sports coat and light-colored pants that bring the outfit together.

He also happens to be wearing loafers that remind me of the pair I accidentally ruined.

"Please tell me those are new shoes," I say after he kisses me.

He laughs. "That's the first thing you have to say to me?"

"Do you want me to compliment your outfit instead?"

He checks me out again, as if one pass wasn't enough to get the full experience. "I'd much rather focus on yours."

I kiss him again. "Thank you for the dress."

He gives me a spin, and I stumble thanks to my stilettos.

"Shall we?" He offers me his arm, and I lock elbows with his.

"What happened to having the party at your house?" I ask as he leads me through the gate.

"I had a different idea."

"Honestly I *was* a bit hesitant about asking everyone to remove their shoes at the door, so I suppose this is better."

He hits me with another smile that makes him look way younger. Less...bothered, even. "I'm going to ask you to close your eyes."

"Um..."

"Trust me."

Reluctantly, I shut my eyes and allow Lorenzo to lead me through the grass. The ground beneath my heels changes from grass to pebbles, and if it weren't for his arm gripping mine, I'd trip.

"Almost there."

The soft sound of water rushing makes my heart stutter. I haven't visited the fountain since the last time Lorenzo was here, so I have no idea why he—

"You can open them now."

I want to, but I'm scared of what I might see. Lorenzo doesn't push me, so I wait for what feels like a whole minute before I open my eyes.

My father's garden instantly brings me to tears. Gone are the dreary, half-dead hedges and long-abandoned flower beds, and in its place are flowers of all types. Healthy hedges surround us on all sides, and the old, weathered bench has been replaced with a new one. A white trellis hangs above, where healthy vines with tiny flowers are woven between the wood slates, providing some shade from the sun above.

Everything about the space is perfect, and it fills me with such immense joy to see my father's garden thriving once more. It's everything I could've dreamed of, and it reminds me so much of how it used to look back when my father took care of it.

Lorenzo shuffles us over to the bench with a golden plaque

screwed to the seat. The metal is engraved with my dad's favorite saying: *Un Muñoz nunca se rinde.*

He wipes a water spot off the plaque. "Maybe one day, we can update the phrase."

"What do you mean?"

"We want our kids to relate to their grandpa's most important lesson too, right?"

My stomach flips. "A bit presumptuous of you to think these hypothetical children would take your last name."

He grins. "It doesn't matter if they share yours or mine, so long as the kids are ours."

I sniffle, fighting against the tears building in my eyes. "How did you pull this off?"

He rubs the back of his neck. "An unhealthy amount of caffeine, working odd hours based on your schedule, and Manny."

I shake my head in disbelief. "What did you offer him?"

He makes a face but is quick to smooth it out. "A weekend with my GNX."

"Am I supposed to know what that is?"

Lorenzo looks at me like he might no longer want to be engaged to me. "It's a car, Lily."

"Wow. I never thought I'd see the day where you finally let him behind the wheel of one of yours."

His gaze drops for a second. "I'm working on it with Doctor Martin."

I hit him with an approving smile. "I'm proud of you, you know?"

"What for?"

"Investing in yourself for a change. You've spent so much time and money helping everyone else, and while that is fantastic, it's nice to see you prioritize your needs too. Life is about balance, and I can see you working to find yours."

Lorenzo blushes, and the sight of his rosy cheeks is glorious. He doesn't let me enjoy it for long because he disappears, only to return with a small drawstring bag.

I pause. "What's that?"

His smile is suspicious. "Open it and find out."

My fingers are shaking as I reach for the bag and am surprised by the weight of it. No longer able to hold off, I slip my hand inside and pull out a gold coin.

I stare at it, my eyes wide as it catches the light.

"You got me...coins?" I close my eyes because I can't cry twice in five minutes.

"I know this is something special you had with your dad, and I'm not trying to take anything away from that or replace his memory. I just know how important he is to you, and if this helps you feel connected to him..." He rubs the back of his neck. "And now I'm overthinking everything and wondering if I overstepped—"

If him being more vocal about his anxiety wasn't reason enough to hug him, then him wanting me to have coins to make wishes is.

I throw my arms around him and kiss both of his cheeks before I press my mouth to his. "Thank you. For the garden and for the coins."

He wraps his arms around me. "I know you said you wasted your last wish..."

"Yeah, I did say that, but it turns out he wasn't the wrong guy after all."

"No?" His grin is infectious, and I match it with my own.

"No. It took him a while, but he came around eventually."

"Thank God he did, or else he would've missed out on being with the love of his life."

My insides melt. "I like the sound of that."

"Better than my future wife?" He reaches for my left hand and brushes his mouth over my knuckles.

"Don't get ahead of yourself now," I tease.

"Are you kidding? We have our sixty-year plan to get started on."

"*Our* sixty-year plan?"

"Yeah. Thirty years isn't nearly enough time together—don't you agree?" His smile is infectious, and I return it with one of my own.

"Why stop at sixty years when you can have forever?"

"I always knew you were smarter than me." His smile is infectious, and I return it with one of my own as I wind my arms around his neck and seal our new arrangement with a kiss.

A passionate kiss that promises a future full of wishes, dreams, and maybe if we're lucky, a family to call our own.

CHAPTER FIFTY-SIX

Lorenzo

After two years of meticulous planning, it is hard to believe that election day is finally here. The November date on my calendar has always been a deadline I was looking forward to, but now that it is finally here, I'm dreading the day from the moment my alarm clock goes off.

The last couple of weeks have been a blur of campaign events, strategy meetings, therapy sessions, and dates with Lily, so time passed by quickly.

Today everything seems to be moving at a snail's pace.

Besides the high school where voting will occur, the town is pretty much shut down for the day since people either need to cast their vote for mayor, watch their kids since school is canceled, or volunteer to man the voting booths.

I plan on dropping by Wisteria High later to vote, but this

morning I keep to my routine by meeting with Doctor Martin at ten a.m. Therapy still sucks, but at least it is starting to suck a little less now that we've moved on from discussing my deceased parents and narcissistic, emotionally abusive uncle.

My compulsions are still a problem, but I'm working harder to combat the obsessive thoughts with Doctor Martin's help. Lily and I even attended another cooking class, and I managed a few bites of my food this time, although I still struggled mentally.

But progress, however small, is still progress, so I'll take it.

After this morning's therapy session, I head to the gym before stopping by Rose & Thorn with a lunch I prepared for Lily, which is a habit I picked up two months ago. Providing for her in the smallest ways scratches an itch I didn't know I had, and it hardly costs me anything at all to bring a smile to her face each day.

Once we eat, Lily and I walk over to the high school, where we both vote. She jokes about having no choice in the matter, and all the volunteers working the booths laugh, accusing me of voter intimidation after I kiss Lily hard on the mouth.

She slides behind the curtain with the goofiest smile on her face and blocks everyone, including me, from seeing her while she fills out her ballot.

Thanks to the computer systems Lake Wisteria had invested in during the last presidential election, results could come in as early as tonight, but Willow told me not to expect any updates until tomorrow morning.

The wait will be torture, but Lily is committed to distracting me in the best ways possible until tomorrow. We hole up in my house for the next few hours, only leaving my bedroom for food, water, and to take Daisy outside.

If I had it my way, Lily wouldn't have to leave at all, but she is still committed to following her mom's rule.

"You can't leave," I say when she starts collecting her clothes from the floor.

"I can't sleep over."

I lean against the headboard and stretch, temporarily distracting her with my toned stomach. "But we're engaged."

"You know my mom's rule—no living with a man until you're married." She mimics her mom's voice, and it's surprisingly accurate.

"We can easily fix that problem."

"Sure, in a year and a half. Maybe two."

My mouth falls open. "What?"

"Why are you so surprised?"

"Two. Years?"

"It's not like we've been together for very long."

"So?" I ask, still shocked by her timeline. "My dad married my mom within two months of knowing her."

She pauses in the middle of fixing her dress. "What? I didn't know that."

"It was quite the scandal back then. No prenup either, not that it mattered since they walked away from the business."

I know Lily is far too interested in hearing more stories about my parents, so she pauses her plan to leave and climbs back onto the bed. She fits perfectly in my arms, and I enjoy the feel of her body pressed to mine.

She looks up at me with a grin. "Tell me more."

I share my parents' story, or more so, the tame version they told me since I was a kid. Back then I thought it was crazy, but now I see that my father's idea had some merit.

He loved my mother, so of course he wanted to marry her so they would always be together.

"Cute," she says after I describe their quick wedding.

"Want to keep up the family tradition?"

She giggles. "Nice try, but nope. I've been dreaming of my wedding for a while, and nothing you say or do will convince me otherwise."

I maneuver my body so I'm on top and have her trapped beneath me. "Nothing at all?"

She raises a brow. "No."

I kiss the corner of her mouth. "Don't make me wait two years."

"You'll be so busy with your new job as mayor, time will fly by."

"Being your fiancé sounds like a better job anyway."

Her lips curl with a tease of a smile. "Be serious."

"I am. I'll always make time for you, no matter what."

Her eyes glimmer like two round jewels. "Promise?"

"You have my word. You come first. *Always*." I seal the vow with a kiss, and she returns it with vigor.

All thoughts of her leaving disappear, and we spend the rest of the night tangled in my sheets, right where Lily belongs.

My hand shakes as the phone vibrates against the bathroom

counter. Willow already called once, right as I was rinsing off my toothbrush, but I didn't answer. I *couldn't*.

Just like I can't now.

My heart beats wildly in my chest, and a sick feeling has spread through my stomach, sending acid climbing up my throat.

Lily enters the bathroom wearing one of the new dresses I bought her. "Is that Willow?"

"Yes." I tear my eyes away from her reflection and look down at the phone.

"Do you plan on answering her?"

I nod, yet I don't move to do so.

Lily reaches for my hand and spins me around so my butt is leaning against the counter.

"What's up?" she asks.

"What if I lost?"

She nods. "If you did, it's okay."

"How can you say that with your entire business on the line?"

"Because you gave it your *everything*, and that's all that matters. I couldn't be prouder of how hard you worked, and I'm sure everyone who knows you would agree." She presses her hand to the side of my face, lending me some of her strength. "You should be proud of yourself, and I know if your parents were here, they'd be saying so with me."

My vision blurs, and I shut my eyes until I'm able to formulate a response.

"I did my best," I say, more for myself.

"You did, regardless of what Willow says."

With one last exhale, I reach for my phone. "Okay."

"Do you want me to stay or go?"

I answer her question by wrapping my arm around her and calling Willow back on speakerphone.

"Well, well. Nice to finally hear back from you. I've been trying to get in contact with you for the last ten minutes, Mayor Vittori."

Lily slaps a hand over her mouth, but not fast enough to muffle her excited squeak.

I laugh.

Fucking *laugh* at her round eyes and arched brows.

Right before the humor fades and the truth settles in.

Mayor Vittori.

"You did it. You pulled it off..." Willow rambles on about my plans for the day, but I'm still in shock.

I'm the mayor, and it feels...unfair to be happy when the people I first ran for aren't here to celebrate.

Tears pool in my eyes, and I blink them away. I won't cry in front of Lily. I refuse to.

Yet no matter how hard I try, one escapes out of the corner of my eye and slides down my cheek.

"Willow, Lorenzo will call you back." Lily hangs up the phone and throws her arms around me.

"Baby," she says.

I tuck my head against her shoulder to hide my face.

She slides her hands through my hair, comforting me with her touch and soft words. "I can't imagine how you feel right now."

Happiness is the first emotion I can pin down for obvious

reasons, followed by overwhelming sadness, knowing that the main reason I ran for this position was because of Trevor. Guilt is there too, along with its constant companion, grief.

"Do you want to go visit your parents and share the news?" she offers.

I nod, still not lifting my head from the crook of her neck.

"No rush." She exudes a calm energy that I desperately need to emulate. "Whenever you're ready, we can go."

Lily and I are on our way to the cemetery when my phone rings. The area code is one I recognize, but the number isn't one I have saved.

I let it go to voicemail, only for them to call again.

"Are you going to answer?" Lily asks.

"If it's important, they'll leave a message."

The ringing ends abruptly, and the song Lily and I were listening to starts up again, only to be interrupted a minute later by a voicemail notification.

I pass her my phone and ask her to play it since I'm driving.

"Hey, Lorenzo." Trevor's voice fills the car, and suddenly the large truck I'm driving feels way too small.

Lily pauses it. "You good?"

I loosen my grip on the wheel. "Yeah." As good as I can be, given the circumstance.

You won. He lost.

But I lost more, and that will always be the case.

"We can listen tomorrow—"

I shake my head. "I'd rather get it over with."

"Okay." She taps on my phone screen.

"Congratulations," Trevor says, his voice surprisingly earnest. "You put up a hell of a fight for the position. Way more than we anticipated, and we weren't as prepared as we should've been."

Lily pauses the recording with a scoff. "They had almost two years."

My shrug might appear casual, but my shoulders are tense and ready for an invisible threat. "They wasted a lot of it by underestimating me."

She reaches for my hand tapping against my pocket and laces our fingers together. "Are you sure you want to keep listening?"

"How much more could he possibly have to say?"

She checks the app. "A minute."

"Fine." I refocus my attention on the road.

Her gaze remains pinned on me before she returns to my phone.

"I can make an educated guess as to why you chose to run for mayor, and in a weird way, I respect it. My father doesn't share the same views as me—he told me as much—and neither does my brother, but that's a whole other issue."

Lily spares me a look, but I say nothing because I don't want to pause again.

"They're both unhappy with my loss, but I'm not. We both know I don't deserve it… You do. Nothing I say can make up for anything that has happened in the past, and that's fine. It's my mistake to live with." I say can make up for anything that has happened in the past, and that's fine. It's my mistake to live with."

My molars grind at hearing that word again.

Trevor laughs to himself. "I'll quit my rambling because I doubt you want to hear it anyway."

Lily holds my hand tightly, lending me some of her strength.

He carries on, and God, I hope we're nearing the end of this conversation.

"All this to say, I'm going to get out of your hair for a while. I've always wanted to travel, and now that my wife is embarrassed to show her face around town, this seems like the best time."

"Thank God," Lily mutters.

"Here's to hoping they find somewhere else to live," I joke half-heartedly.

"With the mayor and his wife being forced to move out of their home, who knows," she replies.

"Serves them right after they tried to kick you out of your business."

A small smile tugs at the corners of her lips, and just like that, Trevor's voicemail is forgotten. Hopefully, with enough therapy, he and his family will become a part of my past that I no longer think about.

I have so much to look forward to, and the best part about it is that the Ludlows can't take it away from me.

Together Lily and I head to the cemetery, where I greet my parents without any flowers this time. My head is such a jumbled mess, I didn't think to bring any, but at least the bouquet I dropped off a few days ago is alive and well, the pink flowers standing out against my mom's marble headstone.

I had their headstones replaced when I moved to town, and had the words *Loving Father* and *Doting Mother* etched into the marble, right below *Beloved Wife* and *Devoted Husband*.

My uncle never bothered to write an inscription, so I did.

I take a seat on the bench beside Lily, which I had recently installed once I knew I'd be staying in Lake Wisteria. If I'm going to pass by every Friday for the rest of my life, I might as well make it comfortable like we did with Lily's garden.

Plus I like the permanency of it.

I circle an arm around Lily, and she smiles up at me before facing the headstones.

"Hi," I say, the word partially cut off by a gust of wind that touches my cheek. Lily's hair and the leaves beside our shoes remain unmoved, but I don't think much of it.

Lily keeps her arms locked around my waist while I share the election results with my parents.

"Your son did it," she speaks aloud, like they are here with us. "I had no doubt he'd be able to pull it off—" I arch a brow. "Okay, I had a little doubt, but it wasn't ever because of *him*. The Ludlows…" A look passes over her face. "They've held on to power for far too long, but finally their time has come to an end."

My eyes water, and I panic at the sensation.

"I'm sorry," I mutter when a tear slips from the corner of my eye, which turns out to be the first of many. "It's just…I miss them so much," I confess while she brushes her hands through my hair.

"I know you do."

"I'd do anything to see them one last time. To be able to tell them how much I love them."

I mourn their absence and the time that was stolen from us, and I mourn the future they'll never be a part of.

My parents won't be here to see me become the mayor or get married to the woman I love. They will never be able to attend Sunday lunches with the Muñoz and Lopez families, and they won't have a chance to pass along their own recipes.

I'll never get to share the joys of fatherhood with my dad, and I'll always wish my mom was around to teach me how to step up and be the partner Lily needs.

But most of all, I cry for the boy who had to grow up way too fast and for the man who will always struggle because of it.

Lily holds me like I could break, and with the way my chest aches, it sure feels that way.

Eventually I gain control over my emotions. I expect for my mind to be cloudy, but the sad fog fades, leaving me feeling lighter than ever before.

Lily doesn't loosen her hold until I confirm that I'm okay. When I pull back, she places her hand on my cheek.

"I love you," she says.

I kiss her before replying, "I love you too."

This time, a stronger wind blows through the cemetery, coming out of nowhere and ruffling her hair and mine.

I'd like to think it's my parents reminding me that they love me too.

We hang out with my parents for a little while longer before I check the time and stand up. "We should get going."

Lily reaches for my extended hand and rises to her feet. "You've got a speech to give and a party to get to."

I'm overwhelmed by another rush of relief. "It's still hard to believe it is happening."

She tilts her head back and kisses my jaw. "Well, believe it, Mayor Vittori, because you did it. You *won*, and if your parents were here, they would be telling you how proud they are of you."

In more ways than one, because in the process of becoming mayor, I earned the best reward of all.

Liliana Guadalupe Muñoz—the people's princess…and my future wife.

X secret garden studio

wws ???
wildflower wishes studio
petal + press

the Pressed Petal

EPILOGUE

Lily

ABOUT TWO YEARS LATER

s much as I'd love to keep watching you work, we do have a plane to catch tonight." Lorenzo's voice startles me.

I drop the tweezer tool I use to arrange flower petals and whirl around to find Lorenzo leaning against the wall, looking comfortable in my workshop despite the chaos surrounding him.

He quit offering to help me organize the space a few months back once he realized I thrive in calm chaos—a term he didn't utilize until we finally moved in together.

I stand and stretch my aching back muscles. "How long have you been standing there?"

The telling grin on his face speaks volumes.

"Maybe I'll take you up on installing that fancy security system," I taunt. "Seems like I have a stalker problem."

"More like you have a *husband* problem, *amore mio*." His sparkling gaze flickers to the diamond wedding band he added to my finger seven months ago.

I toss my work apron across the stool I ditched an hour ago in favor of working on my feet. "What time is it?"

"Four."

I gasp. "We gotta go!"

I'm a frazzled mess as I dart around the workshop, searching for my phone. Lorenzo lunges forward and catches me when I trip over a box of supplies that I accidently left in the middle of a walkway.

"You're a walking, talking safety hazard," he says before searching for my phone. I'm strongly encouraged—okay, *forced*—to sit on a stool and watch him find the device in less than a minute.

"Show off." I rise from the seat. "Now, time to find my keys."

His eyes close with his long exhale.

"Kidding! They're in my purse." I pat the leather shoulder bag pressing into my side.

"You go ahead. I'm going to help clean up a bit before locking up."

"Are you sure?"

He checks his watch. "We have an hour before we need to leave for the airport and you're still not finished packing, so yes. Now get going."

"You're the best!" I hit him with a quick kiss on the cheek, and he returns my affectionate peck by sliding his hands into the back pockets of my jeans and tugging me into his body.

He crushes his lips to mine and kisses me until I forget all about what I originally set out to do.

"See you soon, wife," he says with a rasp while pulling his hands away.

An excited tingle spreads down my spine.

"Now, Lily." He gives my ass a light swat, and I take off for the exit because as much as I want to stick around, I need to get packing.

We have a plane to catch and a honeymoon to start, and commercial flights wait for no one.

"Welcome to Amsterdam," the flight attendant says both in English and Dutch.

"We finally made it!" I let out an excited squeal as Lorenzo and I exit the aircraft and head toward baggage claim.

He wraps an arm around my shoulder and pulls me in for a kiss. "Excited?"

"Are you kidding? I've been dreaming of this day since I did an entire presentation on Holland."

Despite Lorenzo's offer to book a year ago, I wanted to hold off on visiting Europe until our honeymoon. Between him becoming mayor, me focusing on the Pressed Petal, and us planning a three-hundred-person wedding, we couldn't take a two-week vacation. Plus I wanted to finish building our dream cottage, which Dahlia and Julian helped us build from the ground up.

I never thought I'd see the day where Lorenzo asked Julian for his opinion on anything, but turns out the two *can* get along, although I'm not sure they'd ever build another house together. Apparently Julian didn't appreciate the way Lorenzo was always breathing down his neck, making sure everything down to the grout color matched my vision for our future home.

Now that our lives are settled, we finally sat down to plan our honeymoon.

With our schedules fully cleared for the first time since Lorenzo's victory speech, I'm looking forward to some alone time with my *husband*.

Lorenzo doesn't so much as grumble when he lifts my massive, overweight luggage off the conveyer belt, although his arms strain when he has to roll it through the busy train station and carry it up the platform steps once we arrive at the city center.

He curses in Italian more than once while I push his cute little carry-on luggage around with a smile. Once we arrive at our hotel, he lets out a relieved sigh, only to have it cut short when I nearly get mowed down by a bicycle.

He doesn't let go of my hand after that, and he spends the entire check-in and ride up to our hotel room quietly processing the incident.

"I'll be more careful next time, baby," I try to reassure him. "I didn't realize I was standing in the middle of a bike lane."

He locks the door behind us and triple-checks the lock before turning to face me. "This trip is going to send me straight back to therapy."

He has no idea.

"How's your anxiety?" I offer him a compassionate smile because yes, there is a chance he might have to discuss a few new worries with his therapist once we return home.

He shoots me a look. "It *was* better, but now that you almost died from a bicycle…"

I gape at him. "Died? Don't be dramatic."

"Did you see how fast he was pedaling? The person had to be clocking forty miles an hour."

I laugh from the absurdity of that comment. "Uh, no. I was too busy being saved by my husband to notice." I throw my arms around his neck and pull him in for a hug. "You're my hero."

His eyes soften at the corners. "I can't be around to protect you twenty-four seven."

"No, but for the next two weeks, you're all mine, *husband*."

His mouth finds mine as he steals a passionate kiss that ends all too soon. "First *baby*. Now *husband*. What's next?"

"How about *daddy*?" I tease.

He chokes on air. "On second thought, let's stick with those two."

Screw it.

I had this entire plan set up with a photographer, but I don't think I can hold the secret in any longer, especially if I randomly get nauseous during the day. So, with a shaky hand, I reach inside my purse and pull out a grainy black-and-white photo. "At least you have eight months to change your mind."

His face goes completely blank, the span between eye-blinks being few and far between.

"Lorenzo?"

I might've officially broken his brain because he says *nothing*.

"You good?" I ask.

With a shaky hand, he reaches for the photo. "You're…"

"Pregnant." I point at the little dot. "And this right here is Lorenzo Junior." A nervous laugh bubbles out of me.

He draws a circle around our baby. "Isn't it too soon to tell?"

I pat my stomach. "I've got a feeling about it."

He stares at my belly as he slides to his knees in front of me, his eyes full of wonder. My own blur from tears as I watch Lorenzo gently brush his hand across my nonexistent bump.

"This is really happening?" he asks, his voice hoarse from emotion.

"According to the two tests I took and my blood results, yup. We're going to be parents."

The doctor told me such, but now that Lorenzo is in front of me, cradling my hand in his trembling one, the truth finally settles in.

He looks up at me with misty eyes. "Thank you."

I thread my fingers through his hair, pushing the strands back so I can get a better look at him. "I know it happened a bit sooner than we expected—"

He jumps to his feet and crushes me against his chest, only to release me with a curse.

"Shit. Are you okay?" He holds me at arm's length and scans my body for a nonexistent injury.

"Lorenzo. I'm fine." I wrap my arms securely around his

waist and pull him back in. "We can hug, kiss, and have sex like normal. Google it if you don't believe me."

His eyes flicker between my face and my stomach. "Of course I do."

"Good, because I did not pack a bunch of sexy lingerie for nothing."

He tilts my head back. "Can I see?"

"Only if you promise to be on your worst behavior." I grip his chin roughly with one hand and brush the other down his chest.

"You swear the baby will be safe?"

I shoot him a look that dares him to ask me that question again.

Thankfully he thinks better of it, instead choosing to drag me into the shower, where we spend the next twenty minutes celebrating our new titles.

Mom and Dad.

After we bike our way across Amsterdam for two days, Lorenzo and I finally make it out to the tulip fields. I spend the entire bus ride fidgeting in my seat, and on more than one occasion, Lorenzo asks if I need to use the restroom. He does so while glancing toward the back of the bus with a look of sheer terror, and I'm tempted to say yes, just to see how he reacts.

"I'm so excited," I say as the tour guide announces that we have made it to the Keukenhof garden.

I jump to my feet, grab Lorenzo's hand, and yank him

toward the shuttle's exit. We are the first ones off the bus, so we have some peace and quiet before the rest of the guests join us.

Tomorrow we have a private day planned with a photographer, but today I wanted to enjoy a tour with a bunch of fellow flower enthusiasts.

We walk through the colorful fields, and I stop a few times to watch how the tulips sway in the wind, the hypnotic motion stealing my attention more than once.

I catch Lorenzo snapping a few photos of me when I'm not paying attention, and by the time we return to our hotel room that night, his phone has a new background photo of us that a fellow tourist took.

I'm leaning forward to get a better look of the picture when Lorenzo comes up behind me and winds an arm around me, cradling my stomach.

"Replacing our wedding-day picture already?" I joke.

"I couldn't resist."

"But I liked that one." I pout.

"I think I might like this one more."

"What?" I tilt my head to the side so I can get a better look at him.

"It's the first one of our family, so how can I not?"

A heat radiates through my chest, my insides melting at the sound of pure adoration in his voice.

I return to looking at the photo with a smile and take in the way Lorenzo cradles me to his chest, the pose matching how he is holding me now.

When I agreed to our original arrangement, I never imagined we would end up together. At one point, I nearly gave up on finding my own happily-ever-after, but Lorenzo reminded me what it felt like to dream.

It might've taken twenty-plus years for my first wish to come true, but now I have what I wanted most.

A family to call my own, and a husband to share it with.

My father might not be physically here, but I'll keep his memory alive by taking my children to the fountain and telling them all about their grandpa and the gold coins he gave me.

And one day, when they're old enough, I'll tell them exactly what he told me.

To wish is to hope, and that's the one thing no one can take away from you.

Saying goodbye is never easy, but it also reminds me that I created something special enough to be missed, and that in itself is something to be celebrated.

I fell in love with Lake Wisteria back when I wrote Final Offer in 2022, and that love has grown with each book I've written in the Lakefront Billionaires series, to the point where I don't want to leave. So, although this trilogy is complete, I have a feeling I'll be returning to this town because there is something magical about it.

Something that feels like coming home.

I hope these books give you comfort when you need it, just like they brought me while I wrote them. And, no, that process wasn't always the easiest, but it was worth it.

You make sure it is.

It's because of you that these stories exist in the first place, and it's because of you that I'll continue writing more of them.

This might be the end of the Lakefront Billionaires series, but I also see it as the beginning of a new journey. One that I hope you stick around for and one I look forward to sharing more about once the right time comes.

Until the next happily ever after,

DISCOVER LAUREN ASHER'S DREAMLAND BILLIONAIRES SERIES WITH A SNEAK PEEK OF

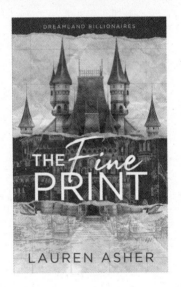

CHAPTER ONE

Rowan

*T*he last time I attended a funeral, I ended up with a broken arm. The story made headlines after I threw myself into my mother's open grave. It's been over two decades since that day, and while I've completely changed as a person, my aversion to mourning hasn't. But due to my responsibilities as my late grandfather's youngest relative, I'm expected to stand tall and unbothered during his wake. It's nearly impossible, with my skin itching like I'm wearing a cheap polyester suit.

My patience wanes as the hours go on, with hundreds of Kane employees and business partners offering their condolences. If there's anything I hate more than funerals, it's talking to people. There are only a few individuals I tolerate, and my grandfather was one of them.

And now he's gone.

The burning sensation in my chest intensifies. I don't

know why it bothers me as much as it does. I've had time to prepare while he was in *a coma* yet the strange sensation above my rib cage returns with a vengeance whenever I think of him.

I run a hand through my dark hair to give myself something to do.

"I'm sorry for your loss, son." A nameless attendee interrupts my thoughts.

"Son?" The one word leaves my mouth with enough venom to make the man wince.

The gentleman centers his tie across his chest with fumbling hands. "I'm—well—uh."

"Excuse my brother. He's struggling with his grief." Cal places a hand on my shoulder and gives it a squeeze. His vodka-and-mint-coated breath hits my face, making me scowl. My middle brother might look dressed to the nines in a pressed suit and perfectly styled blond hair, but his red-rimmed eyes tell a completely different story.

The man mumbles a few words I don't bother listening to before heading for the nearest exit.

"Struggling with my grief?" Although I don't like the idea of my grandfather's passing, I'm not *struggling* with anything but uncomfortable heartburn today.

"Relax. That's the kind of thing people say at funerals." Two blond brows pull together as Cal stares me down.

"I don't need an excuse for my behavior."

"No, but you need a reason for scaring off our biggest Shanghai hotel investor."

"Fuck." There's a reason I prefer solitude. Small talk requires far too much effort and diplomacy for my taste.

"Can you *try* to be nicer for one more hour? At least until all the important people leave?"

"This *is* me trying." My left eye twitches as I press my lips together.

"Well, do better. For him." Cal tilts his head toward the picture above the fireplace.

I let out a shaky breath. The photograph was taken during a family trip to Dreamland when my brothers and I were kids. Grandpa smiles into the lens despite my tiny arms wrapped around his neck in a choke hold. Declan stands by Grandpa's side, caught in the middle of an eye roll while Cal raises two fingers behind his head. My father shows a rare sober smile as he wraps an arm around Grandpa's shoulder. If I try hard enough, I can imagine Mom's laugh as she snapped the photo. While the memory of her face is fuzzy, I can make out her smile if I think hard enough.

A weird scratchiness in my throat makes it difficult to swallow.

Residual allergies from spring in the city. That's all.

I clear my irritated throat. "He would have hated this kind of show." Although Grandpa was in *the* entertainment business, he disliked being the center of attention. The idea of all these people driving out to the edge of Chicago for him would have made his eyes roll if he were still here.

Cal shrugs. "He of all people knew what was expected of him."

"A networking event disguised as a funeral?"

The side of Cal's lips lifts into a small smile before falling back into a flat line. "You're right. Grandpa would be horrified because he always said Sunday was a day of rest."

"There's no rest for the wicked."

"And even less for the wealthy." Declan stops by my other side. He stares at the crowd of people with an unrelenting scowl. My oldest brother has intimidating people down to a science, with everyone avoiding his pitch-black stare. His suit matches his dark hair, which only adds to his cloak-and-dagger look.

I'm somewhat jealous of Declan since people typically talk to me first, mistaking me for the nicest child because I happen to be the youngest. I might have been born last, but I most certainly wasn't born yesterday. The only reason guests take the time to speak to us is because they want to stay in our good graces. That kind of fake treatment is to be expected. Especially when all the people we associate with have a moral compass pointed permanently toward hell.

An unknown couple walks up to the three of us. A woman pulls out a tissue from her purse to dab her dry eyes while her counterpart offers us his hand to shake. I look down at it like he might transfer a disease.

His cheeks flush as he tucks his hand back into his pocket. "I wanted to offer my condolences. I'm very sorry for your loss. Your grandfather—"

I tune him out with a nod. This is going to be one hell of a long night.

This one's for you, Grandpa.

I stare down at the white envelope. My name is written across the front in my grandpa's elegant cursive. I flip it over, finding it untampered with his signature Dreamland's Princess Cara's Castle wax seal intact.

The lawyer finishes passing out the other letters to my two brothers. "You're required to read his individual letters prior to me reviewing Mr. Kane's final will and testament."

My throat tightens as I break the seal and pull out my letter. It's dated exactly a week before Grandpa's accident three years ago that led to his coma.

To my sweet little Rowan,

I choke back a laugh. *Sweet* and *little* are the last words I'd use to describe myself since I'm as tall as an NBA player with the emotional range of a rock, but Grandpa was blissfully ignorant. It was the best thing about him and the absolute worst depending on the situation.

Although you're a man now, you'll always be the same little lad in my eyes. I still remember the day your mother gave birth to you like it was yesterday. You were the largest of the three, with these fat cheeks and a head full of dark hair that I was sadly jealous of. You sure had a pair of lungs in you and you wouldn't stop crying until they handed you over to your mom. It was like everything was right in the world when you were in her arms.

I reread the paragraph twice. It's strange to hear my grandpa talk about my mother so casually. The subject became taboo in my family until I could barely remember her face or her voice anymore.

I know I've been busy with work and that I didn't spend as much time as I should've with you all. It was easy to blame the company for the physical and emotional distance in my relationships. When your mother died, I wasn't sure what to do or how to help. With your father pushing me away, I devoted myself to my job until I became numb to everything else. It worked when my wife died and it worked when your mother met a similar passing, but I realize that it set your father up for failure. And in doing that, I failed you all as well. Instead of teaching Seth how to live a life after great loss, I showed him how to hold on to despair, and it only hurt you and your brothers in the end. Your father parented in the only way he knew how, and I'm the one to blame.

Of course Grandpa excuses my father's actions. Grandpa was too busy to pay close enough attention to the real monster his son turned out to be.

As I write this, I'm living in Dreamland, trying to reconnect with myself. Something has been bothering me over the last couple of years and it didn't click until I came here to reevaluate my life. I met someone who opened my eyes to my mistakes. As the company grew, I lost touch with why I started this all. I realized that I've been surrounded by so many happy people, yet I have never felt so alone in my life. And although my name is synonymous with the word "happiness," I feel anything but.

An uncomfortable feeling claws at my chest, begging to be

released. There was a dark time in my life when I could relate to his comment. But I shut that part of my brain off once I realized no one could save me but myself.

I shake my head and refocus my attention.

Growing old is a peculiar thing because it puts everything into perspective. This updated will is my way of making amends after my death and fixing my wrongs before it's too late. I don't want this life for you three. Hell, I don't want it for your father either. So Grandpa is here to save the day, in true Dreamland prince fashion (or villain, but that's going to depend on your perspective, not mine).

You each have been given a task to complete to receive your percentage of the company after my death. Do you expect anything less from the man who writes fairy tales for a living? I can't just GIVE you the company. So to you, Rowan, the dreamer who stopped dreaming, I ask you one thing…

Become the Director of Dreamland and bring the magic back.

To receive your 18% of the company, you'll be expected to become the Director and spearhead a unique project for me for six months. I want you to identify Dreamland's weaknesses and develop a renovation plan worthy of my legacy. I know you're the right man for this job because there's no one I trust who loves creating more than you, even though you lost touch with that side of yourself over the years.

I *loved* creating. Emphasis on the past tense because there's no way I would draw again, let alone willingly work at Dreamland.

ALSO BY LAUREN ASHER...

LAKEFRONT BILLIONAIRES SERIES
A series of interconnected standalones
Love Redesigned
Love Unwritten
Love Arranged

DREAMLAND BILLIONAIRES SERIES
A series of interconnected standalones
The Fine Print
Terms and Conditions
Final Offer

DIRTY AIR SERIES
A series of interconnected standalones
Throttled
Collided
Wrecked
Redeemed

Scan the code to read the books

ACKNOWLEDGMENTS

To my team, which is made up of incredible editors, alpha and beta readers, sensitivity readers, and proofreaders—thank you for helping me with *Love* (Re)*Arranged*. You were an integral part of this process, and I'm so grateful for all your help, especially when it came down to the wire with my deadlines.

To my agent, Kimberly Brower: Thank you for always advocating what's best for me—and for believing in me when I don't. When you said "all hands on deck" to meet this deadline, I knew you meant it, and I'm so grateful to you and Aimee for helping me pull this off.

And to my publishers, Bloom Books and Piatkus, thank you for helping make this series such a success. You helped give me a platform to tell these stories, and I'll always be grateful for the readers who found me thanks to you.

Also, a big thanks to all my foreign publishers who translate my words for people to read all over the world. I'm so impressed by everything you do, and your editions are some of my favorite.

Mary—Your talent never ceases to amaze me, even after all these years of working together. You give your absolute all to every author you work with, and with each project we complete together, I feel even more lucky to be one of them.

Jos—I've always been a big believer of people entering our lives when we need them most, and you are proof of that. You've accompanied me on this journey—through the good and the not so good—and you've supported me through those times with humor, encouragement, and a little tough love when I'm being hard on myself.

To Kendra—I admire quite a few things about you. Your humor. Your kindness. Your ability to make so many people feel welcomed, including myself. But while writing this book, I admired your honesty. You're a great beta reader, but you're an even better person, and I'm happy and so very appreciative to have someone like you in my corner.

Emily—I just wanted to say I love you so very much. There is so much I could say about our friendship, but ink on paper will never properly summarize the love and happiness you bring into my life each day.

To the guy who knows a guy—Lorenzo wouldn't be the character he is today without your help. Thank you for giving me free political consultations in exchange for spinach dip. I'm sure I'll owe you another one soon.

To the man who loves me and the countless characters who live inside my head: Thank you for being my sounding board, my realism barometer, and my fictional business consultant. While I love writing about other people's happily ever afters, none will ever compare to ours.

ABOUT THE AUTHOR

Plagued with an overactive imagination, Lauren spends her free time reading and writing. Her dream is to travel to all the places she writes about. She enjoys writing about flawed yet relatable characters you can't help loving. She likes sharing fast-paced stories with angst, steam, and the emotional spectrum.

Her extra-curricular activities include watching YouTube, binging old episodes of *Parks and Rec*, and searching Yelp for new restaurants before choosing her trusted favorite. She works best after her morning coffee and will never deny a nap.